READING FLANNERY O'CONNOR IN SPAIN

Reading Flannery O'Connor in Spain: From *Andalusia* to Andalucía

Mark Bosco, S. J. & Beatriz Valverde (Eds.)

The Catholic University of America Press
Washington, D.C.

Copyright © 2020

Universidad de Jaén

The Catholic University of America Press

All rights reserved

Printed in the United States of America. The paper used in this publication meets the minimum requirements of American National Standards for Information Science—Permanence of Paper for Printed Library Materials, ANSI Z39.48–1984.

∞

Reading Flannery O'Connor in Spain: From Andalusia to Andalucía / Mark Bosco, S. J. & Beatriz Valverde (Eds.).— Jaén : Editorial Universidad de Jaén, 2020. — (Estudios literarios. Estudios anglo-germánicos; 1)

218 p. ; 15 x 23 cm

ISBN 978-84-9159-313-3

1. Literatura inglesa 2. O'Connor, Flannery 3. Crítica e interpretación I. Bosco, Mark, ed.lit. II. Valverde, Beatriz, ed.lit.. III. Jaén. Editorial Universidad de Jaén, ed.

821.111

Table of Contents

Flannery O'Connor: Catholic and Quixotic 7
    Mark Bosco, S.J. and Beatriz Valverde

Reaching the World from the South: 23
The Territory of Flannery O'Connor
    Guadalupe Arbona

Another of Her Disciples: The Literary Grotesque 49
and its Catholic Manifestations in *Wise Blood* by Flannery O'Connor
and *La vida invisible* by Juan Manuel de Prada
    Anne-Marie Pouchet

"Andalusia on the Liffey": Sacred Monstrosity in O'Connor and Joyce . . 71
    Michael Kirwan, S.J.

Death's Personal Call: The Aesthetics of Catholic Eschatology 89
in Flannery O'Connor's "A Good Man is Hard to Find"
and Muriel Spark's *Memento Mori*
    Anabel Altemir-Giral and Ismael Ibáñez-Rosales

Quixotism and Modernism: The Conversion of Hazel Motes 107
    Brent Little

A Christian *Malgré Lui*: Crisis, Transition, and the Quixotic Pursuit . . 129
of the Ideal in Flannery O'Connor's Fiction
   Xiamara Hohman

The Other as Angels: O'Connor's Case for Radical Hospitality. 153
   Michael Bruner

"A Purifying Terror": Apocalypse, Apostasy, and Alterity 171
in Flannery O'Connor's "The Enduring Chill"
   José Liste Noya

An Unpleasant Little Jolt: Flannery O'Connor's *Creation ex Chaos* . . . 191
   Thomas Wetzel

FLANNERY O'CONNOR: CATHOLIC AND QUIXOTIC

MARK BOSCO, S.J.
BEATRIZ VALVERDE

"Flannery O'Connor is unique. There is no one like her. You can't lump her with Faulkner, you can't lump her Walker Percy, you can't lump her with anyone." So proclaims the American novelist Alice McDermott regarding the place of Flannery O'Connor in the American canon of literature. When engaging O'Connor and her work today, one's approach ought to be framed by four distinctive features of her life and work: faith, race, gender, and disability. O'Connor was a devout and intellectually formed Roman Catholic who claimed that her religious beliefs grounded her literary vision. She was a person of white privilege during the dismantling of the Jim Crow South trying to reckon with the culture of racism embedded in the class structure of her community. She was a serious fiction writer in a predominantly male world of writers and publishers. And she was a person challenged by the autoimmune disease lupus erythematosus, struggling to focus her energy on her art in the midst of great debilitation. O'Connor lived amidst the social changes that happened during and following World War II, especially as women entered the workforce and the civil rights movement came to dominate the conscience of the United States. Her work vividly portrays narratives of cultural conflict in a nation "haunted" by religious belief.

Critics and fans alike know that O'Connor's religious faith is central to her literary vision. Throughout her life, she immersed herself in the currents of the twentieth century Catholic revival —a hermeneutic that touched upon not only Catholic philosophy and theology, but literary aesthetics, as well. O'Connor maintained: "I write the way I do because (not though) I am a Catholic... However, I am a Catholic peculiarly possessed of the modern consciousness, that thing [Carl] Jung describes as unhistorical, solitary, and guilty" (1988: 90). A writer who came of age during the rise of totalitarian regimes, world wars, and the terror of the Jewish and atomic holocausts, her works question the purpose of humanity, suggesting a higher order account of human commitment. O'Connor's religious imagination, "peculiarly possessed of the modern consciousness," blends the truths of a Catholic medieval metaphysics with modern, existential categories. She believed her faith was her greatest asset in assessing the profound crises of modernity, and found a way to rearticulate the transcendental call to human flourishing in her works. As O'Connor notes in a letter to her friend, Betty Hester, "To possess this [sense of crisis] within the Church is to bear a burden, the necessary burden of the conscious Catholic. It's to feel the contemporary situation at the ultimate level." (1988: 90)

O'Connor's intellectual journey —one which encompassed her entire adult life— began with her graduate degree work at the University of Iowa Writer's Workshop and continued throughout her life. She was well read in the transnational Catholic discourses of 20th century European thought—especially the revival of St. Thomas Aquinas and the many contemporary interpreters of Aquinas, embodied in thinkers like Jacques Maritain and Etienne Gilson. She was taken by the Spanish mystics St. John of the Cross and St. Teresa of Avila. She was drawn to the theologians whose insights echo throughout the Church's Second Vatican Council (1962-1965), such as the Italian-German theologian Romano Guardini and the French Jesuit paleontologist, Pierre Teilhard de Chardin. She read, in translation, the works of the French Catholic literary revival —León Bloy, Georges Bernanos, and Francois Mauriac.

She read John Henry Newman and Baron von Hugel, but also Freud, Jung, and Buber, as well as the 20th century "Crisis Theologians" of the Protestant tradition, Karl Barth and Paul Tillich. As the critic Ted Spivey notes: "what is deepest in [O'Connor's] writing is a tension that exists between her medieval self and her modernist self" (1995: 10). Though not a theologian, O'Connor sought in her art to embody the crisis of meaning in the twentieth century while simultaneously confronting, and perhaps embracing, the contours of her Catholic vision of life. The dramatic settings of her short stories are riveting precisely because they extend outward and upward toward transcendent mystery. Her success in capturing this mystery depended on her ability to shock her readers into acknowledging that the human and the divine literally, and sometimes violently, collide.

A second feature of O'Connor's life and work that shapes our response to her is the ways in which she addressed —or failed to address— race. O'Connor was a Southern white woman of some privilege, living through the last years of the Jim Crow south and the rigid class system of constitutive thereof. She was slow to grasp the magnitude of the developing civil rights movement and its effect on the southern United States. Critics acknowledge that O'Connor was shaped by the racist and segregated world in which she lived, but note the complexity of how race operates in her life and work. Her stories often explore how racism is a learned trait, and suggest that anyone who unconsciously lives with the categories of white privilege is, in fact, always recovering from the latent effects of racism. Recovering from white racism takes a long time, and O'Connor would have included herself as one who journeyed on this path of recovery. Indeed, her stories are shocking and revolutionary in the way they bring home to her readers the assumptions of whiteness. Whether it is Mrs. McIntyre in "The Displaced Person" or Ruby Turpin in "Revelation," her characters are always caught up short by their deformed understanding of status and race.

The intersection, in O'Connor's work, of the religious imagination with the racialized social milieu of the Jim Crow South is what inspires this collection of essays on her work. O'Connor suffered from lupus the last 16 years of her life, and lived with her mother on the family farm in Milledgeville, Georgia: Andalusia. It is said that the name of the farm was chosen because its location was the farthest the Spanish explorers of the sixteenth century traveled before returning to Florida to establish settlements. While, perhaps, colloquial in its origins, this is, nevertheless, a fitting way to connect the American south with the South of Spain. As part of the 2017 *Andalusia in Andalucía*, literary critics from around the world gathered to focus on O'Connor's literary vision in light of three areas of reflection —areas that connect both the Southern Gothic and Southern Spain: first, the relationship of the literary grotesque (a genre that often defines her work, with Spanish baroque aesthetics that have come to define Spain's artistic heritage; second, the relationship between O'Connor's South and the literatures of the broader global South; and, third, the similarities and differences with other writers whose Catholic imagination made their work "counter, original, spare, strange," to borrow a phrase from the Jesuit poet Gerard Manley Hopkins' poem, "Pied Beauty."

Certainly, there is something "counter" about O'Connor's art —something akin to the Catholic Baroque aesthetics of the seventeenth century Counter Reformation. As an artistic and a religious response to a culture reeling from the effects of the Protestant Reformation, the Catholic Baroque offered a theological vision that was as accessible as it was excessive in its sensory overload. It emphasized dramatic, often strained effects typified by bold, complex forms and elaborate ornamentation. Painters as diverse as Caravaggio, Rubens, Velazquez, and Zurbaran —as well as writers of the Spanish baroque age, such as Miguel de Cervantes and Francisco de Quevedo— communicated religious insights in strange, expressive ways, rendered in theatrical or revelatory moments, responding to the spiritual-cultural exigencies of their time. O'Connor is heir to the same strategies of Baroque aesthetics. Her Catholic literary vision fashioned an accessible mode of literary realism that reflected her modernist, formalist credentials, while placing them at the service of an orthodox Christian faith —a faith that often found itself at odds with a complacent and compromising American culture distorted by complacency and privilege. Her parabolic stories deconstruct preconceived notions of righteousness and social order, drawing her characters into the real struggles and costs that constitute attempts to live a coherent and authentic life.

The logic of what might be called O'Connor's baroque aesthetic is asserted in her essay, "The Fiction Writer and His Country":

> The novelist with Christian concerns will find in modern life distortions which are repugnant to him, and his problem will be to make them appear as distortions to an audience which is used to seeing them as natural; and he may be forced to take ever more violent means to get his vision across to this hostile audience. When you can assume that your audience holds the same beliefs you do, you can relax a little and use more normal ways of talking to it; when you have to assume that it does not, then you have to make your vision apparent by shock —to the hard of hearing you shout, and for the blind you draw large and startling figures (1969: 30).

In order to shake the reader out of such false conceptions, O'Connor affects a realistic narrative style that routinely ends in horrendous, freak fatalities, or, at the very least, a character's emotional instability. These grotesque distortions shine a light, in a manner much like a painter's use of chiaroscuro, on a moment that penetrates the self-delusions of her characters.

O'Connor also lived through an extended revival of Southern fiction in the United States. Though never organized as a coherent group, twentieth century American fiction turned out many prize-winning intellectuals, poets, and writers. Beginning with William Faulkner and extending through writers like Eudora Welty, Robert Penn Warren, Caroline Gordon, and Walker Percy, the world O'Connor inhabited was one in which the south was constantly being theorized and discussed. This was, in no small part, because of the growing civil rights movement throughout the United States. O'Connor's sense of place affected how she understood herself. In her essay, "Some Aspects of the Grotesque in Southern Fiction," she notes the irony that "anything that comes out of the South is going to be called grotesque by the Northern reader, unless it is grotesque, in which case it is going to be called realistic." She goes on to suggest that "whenever I'm asked why Southern writers particularly have a penchant for writing about freaks, I say it is because we are still able to recognize one," claiming that "you have to have some conception of the whole man, and in the South the general conception of man is still, in the main, theological." From the standpoint of the southern writer, O'Connor notes "it is safe to say that while the South is hardly Christ-centered, it is most certainly Christ-haunted." The freak, then, can be ascertained as a "figure for our essential displacement that [...] attains some depth in literature" (1969: 44).

As a child of the South, O'Connor witnessed the destruction of rural life during the Great Depression, as both white and black populations moved to the urban north to find work throughout the 1930s and 1940s. She was keenly aware of her region, and the ways in which it struggled with loss and tragedy. This was, for O'Connor, something unique about the American south. She comments on fellow Southern writer, Walker Percy, whose response to an interviewer who asked why there are so many good southern writers—"Because we lost the War," captivated her. His answer, she explains, had less to do with America's Civil War providing good source material than it did with the war's effect on the southern psyche: "What he was saying was that we have had our Fall," O'Connor writes. "We have gone into the modern world with an inburnt knowledge of human limitations and with a sense of mystery which could not have developed in our first state of innocence —as it has not sufficiently developed in the rest of the country" (1969: 59). This sense of human limitation was profoundly religious for O'Connor, for it discouraged presumptuous attempts to elevate the individual as perfectible by his or her own efforts.

The essays in this collection position Flannery O'Connor on a global stage, particularly in light of her Southern Catholic Baroque aesthetics. Her aesthetics are southern because they dramatize a region that is still haunted by religious faith; they are Catholic because her parable-like stories deconstruct the rationalized and distorted preconceptions of faith in order to reevaluate modern religious experience; they are baroque in the excessive yet accessible ways her work moves the reader to mystery and insight. The grotesque —a signature of O'Connor's literary style— that creates a gap between a surface-level realism and the mystery within the complex motivations of her characters. The advent of this "mystery" as a latent force breaking into the the realism and manners of her culture that interrupt the observable social and cultural reality. Each of the following essays locate O'Connor's transnational and global reach in light of these aesthetics, most especially in how her religious faith and the literary strategies she uses draw out the revelatory flashes of insight that become the interpretive center of her stories. This collection offers helpful comparisons of O'Connor with other European writers, especially from Spain and the British Isles, that broaden the intellectual conversation about her work.

In the chapter that opens this volume, "Reaching the World from the South: The Territory of Flannery O'Connor," Guadalupe Arbona examines the broad scope of influence that Flannery O'Connor's narratives have inspired in the works of others. In this essay, she focuses on the case of Spain, a country in which many authors have declared their admiration for O'Connor: José Jiménez Lozano, Esther Tusquets, Antonio Muñoz Molina and Juan Manuel de Prada, among others. Arbona argues that the reason for the appeal of O'Connor's literary production is her textual dynamics, which goes from the particular to the universal, from specific situations to wider visions of human existence. Readers, as Arbona puts it, first feel first attracted to the Southerner's extravagant situations in her stories only to be awakened to universal concerns of human experience by the story's end —experiences like transcendence, migration, social intolerance or different forms of racism. To demonstrate this point, Arbona analyzes three of her outstanding stories, "The Displaced Person" (1955), "The Artificial Nigger" (1955), and "Parker's Back" (1965). In "The Displace Person," two female characters, Mrs. Shortley and Mrs. McIntyre, reject Mr Guizac and his family —Polish immigrants running away from the refugee camps in Europe— on the basis of religious and national difference. Playing with the concept of seeing, both women become blind, but at the same time both find a new vision, identifying themselves with Guizac's suffering. In "The Artificial Nigger," O'Connor deals with racial segregation in the South. Her aim was to dramatize racist white perceptions and feelings towards the African-American community. In this story, the odious racists are depicted in a grotesque way, and it is not until they experience humiliation that they understand the constructed illusions of their imagined superiority. Finally, in "Parker's Back," a story with a strong Biblical background, O'Connor exposes through concrete spaces (geographical and physical) the universal question of whether it is possible to perceive God in the flesh. In these stories, Arbona argues, readers are presented with one reality, but then, in classic O'Connor fashion, are confronted with a different horizon —one which may not have been previously possible.

Anne-Marie Pouchet draws connections between O'Connor and Spanish writer Juan Manuel de Prada (1970-) in her essay, "Another of Her Disciples: The Literary Grotesque and its Catholic Manifestations in Wise Blood by Flannery O'Connor and *La vida invisible* by Juan Manuel de Prada." Similar to O'Connor, Prada considers himself a 'Catholic writer.' Rather than thinking about themes related to the Catholic faith, Prada defines the Catholic writer as one whose religious sensibility pervades his/her literary production. In her study, Pouchet argues that the theological virtues of faith, charity and, most significantly, hope, are interwoven in O'Connor and Prada's work to bring a Catholic ethos to the fore. What is more, Prada's Catholic vision is often achieved through the use of the literary grotesque, much like O'Connor. In this sense, Pouchet analyzes the aesthetics of the grotesque as expounded by the theorist Mikhail Bakhtin and applies this analysis to O'Connor's *Wise Blood*, as is it an important influence in Prada's novel *La vida invisible* (2003). As Pouchet notes, the use of the literary grotesque in both authors is seen in the use of the most abject characters, the outcasts of society, to demonstrate the reality of sin in all its ugliness. These same characters are, however, the ones who mediate the Catholic significance of hope and redemption through expiation and suffering.

O'Connor's scope of influence reached other contemporary authors in Europe as well. In his essay "'Andalusia on the Liffey': Sacred Monstrosity in O'Connor and Joyce," Michael Kirwan reads O'Connor alongside James Joyce and evokes a kind of negative theology operative in their work. Negative, or apophatic, theology is shaped by an approach to the divine through negation —that is to say, what God is not. Both authors manifest a negative theology via their characters, who often assume they are acting faithfully to the norms and manners of religious culture, yet find themselves surprisingly at a loss as to their plight. Both were excellent short-story writers but divergent in both their religious experience and in their feelings towards their respective geographical and cultural contexts. While O'Connor embraced the South and her Catholic faith as essential to her fiction, Joyce's life and work are presented as a Luciferian gesture of refusal of, and exile from, "home, fatherland and church." In their work, however, we find similarities in their sacramental imagination, which produces, in Kirwans' words, "'epiphanies' of grace and revelation." In his comparative analysis, Kirwan focuses mainly on stories from *A Good Man is Hard to Find and Other Stories* (1955) and *Dubliners* (1914), but expands his analysis to their novels as well. In order to carry out this comparative reading and illuminate both contrasts and convergence between O'Connor and Joyce, Kirwan draws from the insights of René Girard's mimetic theory and the link Girard establishes between violence and the sacred. According to Kirwan, reading Joyce alongside O'Connor makes possible an understanding of Joyce's rebellion towards Catholicism not as a denial, but a form of negative theology. To put it in O'Connor terms, it makes possible the demonic groundwork that is needed for grace to be effective.

Continuing along this line of thought, Anabel Altemir-Giral and Ismael Ibáñez-Rosales draw a comparison between O'Connor and another contemporary: Muriel Spark. In "Death's Personal Call: The Aesthetics of Catholic Eschatology in Flannery O'Connor's "A Good Man is Hard to Find" and Muriel Spark's Memento Mori," they note the affinities between Spark and O'Connor in terms of the religious dimensions of their work. Though the two never met, both authors admired each other's literary production. We see this admiration that is expressed in O'Connor's letters and also in interviews with Spark. Both writers share a penchant for violence and shocking moments in their stories in creating an aesthetics of Gothic realism. However, the references to Catholicism in Spark's work are more obscure; the divine doesn't intrude so overtly into everyday life as in O'Connor's stories. Altemir-Giral and Ibáñez-Rosales focus their comparative analysis on different approaches to the experience of death in Spark's novel *Memento Mori* (1959) and O'Connor's story "A Good Man is Hard to Find." In these narratives, the authors argue, each writer conveys a different Catholic eschatological vision connected with death. Born into a Catholic world O'Connor's imagination is permeated with notions of death and salvation, which, in turn, appear as themes underlying most of her fiction. Death also pervades Spark's novel, as we see in the very title of the work —*Memento Mori*, Latin for "remember that you must die." In the novel, characters are reminded about their death through a series of mysterious phone calls, forcing them to face their own mortality. Each reacts differently to this inevitable fact. Spark, a convert to Catholicism, invites her readership to consider that the way we deal with our impending death may be the door through which we transcend our earthly limitations. In a similar vein, O'Connor uses violent death to highlight this eschatological theme in "A Good Man is Hard to Find," a satire about the brutal murder of an ordinary family committed by the Misfit, a character defined aesthetically as the personification of death. Both, Spark's novel and O'Connor's short story, serve to remind readers of death as an inevitable ingredient of life that can lead one to transcend human selfishness and egotism.

The connection of Flannery O'Connor with Spanish Literature that Arbona draws in the first chapter and Pouchet exemplifies with the case of Juan Manuel de Prada in the second, is also reinforced in Brent Little's "Quixotism and Modernism: The Conversion of Hazel Motes," which relates O'Connor's first novel, *Wise Blood*, to what is considered one of the masterpieces of Spanish literature, Cervantes's *Don Quixote*. Specifically, Little reads O'Connor's work in connection with the notion of quixotism, understood as an impractical idealism sometimes rooted in a rigid certainty. Drawing upon Charles Taylor's *A Secular Age*, Little distinguishes between the categories of the "porous" self and the "buffered" self. He argues that Hazel Motes suffers from his own form of quixotism, an idealism marked with an intense certainty that leads him to attempt to preach a "Church without Christ." Little examines the nature of Motes' peculiar quixotism, which he argues is "a distinctly modern variety, for it exalts autonomy and insists that the self should construct its own meaning and morality apart from the influence of a religious past." Such modern idealism —consistent but rigid, sincere but uncharitable— marks Motes' insistence that he is free from any obligation towards others, maintaining his independence from communal responsibilities. His stance manifests, therefore, an extreme dimension of secular modernism. Motes goes through a process of disillusion, in which he realizes that the material world is no longer the sole reality he must grasp. But does such disillusion lead him to reject his modern vision of existence? In this sense, Little's analysis of this quixotism sheds light on a long-running debate amongst O'Connor readers: whether, at the end of Wise Blood, Hazel's self-imposed blindness is a manifestation of a legitimate Christianity. Little casts doubt on this possibility, seeing the overall pattern of Motes' behavior as a problematic form of Christian faith, for his conversion aggravates his disregard for community and his rejection of active discipleship in the world.

Xiamara Hohman also explores the connection between Cervantes and O'Connor. In "A Christian *Malgré Lui*: Crisis, Transition, and the Quixotic Pursuit of the Ideal in Flannery O'Connor's Fiction," Hohman claims that even though scholarship has focused on examining the religious aspects of O'Connor's fiction, little research has been conducted on the ways in which her characters attempt to deal with periods of transition and crisis. Hohman explains why it might be useful to do so, drawing upon Mark Greif's *The Age of the Crisis of Man: Thought and Fiction in America* and providing parallels with her reading of the Spanish philosopher, Miguel de Unamuno. Using Unamuno's understanding of Spanish Catholicism and his love for the literary figure Don Quixote de la Mancha, Hohman draws analogies to O'Connor's characters. Don Quixote, in Hohman's words, "is the character that best exemplifies a man who, unable to deal with the rapid changes of his time, abstracts himself from reality and enters into an enduring but ultimately misguided quest for the ideal." Reading O'Connor alongside Cervantes's masterpiece, Hohman sheds light on the historical discourses of social and political change, on the one hand, and the ways in which O'Connor calls her readership to transcend the moments of crisis and transition, on the other. After the trauma of the second world war, O'Connor's contemporaries offered an existential despair as the only possible response, whereas O'Connor proposed a sober hope that resonates with the character of Don Quixote at the moment he is dying. Hohman discusses the implications of O'Connor's vision of hope for readers at the beginning of the twenty-first century, undergoing its own a socio-political crises.

Michael Bruner's "The Other as Angels: O'Connor's Case for Radical Hospitality," delves deeper into our current crises, reading O'Connor's work in relation to "the inhospitable tenor of our historical moment." In a world with ever-increasing migratory and refugee crises affecting political, cultural, and religious communities, Bruner claims that defining the nature and limits of hospitality has become an urgent task. In this sense, O'Connor's artistic portrayals of hospitality prove to be significant. Bruner also focuses on the role of the Christian churches in our current situation, a role that —in his view— is crucial if people of faith are to heed Christ's call to welcome and embrace the other. In this line of thought, Bruner examines O'Connor's use of the home motif as an instrument to show how Christian hospitality works and to contrast it with what he calls the alleged "Southern hospitality" of O'Connor's era. In her fiction, Christian hospitality, which involves caring for the Other, paying attention to their material needs but also to their moral and spiritual aspirations, serves as an indictment of "Southern hospitality," in which what matters the most is showing good manners. One is hospitable only to the degree that those manners dictates. The Southern tradition of manners, however, when separated from mystery —which serves as a conduit for God's mercy— falls far short of Christ's commandment of establishing an eschatological community of justice and service. Bruner analyzes O'Connor's sense of hospitality in the stories "A Good Man is Hard to Find," "The Turkey," "The Artificial Nigger," "The Comforts of Home," and "Revelation." With the depiction of her sense of Christian hospitality, O'Connor intends to awaken her readers to a different conception of home. As such, Bruner argues, the role of Christian witness in O'Connor's fiction becomes the antithesis of southern hospitality.

In "'A Purifying Terror': Apocalypse, Apostasy and Alterity in Flannery O'Connor's 'The Enduring Chill,'" José Liste Noya reads Flannery O'Connor's work in the shadow of the global order in the post-World War II era: the use of the most destructive weapon ever built, the nuclear bomb and the subsequent Cold War period. The terrible effects of the atomic bombs in Hiroshima and Nagasaki influenced the realpolitik doctrines of the Cold War. The deep, unstable tensions and violent rhetorical bombast pervaded public life as a whole, and the literary domain was not exempted. In O'Connor's work, the reader finds traces of the cultural imaginary of the period. One also finds traces of a psychological and sociological discourse in which the image of apocalypse —both in the sense of destruction of the corrupt old and revelation of the transcendent new— played an important role. "The Enduring Chill" (drafted in late 1957 but not published until 1958) is not a story about the bomb, but its presence is detected in it in its apocalyptic scenarios. The protagonist, Asbury Fox —an example of O'Connor's stock parody of the existentialist, is denied the death he desires, replacing it with a self-humiliating, coercive experience of enforced redemption. In this sense, Liste argues that the devastating nature of an apocalyptic redemption that would follow an atomic cataclysm was refused by O'Connor in "The Enduring Chill." Instead, she offers a sort of religious retreat from annihilation through a transcendent evasion.

The themes of chaos, destruction, and re-creation —along with the role that violence plays in relation to them— are also significant in the final chapter of this volume: Thomas Wetzel's "An Unpleasant Little Jolt: Flannery O'Connor's *Creation ex Chaos*." Here, Wetzel focuses on the Divine Warrior imagery and its presence in O'Connor's fictional world, especially in his analysis of "Why Do the Heathen Rage?," one of the last stories published by O'Connor in her lifetime (and conceived as the opening section of a new novel she was planning to write). Wetzel argues that the vision of Jesus as the Divine Warrior in this story "reflects O'Connor's more mature thinking on the relationship between divine grace and violence," thus opening therefore a new way of examining the presence of violence in her later work. As Wetzel explains, the source for the image of the Bible's Divine Warrior imagery is to be found in the cultural context of the Ancient Near East —specifically in the Divine Warrior Myth or the Divine Combat myth, that echoes throughout religious discourse even today. This myth proposes that creation does not occur peacefully through divine speech; rather, it is the result of a battle between the ancient chaos deity and a young storm god. Upon his victory, the storm deity creates the ordered universe from the remnant elements of the chaotic material, *creation ex chaos*. Humanity thus shares in preserving creation against the forces of chaos as a real battle, both physical and spiritual. Drawing on the biblical sources upon which O'Connor's narratives frequently depend, Wetzel analyzes the presence of chaos in O'Connor's fictional world, and its connections with the Divine Warrior myth and the use of violence to mark divine presence.

Taken together, these essays offer productive ways to think about O'Connor's work in both interdisciplinary terms and global terms. They offer new readings of O'Connor's thematic preoccupations and strategies in connection with the aforementioned distinctive features of her life and work: faith, race, gender, and disability. They examine O'Connor's response in her work to the political tensions of her time —the World Wars, the atomic bombs, the Jewish holocaust, and the Cold War— as well as the social changes that derived from them. They also analyze her response to the crisis of meaning of modernity, rejecting the dominating secular ethics and offering through her Catholic vision a way of rearticulating in her work the importance of human values. In global terms, these essays also analyze comparatively the response that other contemporary and subsequent authors have given to similar socio-political and spiritual preoccupations. In O'Connor's textual dynamics, her concerns are dramatized in a concrete time and place; yet, they can be read beyond Southern boundaries and become universal concerns of human experience with which any reader feels identified. Finally, the essays included in this volume shed light on O'Connor's aesthetics of the grotesque, a vision that accentuates the distortions of modern life for her characters in such a way that they are brought back to themselves in some new insight. All of them challenge readers to think about O'Connor's work in broader frames of reference, opening before us an interdisciplinary reflection that follows in the wake of reading her fiction all around the world.

BIBLIOGRAPHY

O'Connor, Flannery (1969). *Mystery and Manners*. New York, NY: Farrar, Straus and Giroux.

--- (1988). *The Habit of Being*. New York, NY: Farrar, Straus and Giroux.

Spivey, Ted. (1995). *Flannery O'Connor: The Woman, the Thinker, the Visionary*. Macon, GA: Mercer University Press.

Reaching the World from the South: The Territory of Flannery O'Connor

Guadalupe Arbona

In recent years, the work of Flannery O'Connor has received increasing attention in Spain, and not just because the Southern writer lived half of her life in an old farm called Andalusia. This bond with Spain seems to be something that the author herself wanted. In his biography of the writer, Brad Gooch says that the name of the old farm that O'Connor and her mother inherited from their uncle Bernard was Sorrel Farm. In 1946, however, O'Connor met by chance a descendant of the previous owners, the Hawkins, who told her that in the 19th century, the farm had been named after the Spanish region Andalusia. She then begged her mother, Regina Cline, to recover that name for the place, a place where the writer would live until her early death. That way, she established an unconscious connection with Spain, a bond that I intend to examine in this paper.

To go straight to the point, let me start with one of the most significant examples of the influence of O'Connor in Spain. The Spanish contemporary writer, José Jiménez Lozano, winner of the Cervantes Prize in 2002, was soon captivated by her work. In his own words:

> What captivated me as soon as I became acquainted with Flannery O'Connor was her perverse, and caustic intelligence, her admirable

way of narrating and the love she showed for her most laughable characters; but also her serene consciousness of being a writer and her sense of humor in the very midst of those dark stories –sub specie aeternitatis– and perhaps that is the origin of her love for human beings and for the entire world. I was fascinated by her love of life, even in its most mediocre and repetitive daily manifestations (Arbona & Jiménez Lozano, 2007: 153-154).

Jiménez Lozano is fascinated with O'Connor's way of connecting daily life and the entire world:

her complete works, two novels and a collection of stories which make up a relatively compact opus, constitute a narrative which is both harmonious and serene, like a cathedral or a mountain. I have also had the impression of a finished work, in two senses: first, because in these narrations we encounter the world and what is "behind the world", and the most diverse human lives with their helplessness and insignificance, but also their greatness, and it is as though this entire human comedy takes place, as it were, in a very small space surrounding her home (Arbona & Jiménez Lozano, 2007: 156).

In line with Jiménez Lozano, Andrés Trapiello, in his lecture in the Conference "Andalusia in Andalucía" (Sevilla, 2017) talked about how compelling O'Connor's works are for a Spanish audience, despite the Southern and the Spanish traditions being so different. What is more, in Trapiello's view, the structure of her stories is universal and their components —Fall, Redemption and Judgement— eternal.[1]

---

1. "Y sucede que aunque nuestra tradición literaria esté muy alejada de la de Flannery O'Connor (...) y nuestro mundo del suyo, sabemos desde la primera línea de cualquiera de sus relatos, y, de una manera cierta, dos cosas: una, que eso que cuenta es incluso más que real, es verdad, y dos, que eso nos atañe de una manera especial, incluso en el caso de hallarnos en sus antípodas literarias o humanas." (Trapiello, 2017, Unpublished speech; my translation).There are indeed other Spanish writers who admire her works. Cristina Sánchez-Andrade mentioned O'Connor's influence on her work in an interview with Lucy Scholes: "Flannery O'Connor is one of my favourite authors (...) O'Connor has a fascinating biography (...) but she lived on a farm and reared peacocks and I spent some time there doing research (...) people

Following this line of thought, we may ask how is that O'Connor's short stories can be read beyond Southern boundaries? To put it differently: is it true that her narrative, located around the Oconee River, has to do with Hiroshima, as O'Connor herself said? As I will argue in these pages, this dynamic in her work, her intense way of seeing a particular world with strong 'manners,' is precisely what makes her work appealing to the entire world. In this study, I will focus on analyzing the reasons for her readability in Spain. In order to do so, I will take a close look at three of her outstanding stories, "The Displaced Person," "The Artificial Nigger," and "Parker's Back." In this way, I can verify the validity of this dynamic in her work —the movement from the particular to the universal— and demonstrate the way in which O'Connor's writing reaches the world.

For O'Connor, a story fails whenever it does not show something else beyond human poverty and ridiculousness: "When the poor hold sacred history in common, they have concrete ties to the universal and the holy which allow the meaning of their every action to be heightened and seen under the aspect of eternity. To be great story-tellers, we need something to measure ourselves against" (O'Connor, *Collected Works*: 858). Regionalism is not opposed to universal issues; it is rather the means to create great works of literature —Dublin was the means for Joyce, La Mancha for Cervantes or Phaeacia for Homer. "The best American Fiction has always been regional (...) the possibility of reading a small history in a universal light. In these things the South still has a degree of advantage. It is a slight degree and getting slighter, but it is a degree of kind as well as of intensity, and it is enough to feed great literature" (O'Connor, 1988b: 847).

---

tend to associate me more with the Galician writers, and of course I've read them but they're not what I'm most fond of. I would definitely say O'Connor is one of the writers who has influenced me the most" (http://bookanista.com/cristina-sanchez-andrade/) Other Spanish speaking writers who admire her are Esther Tusquets, Rober Saladrigas, Gustavo Martín Garzo, Antonio Muñoz Molina, José María Guelbenzu, Jon Juaristi, Juan Manuel de Prada, Juan Marsé, Alejandro Gándara, Antonio Rivero Taravillo, Fernando Iwasaki and Eduardo Jordá, among others.

The study of "The Displaced Person," "The Artificial Nigger," and "Parker's Back" reveals that the reasons for this positive reception beyond her boundaries is grounded in both her conception and her realization of art, which, taking as their source the particular circumstances surrounding her life, reflect universal concerns and reach mystery. In these stories, every event that happens in her fiction has to do with the suffering of the entire world. In my analysis, I will show how her realist conception of art —"which does not hesitate to distort appearances in order to show a hidden truth" (O'Connor, 1969: 179)— ultimately implies openness to the world in its last horizon, that is, mystery. In addition, following O'Connor's definition of art as the unity of "mystery and manners," I will show how unity is reached in these stories through fictional human experiences that embrace the two extremes (mystery and manners).

"THE DISPLACED PERSON" (1955)

The first version of this short story was published in 1954 in the *Sewanee Review*. The initial version was shorter than the final version —the one analyzed here— and published in 1955 in the first collection of her stories, *A Good Man Is Hard to Find*. I will highlight three aspects in the story that are related to different anecdotes of O'Connor's life. Each of them points at how O'Connor's art is connected to her life. The first one refers to the Polish family that Regina, Flannery's mother, took in as workers in the farm where O'Connor lived after she was diagnosed with her illness. The second anecdote has to do with the documentaries about World War II that the writer watched on TV. Finally, the third is connected with the peacocks she bred and admired throughout her life.

"The Displaced Person" is one of the longest stories by O'Connor. The work narrates the changes in a Southern farm when the owner, Mrs. McIntyre, decides to take in a Polish man and his family as workers. The recommendation comes through a priest who helps people who suffered persecution and prison during World War II in Europe. The main point in the story is the rejection of this new worker, Mr. Guizac, twice. He is an immigrant who came from the Nazi camps of death and horror and gets rejected by two different women. First, Mrs. Shortley, who also works in the farm and is afraid of him, and then Mrs. McIntyre, who admires him in the beginning but then gets to hate him. At the end of the story, Mrs. McIntyre watches the death of Mr. Guizac indolently. Although both women are unable to accept the Guizac family, through death, mysterious territories are revealed to them. All of this happens in the company of proud and beautiful peacocks walking around.

"The Displaced Person" is neatly divided in two parts. The first part (I) tells the story of Mrs. Shortley, from Guizac's arrival to her death, with some flashbacks that complete her story and characterization. In fact, the first version finishes with Mrs. Shortley's story. The second part (II and III) was added later and is centered on Mrs. McIntyre. First, we read about Mrs. McIntyre's past and then about her evolution from her initial gratitude towards Guizac to her hatred. This way, both stories reinforce the rejection of this foreigner coming from a horrific experience of suffering in Europe.

The story is built and told through the sense of sight. First of all, both women are strongly characterized by the blue color of their eyes and their particular way of seeing. Mrs. Shortley has "two icy blue points of light that pierced forward, surveying everything" (O'Connor, 1988b: 285); while Mrs. McIntyre "had little doll's mouth and eyes that were a soft blue when she opened them wide, but more like steel or granite when she narrowed them to inspect a milk can" (O'Connor, 1988b: 288). The narrator wants to tell the reader that vision is not a simple thing; it implies, dramatically, the possibility of denying the act of seeing. For that reason, Mrs. Shortley "ignored the white afternoon sun which was creeping behind a ragged wall of cloud as if it pretended to be an intruder" (O'Connor, 1988b: 285) and is described as a person with "unseeing eyes" (O'Connor, 1988b: 290). Mrs. McIntyre's soft blue eyes can become terribly hard too: "Her eyes were the color of blue granite when the glare falls on it" (O'Connor, 1988b: 311). Even though they can see, they reject what they see.

Although both women's stories start in the same way and both finish in physical blindness, their evolution is different. Mrs. Shortley has such a strong prejudice against Guizac's family that she sees everything except who they are, that is to say, human beings. She sees them as characters of a tale (O'Connor, 1988b: 286), bugs (286), rats (287), murderers ("could have carried all those murderous ways over the water with them directly to this place," 287) and she denies what she really sees, that is: "That they looked like other people" (O'Connor, 1988b: 286). She also perceives their lack of language skills ("they can't talk," O'Connor, 1988b: 287), which is the precedent of a series of absurd conclusions: "if they can't talk, they can't work, and if they can't talk, they can't recognize colors" (O'Connor, 1988b: 287).

Due to this distortion of sight, Mrs. Shortley's inner visions become even worse. While she has the splendor of the tail of the peacock in front of her, she only sees, or rather imagines, the fiction of an obscure threat:

> Then she stood a while longer, reflecting, her unseeing eyes directly in front of the peacock's tail. He had jumped into the tree and his tail hung in front of her, full of fierce planets with eyes that were ringed in green and set against a sun that was gold in one second's light and salmon-colored in the next. She might have been at a map of the universe but she didn't notice it any more than she did the spots of sky that cracked the dull green of the tree. She was having an inner vision instead. She was seeing the ten million billion of them pushing their way into new places over here and herself, a giant angel with wings as wide as a house, telling the Negroes that they would have to find another place (O'Connor, 1988b: 290-91).

She prefers her 'inner vision' to what she might discover in reality. This inner vision converts Guizac and his family first into enemies, and then into evil beings. Those judgments have no basis at all, as Guizac is a good worker, responsible, clean and smart. This prejudice grows to the extent that, when Mrs. Shortley hears that Mrs. McIntyre considers Guizac the agent of her salvation, she says to her: "I would suspicion salvation got from the devil" (O'Connor, 1988b: 294). It is interesting that the narrator does not simplify the question, because despite her corruption of vision, she discovers new things with the coming of these displaced people, having to give more thought to a good many matters. Again, her distorted vision continues in a strange and comic combination of correlations: "The trouble with these people was, you couldn't tell what they knew. Every time Mr. Gizac smiled, Europe stretched out in Mrs. Shortley's imagination, mysterious and evil, the devil's experiment station" (O'Connor, 1988b: 296). Interestingly, her inner vision takes over, denying what she actually has in front of her: "They never have advanced or reformed. They got the same religion as a thousand years ago. It could be the devil responsible for that. Always fighting amongst each other. Disputing. And then get us into it" (O'Connor, 1988b: 297). Her obsession with Guizac is so powerful, that she starts imagining

> [...] a war of words, to see the Polish words and the English words coming at each other, stalking forward, not sentences, just words, gabble gabble gabble, flung out high and shrill and stalking forward and then grappling with each other. She saw the Polish word, dirty and all knowing and unreformed, flinging mud on the clean English words until everything was equally dirty. She saw them all piled up in a room, all the dead dirty words, theirs and hers too, piled up like the naked bodies in the newsreel. God save me! She cried silently, from the stinking power of Satan! (O'Connor, 1988b: 300)

Due to these visions, and her particular way of reading the Bible, especially the prophets and the Apocalypse, she considers herself a new prophet seeing many of the things that Mr. Guizac and many other Europeans had endured: "'The children of wicked nations will be butchered,' she said in a loud voice. 'Legs where arms should be, foot to face, ear in the palm of hand. Who will remain whole? Who will remain whole? Who?'" (O'Connor, 1988b: 301). This last thought means the beginning of her identification with Guizac and, as a result, with the pain and suffering of Europeans. It is true that Mrs. Shortley hates the Polish; but despite this hate, she assumes part of their pain. That is why, at the end of the first section of the story, when she decides to leave the farm with her family, the car with all her belongings is very similar to a mountain of limbs: legs on the top, knees to their necks and elbows under their noses, etc. She has embodied the form of European suffering, grappling against it.

The narrator constantly plays with Mrs. Shortley's vision. At the end, she has a particular way of seeing: "There was a peculiar lack of light in her icy blue eyes. All the vision in them might have been turned around, looking inside her" (O'Connor, 1988b: 303). Even her death is painted as the end of her seeing: "One of her eyes drew near to the other and seemed to collapse quietly and she was still" (O'Connor, 1988b: 304). It is at this very moment when another mysterious way of seeing begins: "her eyes like blue-painted glass, seemed to contemplate for the first time the tremendous frontiers of her true country" (O'Connor, 1988b: 305).

Mrs. McIntyre's evolution is quite different. She changes from admiration towards Mr. Guizac to hatred. In the beginning, she is so happy to have a hard-working person in the farm that she finds hope in having him there, as she has someone she can truly trust. "That man is my salvation!" (O'Connor, 1988b: 294). Of course, he is her salvation in the way she conceives 'salvation.' For her, salvation equals hard work and the capacity to struggle and deal with difficulties. In this sense, she considers Mr. Guizac to be her salvation, because he can manage the farm well. Her point of view towards Guizac changes the day she hears about his intention to marry his cousin in Poland to a half-witted black worker from the farm. Then, her racism prevents her from accepting the help she needs to run the farm. From that point onwards, her way of looking at him changes radically. Her gaze narrows and whenever she sees Mr. Guizac in the spotlight, he is reduced to a tiny being, such is her violence against him: "she narrowed her gaze until it closed entirely around the diminishing figure on the tractor as if she were watching him through a gun sight" (O'Connor, 1988b: 315). If her gaze widens, he is merely an insect for her: "She opened her eyes to include the whole field so that the figure on the tractor was no larger than a grasshopper in her widened view" (O'Connor, 1988b: 315). Either way, violence and resentment are present.

At the end of the story, when Guizac dies, Mrs. McIntyre fails to warn him of the danger he is in when he is about to be run over by a tractor. At this moment, she loses all her senses, including her sight: "A numbness developed in one of her legs and her hands and head began to jiggle and eventually she had to stay in bed all the time (…) Her eyesight grew steadily worse and she lost her voice altogether" (O'Connor, 1988b: 326).

Although the stories of Mrs Shotley and Mrs McIntyre are substantially different, with both women the reader witnesses the same unjust rejection of Guizac. In addition, these characters present some other similarities: first, their increasing shortsightedness, to the point that both women become blind. In addition, they trivialize evil and suffering in different ways. On the one hand, the newsreel that Mrs. Shortley saw about the camps in Europe did not fill her with compassion for Guizac; on the contrary, it gave her an occasion to attack him, since in her view he was infected with the evil that existed in Europe:

> Mrs. Shortley had the sudden intuition that the Gobblehooks, like rats with typhoid fleas, could have carried all those murderous ways over the water with them directly to this place. If they had come from where that kind of thing was done to them, who was to say they were not the kind that would also do it to others? (O'Connor, 1988b: 287).

So in her distortion, victim and executioner are the same. Mrs. McIntyre, on the other hand, thinks that the evil which the Polish family endured is nothing in comparison to her daily burdens. Her admiration for Guizac ends when she no longer sees him as a human being and valuable worker, but as an insect and a burden. In her dream, when the priest reminds her of Guizac's suffering, she just answers: "I'm a logical practical woman and there are no ovens here and no camps and no Christ Our Lord [...] Just one too many" (O'Connor, 1988b: 322).

A final similarity between Mrs. Shortley and Mrs. McIntyre is that, surprisingly, at the end of their stories both women find a new vision. Mrs. Shortley "seemed to contemplate for the first time the tremendous frontiers of her true country" (O'Connor, 1988b: 305); Mrs. McIntyre "felt she was in some foreign country" (O'Connor, 1988b: 326). At the end of their lives, they identify themselves with some aspect of Guizac's sufferings, the vision of disjoint limbs in Mrs. Shortley's case or the fact of being a stranger in her own land for Mrs. McIntyre. The narrator insists that something momentous happens to both women: "She had had a great experience" (O'Connor, 1988b: 305) and "She only stared at him for she was too shocked by her experience to be quite herself" (O'Connor, 1988b: 326).

The violence of these two experiences is contrasted with the proud and quiet presence of the peacocks in the story. Besides the esteem that O'Connor has for peacocks, she uses them as the natural frame for highlighting the significance that she wants to give the story. This is how the peacock's tail is described: "He had jumped into the tree and his tail hung in front of her, full of fierce planets with eyes that where each ringed in green and set against a sun that was gold in one second's light and salmon-colored in the next. She might have been looking at a map of the universe" (O'Connor, 1988b: 290-91). The repetitive presence of the peacocks has to do with the whole universe, as it is shown in their tails and is implicit in their beauty. Throughout the story, peacocks surround both characters, but they ignore them. This oversight is connected to the message that O'Connor tried to convey in the story; however, she was dissatisfied with the result:

> The displaced person did accomplish a kind of redemption in that he destroyed the place, which was evil, and set Mrs. McIntyre on the road to a new kind of suffering (...) Purgatory at least as a beginning of suffering. None of this was adequately shown and to

make the story complete it would have had to be –so I did fail myself. Understatement was not enough. However, there is certainly no reason why the effects of redemption must be plain to us and I think they usually are not. This is where we share Christ's agony when he was about to die and cried out, "My God, why have You forsaken Me?" I needed some instrument to get this across that I didn't have. As to the peacock, he was there because peacocks might found properly on such place but you can't have a peacock anywhere without having a map of the universe. The priest sees the peacock as standing for the Transfiguration, for which it is certainly a most beautiful symbol (…) nothing survive but him, the peacock and Mrs. McIntyre suffering. Isn't her position, entirely helpless to herself, very like that of the souls in Purgatory? I missed making this clear but how are you going to make such things clear to people who don't believe in God, much less in Purgatory (O'Connor, 1988b: 970-71).

This letter, written in Milledgeville on November 25th, 1955, shows her aim when writing this story and that she was inspired by her concrete and familiar life in Andalusia. As Brad Gooch points out, Guizac's family is inspired by the Matysiak polish family who arrived as farm workers to Andalusia in the autumn of 1953 (Gooch, 2009: 241-246). Gooch also relates this story with O'Connor's friend, Erik Langkjaer, whom she called the 'displaced person.' What is clear is that this short story creates a connection between a particular situation and a universal concern. Mrs. Shortley and Mrs. McIntyre are presented as deaf and blind, rejecting what is different. Significantly at the end of the story, both women have to endure what the Polish people had suffered before, the disjunction of limbs (Mrs. Shortley) and the feeling of being a stranger (Mrs. McIntyre in her own farm). Both characters experience the acute pain of the world in their own flesh.

At the same time, the story allows these two women to have a glimpse of a new territory. Those new lands are not shown in the short story. The main characters and the readers can only glimpse them through the women's experience of suffering and imagine them following the premonition of the peacocks' tails. Their beauty foreshadows Paradise.

That is why the priest repeats to the angry Mrs. McIntyre, in a quite silly and strange way: "He came to redeem us" (O'Connor, 1988b: 317).

"The Artificial Nigger" (1955)

O'Connor wrote at least four short stories strongly rooted in segregation problems in the South.[2] These stories have several topics in common. In a sense, they describe the context of racism in those years from a unique perspective. As a matter of fact, O'Connor was living in a environment in which segregation was part of her daily life.[3] However, she wanted to depict some white people's way of thinking and feeling about black

---

2. One belongs to the early stories she wrote when she was in the Fiction Workshop at Iowa University, which is entitled "The Barber" (1948). But we have three other mature short stories. The first one is "The Artificial Nigger," which was first published in the Kenyon Review in the spring of 1955 and afterwards as part of her first book of short stories, *A Good Man Is Hard to Find* (1965). The second and the third are "The Judgment Day" (a rewriting of one of her first short stories entitled "The Geranium") and "Everything That Rises Must Converge" (written in 1961). Both of them are in her second book of short stories, entitled *Everything That Rises Must Converge*, published posthumously in 1965.

3. She was brought up in Savannah, where even the Catholic churches were divided (four for white people and three for black people). In Milledgeville, she and her family stayed at Cline Mansion, which was very close to the graveyard. It was, of course, also divided: the best part for whites and the worse part for blacks. When the famous film *Gone with the Wind* was shown as a premiere in Atlanta, Flannery O'Connor was eleven. It was a huge Confederate-themed celebration with two thousand celebrities and the governors of five Southern States. Meaningfully, as Gooch points out, "The black actress Hattie Mc Daniel, who won a Best Supporting Actress Oscar for her role as Mammy, was not invited to the premiere. The sixty-voice Ebenezer Baptist Church Choir, directed by the Reverend Martin Luther King, SR., entertained at a whites-only Junior League ball associated with the opening event: choir members, including the ten-year-old Martin Luther King, Jr., were dressed as slaves" (Gooch, 2009: 68). Flannery O'Connor liked neither these celebrations about the Civil War nor segregation.

people.[4] That was problematic. Her editors were shocked by her using the word *Nigger*, but she was very clear about her perspective in her creation. She always said that, as she did not understand black people, she would always have to write about them from the outside. Her perspective was grotesque and humorous, but the ones she made appeared grotesque were the white people, both the odious racist characters and the ridiculous liberals. For that, when her editor suggested that she should change the title of the story —as 'nigger' was a degrading way to call a black person— she answered: 'The story as a whole is much more damaging to white folk's sensibilities than to black" (Gooch, 2009: 275).

O'Connor was never engaged in political changes about segregation; she welcomed such changes, however, when they happened. Before the Civil Rights Act was passed, she wrote to William Sessions: "I feel very good about those changes in the South that have been long overdue —the whole racial picture. I think it is improving by the minute, particularly in Georgia, and I don't see how anybody could feel otherwise than good about that" (Wood, 2004: 103). It is impossible to measure up how her writings contributed to these changes. However, they certainly contributed to a better way of knowing human beings, even though her approach was a comic one.

I have chosen to focus my comments on "The Artificial Nigger" because the connection between particular realities and universal concerns is very clear in this story. Concretely, supporters of racial segregation —a terrible phenomenon which occurred in a particular place and time— do not understand the suffering of segregated people until these people become part of their lives. As a result, mercy cannot enter the story if supporters of segregation do not realize they need its presence.

---

4. This outside perspective was admired by Alice Walker: 'Yet the African American novelist Alice Walker —in 1953, a nine-year-old girl living in a sharecropper shack eighteen miles away Eatonton— felt the portrayals accurate when she read O'Connor's stories 'endlessly' in college, 'scarcely conscious of the difference between her racial and economic background and my own" (Gooch, 2009: 243).

Significantly, mercy, a universal need, comes to them through what they consider negligible.

Let me begin this analysis by mentioning some experiences narrated in O'Connor's letters. The first of them is an insignificant anecdote that stimulated the writer's imagination. She went once to a farm with his mother to buy a cow. In order to find the place, they were told that they should look for a farm with an artificial nigger at the entrance. These figures of black jockeys were used as hitching and to indicate the labor done by blacks. O'Connor kept this episode in her mind. In addition, she remembered that her uncle used to call them nigger statuaries. Remarkably, in one of her letters, she offered insight into their meaning: "And there is nothing that screams out the tragedy of the South like what my uncle calls 'nigger statuary'" (O'Connor, 1988b: 953-54). Therefore, for her, the starting point of the story is the tragedy of the South. But not just that:

> What I had in mind to suggest with the artificial nigger was the redemptive quality of the Negro's suffering for us all (...) I wrote that story a good many times, having a lot of trouble with the end (...) I have practically gone from the Garden of Eden to the Gates of Paradise. I am not sure it is successful but I mean to keep trying with other things (O'Connor, 1988b: 931).

The story starts at 2:00AM, the moon lighting a poor shack, as if wanting to dignify it all. At the same time, it seems to be asking permission to enter. Under this light, Mr. Head thinks about what he intends to teach his grandson that day. He plans to take him to Atlanta and teach him a lesson about black people. Nelson sleeps in the corner of the shack. The grandfather is thinking that he will have to wake the child up, but the child gets up on his own to proof his maturity and independence. That is when the reader begins to see the competition between the old man and the young boy. Both of them are very stubborn and think that they are right. The grandfather wants to teach his grandson about the city and the blacks who live there. The child thinks that he already knows everything about the city and its inhabitants, since he was born in Atlanta. The moon tries to shed light on the relationship between the two; a light they are unable to welcome in the beginning.

They set off on their journey. They catch the train to Atlanta at sunrise, and in it they see the first black man. Nelson only sees a man, while his grandfather tries three times to force him to identify him as a 'Nigger.' Who knows better, the boy seeing a man or the triumphant grandfather seeing a black? When they get to the city, they see black people everywhere. The first one is rich, proud, well-dressed, and followed by two elegant African American women. Then they see the black waiters serving people in the restaurant car. As they walk through the city, they see a black shoe shiner. But afterwards, the grandfather, who supposedly knows everything, gets lost. They end up in a black neighborhood consisting of poor shacks filled with African American people who are out of work. The presence of a huge black woman to whom Nelson remains attached is the symbol of the necessity he has of a mother as well as of the link between white and black people. As H. Edmondson pinpoints, the black woman foreshadows the end of the story: "As Nelson looks at her in wonder, he finds a strange comfort, a comfort that anticipates the resolution of the story in which redemption will be channeled through a black man, albeit and artificial one" (2002: 149).

O'Connor wrote to her friend Ben Griffith, "You may be right that Nelson's reaction to the colored woman is too pronounced, but I meant for her in almost physical way to suggest the mystery of existence to him" (O'Connor, 1988b: 931). She also explained that the presence of the black woman is necessary to add tension to the story, adding that "I felt that such a black mountain of maternity would give him the required shock to start those black forms moving up from his unconscious" (O'Connor, 1988a: 78).

The last African American the reader encounters is an artificial one: a little plaster figure that is damaged and whose painted smile has faded. It is easy to see how this sequence of African American characters goes from wealthy and satisfied people to poor —or worse than that, artificial, humiliated members. The narrator manages to involve the readers in the story and make them experience an increasing feeling of injustice and pain at the suffering of black people. Therefore, the drama of the two main characters —Mr. Head and Nelson— moves from an experience of satisfaction and presumption to an experience of necessity and dependence. This day teaches Nelson a lot, but not what the grandfather had imagined. The grandfather in turn realizes that he has a lot to learn. They go through an experience of uncertainty and humiliation as well as an experience of betrayal. Mr. Head betrays his grandson when he gets in trouble and Nelson tastes the bitterness of being betrayed. Both seem to be condemned to live the rest of their lives together with sorrow and wrath in a completely merciless relationship.

Then, unexpectedly, they come upon the statue of the 'Artificial Nigger,' the last black figure of the day. The statue represents the strange, the miserable, the humiliated and the rejected, "the image of humiliation suffering for us all" (O'Connor, 1988b: 931). Furthermore, with this strange statue one can see something else that is not immediate. Running into this statue triggers a change in the grandfather and the grandson, and mystery is the cause. O'Connor describes the moment of the encounter in this manner: "They stood gazing at the artificial Negro as if they were faced with some great mystery, some monument to another's victory that brought them together in their common defeat. They could both feel it dissolving their differences like an action of mercy" (O'Connor, 1988b: 230). This is the mystery of mercy, whose action is only possible when it is felt as truly needed. After that, the moonlight appears again. Why does it appear? And what has changed compared to the beginning of the story? To answer those questions, it is necessary to analyze the differences in the action of the moonlight. At the very beginning, the moon was trying to dignify, to transform things (the pants, the jar, the wood, the cloth...) as if it were waiting for permission to enter, whereas at the end, it already has been granted the permission and gives the setting its 'full splendor.' Everything shines under it because grandfather and grandson have felt their need, so the light can go through.

Something happens by means of that humble 'Artificial Nigger' illuminated by the moonlight. In order to make readers feel immerse in the story, O'Connor wisely uses he five senses; touch (the smoothness or toughness of materials, the big African American woman in the city), hearing (the train an city noises, people shouting…), smell ('the smell of fatback,' the cold coffee in a can), taste (thirst and hunger) and sight (the color of the skin, the alikeness of the two main characters, the moonlight, the sunlight). This way, the reader is asked to enter a complex world and to perceive it as if it were the beginning of another kind of knowledge, as a result of the strange action of mercy.

Coming back to the story as a whole, it is possible to say that the problem at its core is racism, as Mr. Head is proud of having kicked African Americans out of the region. He does not like them and wants to teach his grandson the reasons why they are different. Mr. Head is proud of his imagined superiority. In parallel fashion, we observe how the narrator presents black people, from the rich, well-dressed and satisfied individuals in the train to the damaged statue. Their regressive presence claims for justice. But it is not until the main characters experience humiliation personally that they understand the social problem. The first to do so is the boy; he realizes in the train that he cannot live without his grandfather, as he discovers his essential dependence. The man only understands how sour life can be after his action of betrayal. Then they both are ready to perceive how poor they are and how much they need something different from themselves. Ironically, the narrator allows them to discover mercy and forgiveness through an artificial image of an African American.

"Parker's Back" (1965)

"Parker's Back" belongs to the final period of O'Connor's life and comes after a crisis in her writing: "I've been writing eighteen years and I've reached the point where I can't do again what I know I can do well, and the larger things that I need to do now, I doubt my capacity for doing" (Gooch, 2009: 352). And then another crisis arrived: lupus. This explains that all the writer's notes about this short story are surrounded or crisscrossed with comments on hospitals and treatments. Surprisingly, she acts as always, as if her illness didn't bother her; or rather, as if it were simply the unavoidable conjuncture of her writing. Therefore, she took it in the same way as she took everything that really mattered to her, in a comic way. In May 1964, she wrote Maryat Lee from the hospital and told her that she was able to write thanks to a blood transfer (O'Connor, 1988b: 1207). In this line, she wrote to Catherine Carver a month and a half before her death saying:

> I'm still stuck up in the hospital. I thought I was coming for a week or ten days and I'll have been here a month (...) I have another [story] in the making that I scratch on in longhand here at the hospital at night but that's not my idea of writing. How do those French ladies such as Mme Mallet-Joris write in cafes, for pity's sake? (O'Connor, 1988b: 1210).

Similarly, some days before passing away, she joked with Betty Hester about her writing: "Hate to subject you to this writing (hand) (mine). It's almost as bad as yours" (O'Connor, 1988b: 1217).

From her letters we can get more information about the genesis of the story. In 1961, she wrote: "I am a receptive depository for clippings. The latest I have got to add to my collection is one of man who has just had Christ tattooed on his back" (O'Connor, 1988b: 1145). Four years later, she mentioned the book which inspired her to write the story:

> The spirit moveth were it listest. I found out about tattooing from a book I found in the Marboro list called *Memoirs of a Tattooist*. The old man that wrote it took tattooing as a high art and a great profession. No nonsense. Picture of his wife in it —very demure Victorian lady in off shoulder gown. Everything you can see except her face & hands is tattooed. Looks like fabric. *He did it* (O'Connor, 1988b: 1217).

She further clarifies the meaning: "No, Caroline didn't mean the tattoos were the heresy. Sarah Ruth was the heretic – the notion that you can worship in pure spirit" (O'Connor, 1988b: 1218).

As I said before, "Parker's Back" is a spatial short story; that is to say, space is strongly marked and very meaningful. There are three types of spaces: geographical space (the South of USA), cultural space (the Bible Belt) and corporal space (the body). Those three spaces are the limits of Parker's story and, at the same time, the ways of telling his story. Consequently, everything that happens, happens through space.

Readers are invited to enter the story by the hand of O. E. Parker, the main character. His geographical place is Georgia and his family belongs to a low socio-economic status. Parker was fourteen when he discovered that life and body can be colored with tattoos. In a fair, he saw for the first time a man all covered with tattoos:

> Parker had never before felt the least motion of wonder in him. Until he saw the man at the fair, it did not enter his head that there was anything out of the ordinary about the fact he existed. Even then it did not enter his head, but a peculiar unease settled in him. It was as if a blind boy had been turned so gently in a different direction that he did not know his destination had been changed (O'Connor, 1988b: 658).

As he cannot afford them, he decides to join the Navy to earn money and get his body tatooed. The years spent in the Navy open him up to the world: "He stayed in the navy five years and seemed a natural part of the grey mechanical ship, except for his eyes, which were the same pale stat-color as the ocean and reflected the immense spaces around him as if they were a microcosm of the mysterious sea" (O'Connor, 1988b: 658). Parker gets his body tatooed all over the world but this does not calm his dissatisfaction. As a consequence, he goes back to the South and, following a sudden instinct, marries a strict Protestant woman. He ends up living in a poor farm in the South and working for a female farmer.

Poverty, hunger and resignation are the components of this land. In this first space we can see the dynamics of any work by O'Connor: stories rooted in the South, but at the same time open to a greater horizon. In this story, openness to the world has a starting point: the search for new designs. This search is reactivated through Parker's dissatisfaction after getting each tattoo.

Parker's territory is cultural. I mean cultural as a synonym of a way of living and understanding. "Parker's Back" is settled in what is called the 'Bible Belt,' that is, the stories of the Bible that illustrate or accompany daily life. They are the cultural grounds of every story. In fact, Harold Bloom said that one important aspect of O'Connor writings was to recognize the Bible as the poetry of the people. References to biblical stories are constant. First, we find them in the hidden and secret names of Parker: Obadiah and Elihue. Obadiah means 'Servant of Yahweh,' and Elihue means 'Yahweh is God' or 'He is God.' Parker seems to be called to serve God. God will be in his body and that will let him be born again. His wife's names are even more significant: Sara Ruth. Sara is the wife of Abraham and the one who ridicules God's promise. Ruth is in the genealogy of Jesus. She is considered one of Jesus' grandmothers, as she slept with Boaz and made possible the birth of King David. Both biblical references are meaningful in the story. This American Sara hits the representation of God tattooed on his husband's body at the end of the story, restricting metaphorically with this attack His freedom to reveal Himself in the form He chooses. She is also in a sense a recreation of Ruth, as she does an important contribution to Parker's longing for God.

Second, we can see other biblical references that are continuously mentioned in the story: Jonah and the whale, Jesus as the Good Shepherd. Third, the Bible is present in the expressions used by different characters. Sarah Ruth is the daughter of a Straight Gospel preacher, so she thinks in biblical terms: Hell and Paradise, vanity of vanities, idolatry, Judgement seat of God, etc., are present in her discourse. In addition, the Bible is one of the possibilities that Parker considers for the first tattoo in his back, but it is rejected by Sarah Ruth.

Finally, a new biblical reference is present in the most compelling and important idea in the story: the biblical debate about whether God can be seen or not. Representations of God were banned for Jews in the Old Testament, a prohibition that is partly accepted by Protestants. The origin of this prohibition was the fear of idolatry (*New Jerusalem Bible* Ex 32, 1, 34; Ex 20, 2-5) and it used to be a tenet of Protestantism (Dt 4 12-13). On the contrary, the prophet Isaiah expressed his desire to be in front of God, and the New Testament is in fact the story of Revelation, the story of a man who says that he is God.

O'Connor's short story is set within this biblical background; but at the same time, it expresses the human desire for a visual and touchable God. Through an extravagant story, locally grounded, O'Connor is opening the story to a rich and complex world, the world of the Bible. Furthermore, the story poses the following question: Is it possible to see God? That is one of the questions that have moved, and still move, humankind since Plato, as we can see in a song by U2: "But I still haven't found what I'm looking for" (U2, *The Joshua Tree*, 1987).

The third space is Parker's body. As seen before, he was fascinated when he saw for the first time the tattooed man in the fair. He likes the 'intricate design of brilliant color' and the lively movement that is created in the man's body: "the arabesque of men and beasts and flowers on his skin appeared to have a subtle motion of its own" (O'Connor, 1988b: 657). So he covered his body with objects (a shell, a hand of cards, an anchor hearts...), names (his mother's name), animals (a serpent, an eagle, hawks, a cobra...), people (queen Elizabeth II and king Philip). He looks for color, movement, and life. He gets excited when he is planning to get a new tattoo; but when he gets it, he feels dissatisfied again, looking forward to the next tattoo. By the time he marries Sarah Ruth, only one place in his body is free of tattoos: his back. He is so obsessed with the future design for his back that he has an accident. He crushes his tractor and so decides to have God tattooed on his back. When he enters the tattoo shop, he has to choose between quite different images of God: 'The God Shepherd,' 'Forbid Them Not,' 'The Smiling Jesus,' 'Jesus and the Physician's Friend,' and a Dead Christ. He finally decides to tattoo "a flat stern Byzantine Christ with all demanding eyes" (O'Connor, 1988b: 667). But the making of the decision is described in a dramatic way: "On one of the pages a pair of eyes glanced at him swiftly. Parker sped on, then stopped. His heart too appeared to cut off; there was absolute silence. It said as plainly as if silence were a language itself, GO BACK" (O'Connor, 1988b: 667).[5]

The tattoo takes a day and a half to be done; and despite the tattooist and his friends' mockery and his wife's anger, Parker finally obtains the colors and the sensation of movement that he was looking for. If at the beginning Parker's body was described as chaotic —"The effect was not of one intricate arabesque of colors but of something haphazard and botched" (O'Connor, 1988b: 659)— at the very end of the story, it is seen as lightly, full of colors and as a perfect arabesque: "Whose there? (...) Parker bent down and put his mouth near the stuffed keyhole. 'Obadiah', he whispered an all at once he felt the light pouring through him, turning his spider web soul into a perfect arabesque of colors, a garden of trees and birds and beasts" (O'Connor, 1988b: 673). It can be said that his flesh is the space of an evolution from chaos to beauty. Reading further, we could say that this evolution embodies his soul's evolution. But if corporal space is meaningful in general, so is the part of the body that appears in the title, the back. First of all, it is the weakest part of the body. The back is also the first part that can be reached when someone is being chased. In fact, Parker's evolution is described as if God were pursuing Parker, as if he had the feeling that there was someone constantly looking at his back. At the same time, it has a biblical meaning. In the Bible, prophets are the servants of God and the back is a special place for at least one of them, Isaiah: "I gave my back to those who struck

---

5. It is important to take into account that "Parker's Back" is one of the last stories O'Connor wrote. As I pointed out before, she was in hospital when she was writing this story and often commented on the treatments she was going through or her awful handwritting because of her illness. She probably knew she was going to die and it is likely that she chose a triumphant Christ for that reason. It was a compelling moment in her life that might have left some mark in her story.

me (...) I did not hide my face from insult and spitting. The Lord GOD helps me" (Isaiah 50:4-7). These words are interpreted as a foretelling of what will happen to Jesus, who is called the "servant of Yahvé" and who, in his Passion, is the One who is scourged in his back. So is Parker, whipped in his back by his wife.

But the back has another meaning in English; it is closely related to the action of going to the origin, of going "back." At the end of the story, Parker goes back to his beginning. He recovers his name and as a newborn child, he discovers his essential dependence: "The eyes that were now forever on his back were eyes to be obeyed. He was as certain of it as he had ever been of anything. Throughout his life, grumbling and sometimes cursing often afraid, once in rapture, Parker has obeyed whatever instinct of this kind had come to him" (O'Connor, 1988b: 672). "There he was —who called himself Obadiah Elihue— leaning against the tree, crying like a baby" (O'Connor, 1988b: 675).

We can conclude, therefore, that two of the three spaces in this short story (the South of the United States and Parker's back) are open to bigger and wider spaces (the world and God's tattoo), while the third, the Bible Belt, is open to a new possibility: God reveals Himself in human terms. In this third case, therefore, the focus shifts to a universal concern, pointing towards the possibility of perceiving God in the flesh. Here, the etymology of "universal" may be enlightening; the first two spaces (region and body) are opened to the world; that is to say, they accomplish the first meaning of universal, which means "related to the universe." The universality of the third space mentioned suggests another meaning. The word universal can be divided in 'unus' (from one) and 'versus' (from 'vertere,' to turn); in this sense, it means that the 'unus' (God) turns towards a particular person, Parker.

Although it is difficult to separate "manners" from "mystery" as I have done —probably O'Connor would not have liked it—, it is nevertheless possible. Manners alone are grotesque and ridiculous, if not harmful. O'Connnor made ferocious and grotesque images of stubborn and proud characters, such as two mean farmers who think that World War II was a trivial matter; a racist man trying to teach hate and differences between races to his grandson or a ridiculous man searching God in tattoos. They could have become obtuse, had they not been given bigger horizons. These final openings to greater horizons is what has made O'Connor so widely read.

Through this reading, we can understand that the movement from specific situations to wider visions is an inner characteristic of O'Connor's writings. This attracts the readers, who first feel curious about Southerners and their extravagant situations to focus afterwards on contemporary problems (immigration, different forms of racism, body language) and are finally awakened to wider issues of human experience. Furthermore, the analysis of these three texts confirms that the more united these two terms —the particular and the universal— in her textual dynamics, the better the short stories are. In literature, two plus two are more than four, she said, meaning that in literature through mere "manners," we can reach universal concerns. We can certainly say that this happens in her writing, and that it is the mark of a great piece of literature.

BIBLIOGRAPHY

Arbona, Guadalupe and Jiménez Lozano, José (2007). "Understanding a Literary Complicity. José Jiménez Lozano and Flannery O'Connor: A Conversation with José Jiménez Lozano," in *Flannery O'Connor Review*, 5: 153-167.

The New Jerusalem Bible (1985). New York, NY: Longman & Todd.

Bloom, Harold (1986). *Flannery O'Connor*. New York, NY: Chelsea House Publishers.

Gooch, Brad (2009). *Flannery: A Life of Flannery O'Connor*. New York, NY: Little Brown and Co.

Cash, Jean (2002). *Flannery O'Connor: A Life*. Knoxville, TN: University of Tennessee Press.

Edmondson III, Henry T. (2002). *Return to Good and Evil. Flannery O'Connor's Response to Nihilism*. Lanham, MD: Lexington Books.

Jiménez Lozano, José (1988). *Una estancia holandesa*. Barcelona: Anthropos.

--- (2006). Prólogo-coloquio con Guadalupe Arbona. In *Flannery O'Connor, Un encuentro tardío con el enemigo*. Madrid: Ediciones Encuentro.

O'Connor, Flannery (1969). *Mystery and Manners*. New York, NY: Farrar, Straus and Giroux.

--- (1988a). *The Habit of Being*. New York, NY: Farrar, Straus and Giroux.

--- (1988b). *Collected Works*. New York, NY: The Library of America.

http://bookanista.com/cristina-sanchez-andrade/

Wood, Ralph C. (2004) *Flannery O'Connor and the Christ-Haunted South*. Cambridge: Eerdmans Publishing Company.

Another of Her Disciples: The Literary Grotesque and its Catholic Manifestations in *Wise Blood* by Flannery O'Connor and *La Vida Invisible* by Juan Manuel de Prada

Anne-Marie Pouchet

> Meanwhile, Simon Peter was still standing there warming himself. So they asked him, "Aren't you another of his disciples?"
> He denied it, saying, "I am not."
>
> John 18:25-27 (New International Version)

Unlike Peter who promptly denied Christ in the abovementioned epigraph, contemporary Spanish author, Juan Manuel de Prada, who declared himself a Catholic writer in 2003, has publicly acknowledged his debt to American writer, Flannery O'Connor. In a 2006 interview expounding on what it meant to be a Catholic writer, with Petrine conviction, Prada explained that, much like O'Connor's own practice, he believes that a Catholic author need not write on themes obviously related to the Catholic faith but rather that one's Catholic sensibility as a writer will necessarily pervade one's literary production. Being Catholic is not only a matter of dogmas and beliefs but a cultural construct, a cultural imagination. One can be imbued with this culture, passed on from generation to generation through practices and attitudes. It is not surprising to learn that O'Connor's Catholicism has sometimes been dismissed over the years of critical reception as irrelevant to her writing. Yet, given Prada's own definition of a Catholic writer, it is also not difficult to perceive how the theological virtues of faith, charity and above all, what Prada names as the touchstone of Christianity, hope, are intertwined symbolically in both writers' works to bring the Catholic ethos to the fore.

Oddly enough, Prada's Catholic imagination, like that of O'Connor, is often achieved through the use of the literary grotesque, where deprivation of what is considered godly leads to the most abject of characters and fateful endings. The dehumanization and animalization of characters who have rejected a God-faring life or who appear abandoned by any such loving Deity seem to lend credence to the Christian outlook that Hell is an absence of God and that turning away from the Christian faith leads to despair, disfigurement and hopelessness. Yet, in O'Connor's *Wise Blood* (1952) and in several of her heartrending short stories, there is, in the midst of the most poignant of human suffering, the intimation of Christian grace, expiation and the possibility of redemption through hope and the charity of the less obvious other.

Using the work of Mikhail Bakhtin's understanding of the literary grotesque —especially the grotesque body— offers us a fruitful comparison between O'Connor's Wise Blood and its influence on Juan Manuel de Prada's novel *La vida invisible* (2003). The relationship between O'Connor and Prada will be explored not only in their aesthetic of the grotesque, both as a literary tool and an instrument of a dark wit, but also in a manner that the marginalized and outcasts of society communicate the quintessential Catholic message of hope and redemption through expiation and suffering. Furthermore, Prada's "Calvarian" journey as an outspoken Catholic author in modern day Spain offers us a perspective on why O'Connor's presence has not been felt in any major way among Spanish letters.

Prada: A Catholic Writer in His Own Right

Juan Manuel de Prada is a prolific writer of varied and complex works. His collection includes historical novels, detective novels, biographies, short stories and writings that defy literary genre. Yet, his Catholicism only becomes explicit after his reconversion to the faith. Prada's subtle and implicit use of what is akin to O'Connor's aesthetics of the grotesque can be found in some of his previous works, but it culminates in all its depth and complexity in *La vida invisble*.

Prada's first creative work *Coños* (1995) is an homage to women and literature, more specifically to Ramón Gómez de la Serna's work *Senos* (1917). It is a series of burlesque odes to female genitalia, clothed in elaborate and ornate neo-Baroque language. It evokes the poetry of Baudelaire for its beauty and vulgarity. Coños is a farcical mortal sin against the moral concepts of the body as a temple of the Holy Spirit and the responsibility of the artist to portray the same with the respect that reflects the integral beauty of the body (Pope John Paul II *Theology of the Body* (1997)) and recalls the voyeurism of Hazel in *Wise Blood* as his sinful curiosity as a ten-year old leads him to an image of an obese naked woman in a box at the Carnival show. Prada positions himself as the white, European male subject who objectifies and others the fragmented female body, who renders her as nothing more than a vulgar cunt, which he happily describes and adores with a dark wit reminiscent of O'Connor. The use of the grotesque is abundantly seen in his choice and treatment of the vagina. He even dabbles in literary necrophilia with the sordidly humorous reference to "The mummy's cunt" ("El coño de las momias"), and "Cunts in the morgue" ("Coños de la morgue.") (Acín 14).

Prada's characteristic irreverence is evident throughout this work in his use of blunt terminology. He claims to imitate and pay homage to *Senos* (Breasts), by de la Serna, who highlights in his work a woman's distinguished and beautiful attributes, symbolic of motherhood, nurturing, and sexual attraction. Instead, in *Coños*, Prada degrades female physical attributes in Rabelasian fashion, using one of the most vulgar and degrading terms to describe female genitalia: cunt. As a neo-Baroque wordsmith, Prada intentionally uses the cunt as an expression of grotesque humor.[1]

In his revisionist historical novel, *Las máscaras del héroe* (1996), Prada demystifies various historical and literary Bohemian figures of the first decades of twentieth-century Spain immediately preceding the Civil War. Prada's Catholic pen becomes apparent in his use of Judeo-Christian and Catholic symbols and imagery and his dark wit marries this sensibility to the grotesque. His penchant for going against the grain leads him to portray more liberal thinkers and writers in a less complimentary light, while exalting the founder of the Falange, José Antonio, to the status of a poet. The past spiritual life of Gálvez, his anti-hero protagonist, as a seminarian, mirrors the strict spiritual upbringing of O'Connor's character, Hazel Motes. Gálvez, like Motes, has an alter ego, his apathetic and nihilistic biographer, Navales. Their problematic symbiotic relationship, like that of Hazel and Enoch, lends structural and thematic unity to the novel. As the moral degradation of Gálvez takes place, it is mirrored in Navales who plunders Galvéz's work for his own material gain in true Judas fashion. The anti-religious stance of Hazel is reflected in the anticlerical and anti-Catholic atmosphere portrayed in *Las máscaras*. Gálvez describes the seminary, for example, as a den of iniquity and sexual repression. History and the relativity of truth, identity, filiation and betrayal are themes at work throughout. Navales looks to the picaresque Gálvez as a spiritual father of sorts, a Jesus-like figure who valorizes the Falangist José Antonio. Prada blurs the lines of heroism and antiheroism. While he makes the founder of the Falange a Messianic figure, a martyr who will save Spain from its alienation and chaos, it is only after the disappearance of the marginalized Gálvez that Spain's impending authoritarian dictatorship would usher in the era of Fascism.

---

1. Acín highlights the conservative paper ABC (27-IX-1996)'s description of *Coños* as work with an impossible title.

Like O'Connor had done is stories she has written, Prada interweaves his protagonist, Pedro Luis Gálvez, in the short story collection *El silencio del patinador* (1995), into his novel *Las máscaras del héroe*. In these stories and elsewhere in the collection *Desgarrados y excéntricos* (2001), and his novel *Las esquinas del aire* (2000), Prada explores the idea of a search for immortality through writing. In line with his neo-Baroque grotesque style, his protagonists are the marginalized, less known fictional and real writers whom he seeks to rescue from oblivion. Like O'Connor, he seeks out those on the margins of society and those in desperate need of salvation, such as the amoral Gálvez, the exiled lesbian Ana María Sagi, and the demented Armando Buscarini. These works are imbued with a lonely and often sordid and decadent atmosphere of madness, death, sickness, prostitution, decrepitude and oblivion. They delve into Prada's own preoccupation with immortality as a writer and appear to express his fear of a lack of acceptance from the liberal Academy.

In his prize-winning novel *La tempestad*, Juan Manuel de Prada unveils a text that explores knowledge and truth and the knowledge of truth. The narrator-protagonist, Alejandro Ballesteros, who also appears in Prada's later works *Mirlo Blanco, Cisne Negro* (2016) and *Lucía en la Noche* (2019) embarks on a journey to study Giorgione's painting *La Tempesta*. He experiences his own tempestuous epiphany of self, as his four-day trip to Venice is a roller coaster of events: a murder, falling in love and then being rejected. Through his use of ekphrasis, Prada comes to terms with the fact that logic and reason alone cannot bring one to the full truth and that a personal vision is always partial. His Catholic outlook informs just one of the many interpretations of the painting: as a representation of the exile from the Garden of Eden precisely for wanting to possess the fullness of knowledge. This original sin gave way to an imbalance in nature, including storms. The separation of man and woman is evident, causing them to look at each other with desire and not as a complement. The woman breastfeeds the child, symbolic of the pain in bearing and rearing children and the man is in worker's garb, symbolic of his own punishment promised by God for eating the forbidden fruit. The child is Cain, an assurance that both sin and suffering will continue. The absence of the Savior in the painting lends a fatalistic tone as suffering has become the destiny and constant companion of humankind, represented by Ballesteros' own life of drudgery without any sign of love or hope.

O'Connor is one of a number of influences on Prada's brand of Catholic writing. His work reveals the influence of the medieval grotesque, his own neo-baroque concerns and his attempts at a personal *counter-neo-reformation*. His response to the perceived anti-Catholic and progressive intelligentsia and media is perhaps most evident in his collection of newspaper pieces *La nueva tiranía* (2009), where he challenges what he terms the Progressive matrix, the very Spanish tradition of the novela picaresca, as well as the postmodern reality in which he writes. All of these elements play key roles in his trajectory as a contemporary Spanish, Catholic author. Nevertheless, his discipleship of Flannery O'Connor is undeniable and one which he has proudly embraced.

THE LITERARY GROTESQUE OF THE CATHOLIC WRITER

Many secular readers wonder at the dark and grotesque Catholicism of some Catholic writers. Writers in the vein of O'Connor and Prada exercise their freedom not to show their Catholic slip, but rather subtly be informed by a worldview that can be considered Catholic. Sana Goia points out that,

> Surprisingly little Catholic imaginative literature is explicitly religious; even less is devotional. Most of it touches on religious themes indirectly while addressing other subjects —not sacred topics but profane ones, such as love, war, family, violence, sex, mortality, money and power. What makes the writing Catholic is that the treatment of these subjects is permeated with a particular worldview (Goia, 2013, 7).

Prada has explicitly rejected the image of a sanctimonious Catholic writer. In this vein, he cites the example of the American writer, Flannery O'Connor, as a Catholic writer who deals with the darker and more sordid aspects of life. He claims that writing from a Catholic perspective necessitates writing about the world, about evil, about the Devil and his presence in a fallen world. Although this writing may descend into the abject, it does not remain on Calvary with scourged, bloodied and bruised bodies, but rather points to the Resurrection through the salvific action of grace.

Prada admits that he was taken aback by the harsh nature of O'Connor's writings, which he describes as harrowing and heartrending. But he is also quick to recognize that the Catholic writer is a witness of his or her time and must often deal with the vestiges of sin and evil. Like other great Catholic writers from the French and English tradition, such as Mauriac and Chesterton, the Spanish writer thinks it fitting that if one deals with Redemption, one must deal with that which needs to be redeemed, and which would take the reader into the depths of sordidness and the grotesque.

Bakhtin discusses the literary grotesque at length in his treatise on Rabelais, "The essential principle of grotesque realism is degradation, that is, the lowering of all that is high, spiritual, ideal, abstract; it is a transfer to the material level, to the sphere of earth and body in their indissoluble unity" (Bakhtin, 1984: 19). The Rabelaisian grotesque challenges pre-conceived truths, hierarchies and notions through parody, hyperbole, exaggeration and excess. But it is also prelude to rebirth, renewal, and redemption. O'Connor herself indicated that her writing is rooted in redemption but admits that "I have found, in short, from reading my own writing, that my subject in fiction is the action of grace in territory largely held by the devil" (O'Connor, 1969: 118).

Through the use of the literary grotesque, these two writers create the most abject characters, explore the seedier side of the circus and brothels and living on the street, reminiscent of the Rabelaisian marketplace, in order to demonstrate the reality of sin in all its ugliness and deformity. Yet, as part of the doubling associated with Bakhtin's reading of the grotesque, we are presented with the educated, the soldier, and the false preacher with theological doubts in *Wise Blood*, and in Prada's case, the writer who travels to the United States in *La vida invisible* as victims of the evil who, as Bakhtin explains, descend from the high to the low and become sullied with the filth and stench of sin. The degradation and decay associated with the animalization and moral degradation of characters in O'Connor's Wise Blood and Prada's *La vida invisible*, ultimately lead to new life through grace and expiation in the devil's territory.

Goia insists that the Catholic writer only needs faith, hope, and ingenuity to succeed —faith in the power of his craft and its duty and capacity to communicate the most important values and the beauty of its purpose in spite of, in the midst of, and precisely because of, the fallen nature of humanity. He employs his ingenuity to achieve this. Furthermore, Goia points to what Prada refers to as the cultural identity of a Catholic, as a source of his personal identity as a writer.[2] Imbued with a spiritual tradition so rich in ritual, signs and symbology, the Roman Catholic writer is well equipped to write aesthetically pleasing literature as he draws upon this identity.

---

2. "Firstly, there is your cultural formation, a tradition in which you are born and grow up. Undoubtedly, when you are born into a Catholic family, not only are you taught about the dogmas of the religion, but there is, above all, a specific cultural tradition, which, in my view, is the richest of all that make up Western Cultural heritage. Then, of course, there is the personal quest." (trans.) Juan Manuel de Prada, "¿Un escritor católico? Interview by Anne-Marie Pouchet. *España contemporánea*, XIX, 1 (2006):81.

cf "The Catholic writer must have the passion, talent, and ingenuity to master the craft in strictly secular terms while never forgetting the spiritual possibilities and responsibilities of art. ... The Catholic writer has the inestimable advantage of a profound and truthful worldview that has been articulated, explored, and amplified by two thousand years of art and philosophy, a tradition whose symbols, stories, personalities, concepts, and correspondences add enormous resonance to any artist's work. To be a Catholic writer is to stand at the center of the Western tradition in artistic terms." (Goia, 2013: para. 54)

For Prada, it is hope, Goia's third ingredient that is most important as a touchstone of Christianity. While Goia concentrates on the efficacy and success in Catholic writing that must be based on this virtue, Prada imbues his writing with hope in the midst of sin and depravity as a vehicle for the search for redemption. Through the action of grace, whether designated *Wise Blood* in its true sense or *La vida invisible* (the invisible life), grace stirs conscience and leads to actions based on an underlying hope.

Given that Prada admits that the themes of guilt and grace are present in his work, it is not surprising that he, like O'Connor, would find the literary grotesque and grotesque realism fitting vehicles to communicate the aloneness of the writer seeking to share a view of reality twisted by the ravages of sin, but yet in the reach of redemption. Stylistically, he represents grace in its absence through the grotesque, albeit in a less violently physical way than O'Connor, but with the same objective. "Often the nature of grace can be made plain only by describing its absence" (O'Connor, 1969: 241). From a state of grand deprivation and depravity, the journey from sin to expiation through grace to redemption, leaves the reader at the end of *Wise Blood*, with the pinpoint of light, a glimmer of hope, Prada's touchstone of Christianity.

WISE BLOOD AND LA VIDA INVISIBLE AS GROTESQUE CATHOLIC NOVELS

The distortion that is the nature of the grotesque, eliciting both horror and empathy, is a perfect fit for the Catholic writer to highlight the horror of sin and appeal to God's mercy. As Goia says, the Catholic writer prefers to write about the sinner rather than the saint. The sinner provides more interesting raw material for the writer. If one is writing about sinners then one will have to write about sin in all of its depravity. What both O'Connor and Prada do, albeit in different ways, in *Wise Blood* and *La vida invisible*, is to speak to the baser instincts and repulsive aspects of human degradation as subjects in sin and as instruments of atonement. Grotesque realism evokes pity and revulsion. The human subject in his transgressions evokes pity and a response of grace that reveals a beauty in the midst of ugliness and death, a grace that if rejected, leaves man in despair and degradation.

Prada expressed in his 2006 interview that perhaps his literary trajectory reflects his own path back to his religious faith. The grotesque, inhuman, troubled and searching Hazel Motes of *Wise Blood*, and his alter ego, the animalistic, instinctual and degraded Enoch, are mirrored in Prada's *La vida invisible*, where once again there is a contrasting —the writer Losada and Tom, who give in to baser instincts, and their despoiled victims, Fanny and Elena. The intertwining fates of the characters of both writers demonstrate the price of sin. In these works we have a complex network of relationships and circumstances that reveal a Catholic understanding of sin, the wages that sin attracts, expiation, and the grace of redemption.

The gloomy southern grotesque associated with O'Connor's *Wise Blood* is contemporized in Prada's *La vida invisible*. The freakishness of the grotesque found in Wise Blood is replaced by the marginal and desperate in *La vida*. While Gleeson-White points to "barren landscapes, penetrating heat, and closed spaces, with themes of miscegenation, sexual deviance and bloody violence" (Gleeson-White, 2001: 108) of the southern grotesque, Prada uses the quintessential symbol of modern terrorism, the attacks of the Twin Towers on September 11th, 2001. As a backdrop to the novel, this evokes an atmosphere which Prada describes as steeped in shadows, suspicion, desperation and a search for redemption. O'Connor's settings are filled with morally depraved and physically deformed characters. Enoch, his mummified "Saviour," the falsely blind preacher and his urchin-like daughter, Hazel Motes, blinded and beaten, —all evoke a circus-like atmosphere reminiscent of the Rabelaisian marketplace. Wise Blood emphasizes the brute violence of one individual towards himself and others, while the terrorist attacks that form the background of *La vida* showcases a form of collective violence towards a community. The novels take readers from high to low, from the lofty ideals of religion, or self-affirmation, to the sordid depths of brothels, preachers' dens of sexual deviance, the zoo and circus with their caging of animals and humans, and the mental institution where the entrapment of the mind and the sterility of the walls leave the reader with a tremendous sense of dread and melancholy. Both O'Connor and Prada, through their Catholic lens, portray modern society as one that without God has lost its soul, but where a providential hand still lends the hope of expiation and salvation.

Apart from its seedy settings, the grotesque takes shape in deformed and twisted bodies and morals which hearken back to a Catholic understanding of the Original Sin, an idea that the perfection of Creation was corrupted by the first transgression. Not only did Original Sin usher in death and a suspension of preternatural perfections, but it also left humankind a weakness of the will and a tendency towards sin. That imperfection permanently tarnishes both the human body and nature. The deformed body of the grotesque is not a punishment of the individual who bears the deformity, but a symbol of the inheritance of sin that has been bequeathed to the human race. Bakhtin explains in *Rableais and His World* that in "the grotesque concept of the body, a new, concrete, and realistic historic awareness was born and took form: not abstract thought about the future but the living sense that each man belongs to the immortal people who create history" (1984: 367). This 'ancestral body of mankind' or 'communion of saints' seeks out and responds to, but only through free will, the salvific power of grace. Bakhtin emphasizes that this grotesque collective body, is one that is never completed but always in a state of potency, in an act of becoming. As death signifies only the end of the individual body and not the ancestral one, the actions of one body affects the collective. St Paul remarks, "We know that the whole creation has been groaning as in the pains of childbirth right up to the present time. Not only so, but we ourselves, who have the first fruits of the Spirit, groan inwardly as we wait eagerly for our adoption to sonship, the redemption of our bodies. For in this hope we were saved" (Romans

8: 22-24; *Holy Bible*). Therefore, at the end of *Wise Blood*, while the reader may despair for Hazel's salvation, his mortification seems to have borne fruit for him and others as he leaves a pinpoint of light for Mrs. Flood.

The unconscious search for Christ, or *Christ-hauntedness* as O'Connor terms it, is a reflection of man's deep desire for Christ, so aptly portrayed in Wise Blood by Hazel Motes. Muller posits that "Hazel Motes is presented as the epitome of the grotesque protagonist" (Muller, 1972: 23). The deformation of the body, whether manifested in Hazel's self-inflicted blindness, his corpse with his head bashed in, or the broken corpse of his double, Enoch, as a gorilla, or in *La vida invisible*, the raped and desecrated body of Fanny, or Elena's abject prostitution, the locus of man's lust. All cry out in their ugliness and desolation, as St. Paul points out, and as Prada notes of the United States after the tragic terrorist attacks, seeking expiation.

Prada and O'Connor employ the grotesque in these works to demonstrate how sin, both Original and individual, bring humanity down to its lowest level. The absence of God leads one to the level of the flesh and baser instincts. Enoch reverses the evolutionary process and has taken on a gorilla persona, leaving all rational and compassionate behavior behind. Hazel Motes is a deformed, misshapen shadow of a corpse. Fanny is desecrated, becomes a murderer and has lost her mind, while Alejandro discovers that his selfish, lustful actions have disastrous consequences.

The decay and decadence of the human soul and the somber outlook of both novels, which show the suffering under the vestiges of sin, are mitigated by the use of hyperbole so typical of grotesque humor. The excess of violence, lust and deformation causes the reader to recoil in horror and to smile at the same time. "Melodrama is by definition bloody, but there is in blood both redemption and wisdom. One may be disgusted by blood, one may be morbidly attracted, but one cannot remain neutral, impassive and lukewarm." (Sonnenfeld, 1982: 99) They both use their humor as a form of degradation. There is a horrific scene in *La vida* where the evangelical preacher, Burkett, gives in to his latent lust on beholding the voluptuous Fanny, who has come to his congregation hoping to be cleansed of her carnal sins and seeking redemption. Burkett cannot resist his desire for Fanny, and desecrates the name of God and religion when he succumbs to temptation as he feigns a ritual to exorcize Fanny of her demons. She opens up her womb to him to make motherhood possible even after having given herself to so many other men. Burkett takes advantage of Fanny's vulnerability and naivety. He not only acts out of lust, but also out of pride —two cardinal sins— when he has anal sex with Fanny. Through this act he claims her alternative virginity.

Prada reiterates that sin brings with it its own punishment, which can serve as atonement, and with a humble disposition and correspondence to grace, can lead to redemption. This redemption, however, can only come from Christ. While others along the way can help and guide, within the communion of saints, such as Fanny for Tom, and Tom and Elena for Alejandro, real salvation can only come from the personal acceptance of one's fallen nature, a willingness to atone and a dependence on the divine life, *la vida invisible*, or even arguably, true *wise blood*. These are metaphors for grace. This is a gift bestowed and not one that comes from humanity itself. Therefore, as Bakhtin points out, this degradation, through sin in the case of the Catholic grotesque, is regenerative, life giving. Despite his persistent anti-Christian stance, even founding the Church without Christ, Hazel Motes saves no one, convinces no one and only attracts an emotionally and sexually needy Sabbath Hawkes and a con-man impersonator. It is only after a life of reflection and extreme mortification, reminiscent of his father's teachings that Hazel dies with a sliver of hope. In both Prada's and O'Connor's work there is, in the midst of the most poignant of human suffering, the intimation of Christian grace, expiation and the possibility of redemption: blindness leads to light, atonement leads to death and peace, grace found in the midst of the grotesque makes new life and new hope possible.

The constant fight between the flesh and the spirit and the duality of the human person, rational and irrational, is played out in the ambivalence of the Catholic grotesque. As human beings, self and destiny are entwined in communion and bodies are merged, as Bakhtin points out, in a tendency toward duality. He explains that "the events of the grotesque sphere are always developed on the boundary dividing one body from the other and, as it were, at their points of intersection. One body offers its death, the other its birth, but they are merged in a two-bodied image." (1984: 322) Both O'Connor and Prada express the Catholic grotesque in the intertwining fate of the characters demonstrating the price of wallowing in sin in the absence of grace.

The cycle of sin-expiation-grace-redemption is constructed in the novels on a series of doubles that serves to make the work more aesthetically pleasing, as well as to reinforce the universality of sin and the possibility of redemption. In *Wise Blood*, Hazel Motes is presented as the more rational, but just as morally reprehensible and cruel as his alter ego, the instinctual and animalistic Enoch. 'As Hazel Motes becomes a parody of mind, so his disciple, Enoch Emory, is a caricature of body' (Hedin, 2009: 44). They both seek the pleasures of the flesh and some meaning in life, but while Hazel seeks to use his head to disprove Christ, Enoch depends on his instinctual wise blood to act as a guide for his own form of salvation. Enoch is highly symbolic of the physically and mentally grotesque, given to baser instincts of food and sex and is more comfortable with his animal self, even his Savior figure is a disfigured mummified creature. Hazel, morally grotesque, uses his rational thought to coerce and seduce with no moral accountability, since he does not believe in sin. When both fail, Enoch becomes Gonga, the gorilla in a moral and physical reversion while Hazel reverts to childhood moral religious habits of self-mortification to achieve light. He expiates for his meaningless and cruel life with his loneliness, self-inflicted blindness, and physical battery unto death.

Another double of Hazel is Asa, the false preacher who pretends to have blinded himself and lives in self-loathing. While Hazel admires him, he preaches a different gospel, that there is no such thing as sin and therefore no need for redemption, as all men are clean. Hazel Motes wildly rejects Christ. When his senses are intact, he lives in self-loathing. His sensorial and sensual life leads him to reject Christ, his existence and his message. On the other hand, with his self-inflicted blindness and fasting, mortifying the senses leads him to a spiritual life and end. Ambivalence is evident as Hazel Motes fights believing in Christ, expounding atheism and even founding a Church without Christ, but also without followers. The duality of his religiosity and his virulent anti-religiosity leave him lonely and unsatisfied. He becomes a recluse, much like a religious monk, and he dies blinded and bludgeoned, but leaving a little light behind him.

Hazel learns to accept his uncleanliness and the fact that he is not perfect. But this comes through sight-giving blindness and physical hardships. With these actions he seeks consciously to atone for his uncleanliness. The car he buys before his fairly reclusive life, which is old and barely running, is a symbol of his own self and spiritual state. With full sight, he blindly believes that the car is perfect and uses it as an instrument to kill his other double, the conman ironically named Solace, who formed a Church without Christ of his own as a purely commercial venture. When his car, his Church, and even the bodily pleasure he felt with Sabbath, are taken away from him, he is left with no choice than to face himself. He receives the grace he needs, the wise blood, even in blindness and death.

Prada's *La vida invisible* follows O'Connor's lead with a series of doubles all tied to the Catholic web of sin, grace, atonement and salvation. Alejandro Losada, writer and narrator of the novel leaves his fiancé behind to gather biographical information about the 'pin-up' girl, Fanny, from Tom, her once tormentor turned savior. The writer comes to Chicago as an observer. With a privileged glance, he gathers and compiles information. During his mission, he succumbs to lust and vanity and sleeps, with Elena Salvador, a young teacher and his fan. His sin brings guilt, and the narrator in his remorse assumes the guilt of Elena's degradation, even though she is pregnant with another man's child. Alejandro feels tortured as Elena sinks even deeper into prostitution and mental instability, much like Fanny, her own double. The denigrating effect of sin leaves a sombre shadow on the novel. Alejandro loses his girlfriend; Elena suffers abuse from her clients in spite of her pregnancy; Fanny has gone crazy and has become an assassin Tom, Alejandro's double, pays for his cruel mistreatment of Fanny, from whom he extorts sexual favours. Yet, in the midst of this sordidness, grace is there, the invisible divine life which ever so gently to atonement. There is a happy ending for the two couples. Tom and Fanny reach a stage of mutual love and support, as he takes care of her at the mental institution. Alejandro and Elena celebrate the new life of the baby, and manifest the Christian hope of new life in spite of past sins.

Yet it clear that this happy ending comes at a very high price. Prada, like O'Connor, emphasises the grotesqueness of sin and its consequences. Fanny's beautiful body is twisted, contorted, desecrated by her father, a gang rape, her many clients as a prostitute, and by a pastor in whom she sought refuge. Her mind is tormented by these experiences. Fanny tries to achieve her own salvation by assassinating her father, snuffing out the incest he represents, and seeking to begin the process of freeing herself from her own sins. Getting rid of her own lineage means having to forge a new one. Fanny's other escape is madness, which makes her hallucinate a serpent. This serpent is both a phallic symbol, typical of the literary grotesque, and a symbol of the devil both in the novel and the Garden of Eden. Her madness inspires her to stay away from the evil ones, both human and angelic, and their deeds.

What Prada emphasizes in *La vida invisible* —in spite of its sordid and abject content— is the hope of redemption. Although all the main male characters commit reprehensible crimes, Prada demonstrates the mercy of God. Within the Christian worldview, God offers many opportunities for his children to.change their lives. Guilt and remorse can open one to grace and repentance. Both Alejandro Losada's and Tom Chambers' trajectory demonstrate this expiatory journey towards redemption.

The struggle of the Catholic writer

The Petrine-Christ-like relationship that O'Connor and Prada share includes shouldering the emblem of Christianity —the cross of being Catholic. It seems to have become an accepted form of discrimination to disregard the Catholic writer for the mere fact of being Catholic. It is important, though, to reiterate that scholars of Catholic writers do not laud them because they are Catholic. They recognize that they are Catholic and that they benefit from and make good use of their cultural, spiritual and personal tradition, the beauty and history of two millennia of great artistic and cultural heights. But as Goia points out, Catholic writers need to be good writers. "The goal of the serious Catholic writer is the same as that of all real writers —to create powerful, expressive, memorable works of art" (Goia, 2013: para. 51). Flannery O'Connor observed, "The Catholic novelist doesn't have to be a saint; he doesn't even have to be a Catholic; he does, unfortunately, have to be a novelist."(O'Connor, 1969: 172) Endowed then with the advantage of so much beauty, knowledge and history on their side and their concept of truth which pervades all things, it is incumbent on the Catholic writer to write literature that addresses reality seen through the light of truth and beauty or emphasize the ugliness of its absence, with an eternal perspective, "a Catholic vision" (Sayers, 2004: para.4). and "another invisible and eternal dimension" (Goia, 2013: para. 51).

This eternal dimension may provide the lens through which one sees reality but in both Prada's and O'Connor's case, they insist that it is reality in all its shame and glory that must be depicted. The lofty needs to be seen amongst the sordid, the high through the low, and the supernatural through the natural. In this sense, the Catholic novel can become a written embodiment of the incarnation —the Divine made one with flesh. The intense presence of the abject and the wretched may be seen as a stumbling block for some who expect happier and more optimistic content, but the virtue of hope is highlighted by some Catholic novels in the midst of despair, grace in the midst of sin, suffering as expiation and salvation in the face of damnation. O'Connor admits that "when we look at the serious fiction written by Catholics in these times, we do find a striking preoccupation with what is seedy and evil and violent" (O'Connor, 1969: 178).

Yet this violence and evil is not extraneous. Both O'Connor and, Prada defend the fact that the journey from sin (fall), to grace to expiation (suffering and atonement) to redemption are theological truths of the Catholic faith. The grand obstacle that the Catholic writer faces, and not merely among non-Catholics, is pointed out by Valerie Sayers when she writes, "Here we are in an age defined, simultaneously, as post-religious and hyper-religious. In such a time every writer is acutely aware that, as Elie says, "the religious question of our time is whether religion itself is legitimate." (Sayers qtd in O'Brien Steinfels, 2004 :130) This leads to Paul Elie's conclusion that the defining characteristic of the Catholic writer is aloneness. The Catholic writer fights against the commonplace belief that sin does not really exist or is at best relative, that there is no redemptive value in suffering, that comfort and luxury are what ought to be sought after, that one no longer has personal responsibility for one's acts and the consequences for one's soul, the souls of others and of humankind (the responsibility of the communion of saints). Catholic writers find themselves isolated, and often resort to the grotesque and shocking in order to communicate their worldview, and show the reality of the world without Christian hope. O'Connor's statement that the Catholic writer "may resort to violent literary means to get his vision across to a hostile audience, and the images and actions he creates may seem distorted and exaggerated to the Catholic mind" (O'Connor, 1969: 50) also applies to some degree to Prada's *La vida invisible*. As Goia points out "Catholic literature is rarely pious. In ways that sometimes trouble or puzzle both Protestant and secular readers, Catholic writing tends to be comic, rowdy, rude, and even violent" (2013: para. 10).

It is hard to conceive of the formerly dominant as a marginalised group and yet for some time, being labelled a 'Catholic writer' has been a disadvantage. At a conference on Flannery O'Connor in June 2017 in Seville, Spain, three contemporary Spanish writers chaired the first session. Much to the chagrin of a largely American audience, they revealed that Flannery O'Connor was little known in Spain. What was more surprising was the reason that her renown was so insignificant. The fact that she was a Catholic writer worked against her favor. In general terms, America is considered Protestant and Spain Catholic, so this was disconcerting to many of the Flannery followers. They were admirers of the Southern writer for her literary talent, wit, originality and outlook, but to be told that her little success had less to do with a language barrier than with religion was hardly acceptable.

Considering Spain's history with Catholicism and particularly its recent history, an anti-Catholic stance among the intelligentsia is quite believable. The Francoist *nacional-catolicismo* gave the Catholic Church power and authority over public and private life in Spain during the fascist Franco dictatorship from 1939-1975. The reaction against Catholic hegemony is to be expected although perhaps to be regretted. Any marginalisation needs to be questioned, any extremism interrogated.

Furthermore, as Ripatrazione explains, the identity of the Catholic writer is splintered. While there are the general characteristics of the Catholic novel and novelist, they do not speak with one voice. There is diversity as in any other form of categorising writing, but unifying threads mau allow these writers to be categorised or to categorise themselves:

> There is no singular and uniform Catholic worldview, but nevertheless it is possible to describe some general characteristics that encompass both the faithful and the renegade among the literati. Catholic writers tend to see humanity struggling in a fallen world. They combine a longing for grace and redemption with a deep sense of human imperfection and sin. Evil exists, but the physical world is not evil. Nature is sacramental, shimmering with signs of sacred things. Indeed, all reality is mysteriously charged with the invisible presence of God. Catholics perceive suffering as redemptive, at least when borne in emulation of Christ's passion and death. Catholics also generally take the long view of things —looking back to the time of

Christ and the Caesars while also gazing forward toward eternity (Goia, 2013 para. 8).

Yet not all of the resistance to Catholic writing is based on the sins of Catholic past. Often it is precisely an outlook and philosophy that marginalises Catholic works of fiction. Despite their artistry, wit, the message is fundamentally essentialist in a world of constructionism. "O'Connor saw her special problem as a writer to be rooted in the fact that the age speciously believed in its own capacity for achieving wholeness exclusive of the divine. A situation she found truly grotesque" (John Desmond *Risen Sons* quoted in Srigley, 2004: 60).

Unlike in past eras, contemporary Catholic writers often find themselves in an environment hostile to their religion, and consequently artistic and thematic considerations are side lined once they identify themselves as Catholic. Goia exposes the decline of a Catholic literary culture as follows:

> First, many important writers publicly identified themselves as faithful Catholics. Second, the cultural establishment accepted Catholicism as a possible and permissible artistic identity. Third, there was a dynamic and vital Catholic literary and intellectual tradition visibly at work in the culture. Fourth and finally, there was a critical and academic milieu that actively read, discussed, and supported the best Catholic writing. Today not one of those four observations remains true (Goia, 2013: para. 22).

In these modern times, despite a society supposedly committed to tolerance, Catholic writers are often viewed with suspicion and disdain, partially because the Church is viewed by many in academia and elsewhere to be backward and opposed to progressive views, and Catholicism is perceived as a comfort to the poor and uninstructed who are brainwashed.

Catholic writers who embrace their Catholicism, such as Flannery O'Connor and Juan Manuel de Prada, are sometimes not recognised for their literary talents because of an unfortunate anti-Catholic bias. As O'Connor has pointed out, the important thing about a Catholic novelist is that he or she be a novelist and a good one.

Proclaiming themselves Catholic writers may have the opposite effect of what was intended: instead of spreading a message of hope in a world of despair, their identifying title may chase away many from reading what is very good Catholic literature. And it is a pity because Catholic Novels matter.

Bibliography

Acín, Ramón (2003). Dos anotaciones al margen: Modernidad y valor de la mirada en *Coños* de J.M. de Prada. In José Manuel López de Abiada, Augusta López Bernasocchi (Eds.), *Juan Manuel de Prada: De héroes y tempestades*. Madrid: Editorial Verbum, pp. 11-24.

Bakhtin, Mikhail (1984). *Rabelais and His World*. Translated by Helene Iswolsky. Bloomington, IN: Indiana University Press.

Desmond, John (1987). *Risen Sons: Flannery O'Connor's Vision of History*. Athens, GA: University of Georgia Press.

Elie, Paul (2001). "The Last Catholic Writer in America?" edited by John Wilson, in *Books and Culture*, November/December.

Gentry, Marshall B. (1986). *Flannery O'Connor's Religion of the Grotesque*. Jackson, MS: University Press of Mississippi.

Gleeson-White, Sarah (2001). "Revisiting the Southern Grotesque: Mikhail Bakhtin and the Case of Carson McCullers," in *The Southern Literary Journal*, 33, 2: 108-123.

Goia, Dana (2013). "The Catholic Writer Today," in *First Things*. http://www.firstthings.com/article/2013/12/the-catholic-writer-today. Accessed 13 August 2017.

Hedin, Josephine (1970). *The World of Flannery O'Connor*. Bloomington, IN: Indiana University Press.

Muller, Gilbert H. (1972). *Nightmares and Visions. Flannery O'Connor and the Catholic Grotesque*. Athens, GA: University of Georgia Press.

O'Brien Steinfels, Margaret (2004). *American Catholics, American Culture: Tradition and Resistance*. New York, NY: Sheed & Ward.

O'Connor, Flannery (1969). *Mystery and Manners*. New York, NY: Farrar, Straus and Giroux.

--- (2003). *Spiritual Writings*. Maryknoll, NY: Orbis.

--- (1957). "The Church and the Fiction Writer," in *America*, March 30: n.p. https://www.americamagazine.org/issue/100/church-and-fiction-writer. Accessed 21st December, 2018.

--- (1952). *Wise Blood*. San Diego, CA: Harcourt.

Pouchet, Anne-Marie (2006). "¿Un escritor católico? Entrevista a Juan Manuel de Prada," in *España contemporánea*, XIX, 1: 81-98.

Prada, Juan Manuel de (2007). *El séptimo velo*. Barcelona: Seix Barral.

--- (2003). *La vida invisible*. Madrid: Espasa Calpe.

--- (1996). *Las máscaras del héroe*. Madrid: Valdemar.

--- (2012). *Me Hallará La Muerte*. Madrid: Ediciones Destino.

Ripatrazone, Nicholas (2013). *The Fine Delight: Postconciliar Catholic Literature*. Eugene, OR: Wipf and Stock Publishers.

Sayers, Valerie (2004). "Being a Writer, Being Catholic. Sometimes the Twain Can Meet," in *Commonweal*, 2001-05-94.

Sonnenfeld, Albert (1982). *Crossroads: Essays on the Catholic Novelists*. York, SC: French Literature Publications Company.

Srigley, Susan (2004). *Flannery O'Connor's Sacramental Art*. Notre Dame, IN: University of Notre Dame Press.

The Holy Bible, New International Version (1984). Grand Rapids, MI: Zondervan House.

"Andalusia on the Liffey":
Sacred Monstrosity in O'Connor and Joyce

Michael Kirwan, S.J.

I. Introduction

Flannery O'Connor writes that 'the devil accomplishes a good deal of groundwork that seems to be necessary before grace is effective'.[1] In the light of this statement, I propose to read O'Connor alongside James Joyce; both Catholic authors, with explicit recourse to a Thomist aesthetic and to the Ignatian spiritual tradition. I will read them through the mediation of the French cultural theorist René Girard, a committed Catholic, whose work is best regarded as a theologically-inflected cultural anthropology.

O'Connor and Joyce each excelled as short-story writers, whose sacramental imagination produced 'epiphanies' of grace and revelation in, respectively, *A Good Man is Hard to Find* (1955) and *Dubliners* (1914). And yet they diverge, strikingly. O'Connor embraced, as essential to her fiction, her geographical and cultural context, and also her Catholic faith, in which 'dogma safeguarded mystery'. Joyce's life and work, on the other hand, are presented as a luciferian gesture of refusal of, and exile from, 'home, fatherland and church' —the "nets" which restrain the artist's free flight. We should certainly heed the judgement of Geert Lernout

---

1. Flannery O'Connor, from 'In The Devils Territory'; O'Connor, 1961 [1957]: 117.

(2010), that it may not in fact be helpful to describe Joyce as a 'Catholic' writer, insofar as his essential stance is adversarial to the Church and the Catholic faith. Joyce's fiction is anchored, not in Christianity, but in modernist myth-making— of Ulysses, of course, but also the myth of Daedalus: 'Old father, old artificer, stand me now and ever in good stead' (Joyce, 2015: 385).

This is not to deny the vital significance of Catholic symbolism and doctrine in Joyce's writing. Valentine Cunningham takes up the description of supersaturation (used by Cranley in *A Portrait of the Artist*) to suggest 'a severely overdone baptism... Joyce's texts come soaked in religion, supersaturated indeed in the specifically Christian, the Roman Catholic, the Irish Roman Catholic' (Cunningham, 2007: 499).

A comparison of O'Connor and Joyce will lead us to ask whether James Joyce's spiritual rebellion is best understood, not as outright denial, but as a form of negative theology— or even, as O'Connor would have it, the demonic 'groundwork' which needs to be done 'before grace can be effective'. O'Connor shockingly confronts and explores radical evil in its naked form, so to speak. 'Evil', in Joyce's stories, is rather the result of suffocating social or historical constraints. In the opening story of *Dubliners*, the young narrator declares that the word "paralysis" 'sounded to me like the name of some maleficent and sinful being. It filled me with fear, and yet I longed to be nearer to it and to look upon its deadly work' (Joyce, 2015: 3).

O'Connor is one of the most striking and yet enigmatic of twentieth-century Catholic writers. The spiritual conflicts she so graphically —'grotesquely'— depicts require us to make a decision about her 'shock and awe' approach. For her devoted aficionados, the violence is justified because its depiction is very closely at the service of O'Connor's moral and spiritual imagination. For her critics, this higher purpose is not described sufficiently or convincingly. There is, ultimately, no significant distinction between her version of 'Southern Gothic' and the nihilistic bloodbaths of, for example, Quentin Tarantino (who has indeed acknowledged O'Connor's influence).

As for the labels routinely applied to O'Connor— 'grotesque', 'gothic'; these possibly tell us less about her fiction, than about our own allergy to her society and its times. Would a writer from New York be similarly described? And yet, the 'grotesque' elements of her 'Gothic' writing, cruel yet darkly humorous, have affinities with other imaginative styles: the surrealist Spanish imagination, for example, or, as I hope to indicate in this chapter, with Joyce's modernist experiment.

O'Connor's fiction is neither pretty nor consoling. Her stories deal head-on with religious fanaticism (*Wise Blood*, 'The River'), with racism and xenophobia ('The Artificial Nigger', 'The Displaced Person'), with cynical misogyny ('Good Country People'). Her short story, 'A Good Man is Hard to Find', depicts the execution of a family, shot dead in cold blood by an escaped criminal who rejoices in the nickname of "the Misfit". As noted, Quentin Tarantino has cited O'Connor as an influence. Perhaps this clarifies our question: what distinguishes the horrific scenarios of O'Connor's fiction from the gratuitous and seemingly nihilistic violence of Tarantino's films? The answer, to repeat, must surely be the religious and moral purpose which underpins her attempt to engage the attention of the 'wingless chickens'— a readership, incapable of relating to a transcendent dimension.

Personally, I would be interested in arguing the case with regard to Tarantino, as to whether his films are indeed irredeemably nihilistic. *Pulp Fiction* contains the narrative of the 'conversion' of Jules (played by Samuel L. Jackson), who resolves to give up the life of an L.A. gangster, and to 'walk the earth' in search of God's plan for him— much to the incredulous disgust of Vincent (played by John Travolta). The restaurant hold-up scene, in which Jules resolves to 'try to be the shepherd', and therefore refrain from shooting his way out of the final Mexican stand-off, is richly, darkly comic. But does this preclude any serious consideration of its religious content?

The resonances with the contemporary master of cinematic violence, much of it racially inflected, is uncomfortably topical. Tarantino's 2016 film *Hateful Eight* —even by his standards a cynical, blood-splattered affair— is set in the aftermath of the American Civil War, and seethes with racial toxicity. Flannery O'Connor's stories depict vulnerable and fearful characters and their communities, under conditions of economic precariousness, bitter racial tension, and febrile religiosity. O'Connor's world continues to assert its presence, in the thirty per cent approval ratings for an 'outsider' President, who speaks for them in their resentful alienation. The incomprehension of liberal and mainstream politicians towards this demographic —for "grotesque" read "deplorable"— marks the chasm which has gaped open in the American body politic.

Here we will draw, naturally enough, on the insights of René Girard, the French-American cultural theorist who uncovered precise and disturbing links between human violence and sacred transcendence. He has probed into our readiness to make our lynchings and persecutions acceptable, by re-describing them as sacrifices. With Girard as an intermediary, I propose an instructive contrast of O'Connor with James Joyce. O'Connor, as we have noted, was rooted in her Southern geographical and cultural context, embracing a Catholic faith in which 'dogma safeguarded mystery'. Joyce's life and work, on the other hand, are a luciferian gesture of refusal, exile, and conscious self-damnation. Throughout, dogma is present almost exclusively as parody or blasphemy. Joyce's protagonist in *A Portrait of the Artist as a Young Man*, Stephen Dedalus, proudly echoes Satan's declaration: 'I will not serve that in which I no longer believe' (Joyce, 2015: 380).

II. Girard: a 'world off-balance'

What light does René Girard shed on these two apparently divergent writers? In his first book on selected European novelists (1961), Girard distinguishes between 'romantic' and 'novelistic' fiction. Does a writer merely *depict* the process of conflictive desire and its corrosion of human relationships, causing them to descend into violence? Or does he or she *reveal* the hidden meaning of this vortex, thereby offering a possible escape, a 'resurrection from the underground'?

Only the second of these is truly effective in getting to the heart of human dysfunction, and pointing to the grace which alone overcomes it. The authors who manage to achieve this insight form the 'canon' of Girard's literary criticism: primarily the five novelists considered in *Deceit, Desire and the Novel* (Cervantes, Flaubert, Proust, Stendhal and Dostoyevsky), and above all Shakespeare, whose drama Girard explored in a collection of essays entitled *A Theatre of Envy: William Shakespeare* (1991). Not all of these authors are explicitly religious, but Girard maintains that each undergoes a personal transformation which is parallel to a religious conversion: and that in each case this conversion becomes a structuring principle of their most important writing.

For Girard, therefore, the adjective 'novelistic' (romanesque) denotes a higher level of literary insight than is to be found in romantic (romantique) literature. The first is a source of truth; the second, because it describes and depicts false imaginings about the autonomy of human nature, rather than exposing them, is mendacious. 'Romantic' writing perpetuates the 'Romantic Lie'— hence the title of Girard's book in its French original: Mensonge romantique et vérité romanesque.

> Great novels always spring from an obsession that has been transcended. The hero sees himself in the rival he loathes; he renounces the "differences" suggested by hatred. He learns, at the expense of his pride, the existence of the psychological circle. The novelists' self-examination merges with the morbid attention he pays to his mediator. All the powers of a mind freed of its contradictions erupt in one creative impulse. This victory over desire is extremely painful. Proust tells us that we must forego the fervent dialogue endlessly carried on by each of at the superficial levels of our being. One must "give up one's dearest illusions." The novelist's art is a phenomenological *epoche*. But the only authentic *epoche* is never

mentioned by modern philosophers; it is always victory over desire, victory over Promethean pride (Girard, 1961: 300).

The next stage in Girard's theory is his description of what happens when the subject, falsely convinced of its own abiding autonomy, asserts its identity in interaction with others. Such an endeavour, grounded as it is on vacuity, is destined to end badly. The 'stable' desiring self turns out to be insecure and volatile. Girard sees his chosen authors as obsessed with 'violence as a subtle eroder of the differential it seeks to inflate' (an obsession he shares). The closer two antagonists are to one another, the more they need to insist upon their distinctiveness. Their convergence is a recipe, not for mutual peace and co-existence, but for an escalation of conflict.

In one sense René Girard offers a sustained reflection on two scenarios or configurations of violence: firstly, the 'Master-Slave' dialectic, put forward in its classic form by Hegel, according to whom the most fundamental life-struggle is a struggle for 'recognition' between two subjects;[2] secondly, the phenomenon of 'scapegoating', by which the mutual antagonisms of a group are channelled onto a vulnerable individual or subgroup, whose victimization acts as a catharsis and stabilizes the social order once again. Both forms of violence are present in the chilling conclusion to Joyce's story 'Counterparts', in which Farringdon, a clerk, comes home after a bad day at work, where he has had a dreadful altercation with his bullying boss. His attempt to get drunk after work has left him penniless and furiously discontented: his wife, 'a little sharp-faced woman who bullied her husband when he was sober and was bullied by him when he was drunk' (Joyce, 2015: 74) has gone out to church, so he vents his fury upon his little boy:

…"Take that, you little whelp!"

---

2. Like many French intellectuals of the mid-twentieth century, Girard was very impressed with Alexandre Kojève's famous lectures on Hegel's *Phenomenology of Spirit*, delivered in Paris between 1933 and 1939.

> The boy uttered a squeal of pain as the stick cut his thigh. He clasped his hand together in the air and his voice shook with fright. "O, pa!" he cried. "Don't beat me, pa! And I'll ... I'll say a *Hail Mary* for you ... I'll say a *Hail Mary* for you, pa, if you don't beat me ... I'll say a *Hail Mary*. ..." (*ibid*)

The Master-Slave trope, understood here as the desperate struggle of each of the combatants to assert or reassert difference (hierarchy), as a fundamental drive of their identity, is powerfully present in O'Connor's 'Everything That Rises Must Converge'. What Girard calls the 'crisis of degree' —i.e. the crisis that ensues when degree or difference is eroded— is comically rendered when the woman, referred to throughout as 'Julian's mother', is travelling on a bus with her truculent son. Suddenly she is confronted by a black woman, wearing an identical hat (as it happens, of hideous design). Given her deeply entrenched paternalistic racism, the scene is excruciating. The situation deteriorates catastrophically, however, when she gushes over the black woman's 'cute' little boy, and tries to give him a nickel. Such largesse, of course, is intended to reassert her social and racial superiority. The furious reaction of the boy's mother is the inevitable refusal of such a power play:

> The huge woman turned and for a moment stood, her shoulders lifted and her face frozen with frustrated rage, and stared at Julian's mother. Then all at once she seemed to explode like a piece of machinery that had been given one ounce of pressure too much. Julian saw the black fist swing out with the red pocketbook. He shut his eyes and cringed as he heard the woman shout, "He don't take nobody's pennies!" When he opened his eyes the woman was disappearing down the street with the little boy staring wide-eyed over her shoulder. Julian's mother was sitting on the sidewalk ... her legs were stretched out in front of her and her hat was on her lap (O'Connor, 1990: 418).

The double-bind of the situation, of course, is that the black woman must resort to violence in order to affirm her non-inferiority (that is, her equality). She is trying to claim both difference and equality at the same time; but she can do so only by an act of physical violence, mirroring the real but non-physical violence of Julian's mother. They are therefore violent 'doubles' —and not by virtue of the identical hats.

The 'Master-Slave' dialectic has become a tool of therapeutic and political analysis— for example, in the theory of post-colonialism[3]— but for Girard, the problem is ultimately a metaphysical one. In Parker's Back, Parker's 'devotional' (or idolatrous?) tattoo of an icon of Jesus, to which his wife reacts hysterically, makes clear that we are in a realm beyond straightforward socio-political explanation. "The Misfit" in 'A Good Man is Hard to Find', declares to the grandmother, just before he shoots her, that 'Jesus thrown everything off balance'. He blames God for the disruptions in his life which have turned him into a murderer. Is this merely the self-rationalization of a sick killer, or does he utter some prophetic truth? O'Connor's assertion, quoted above, that 'the devil accomplishes a good deal of groundwork that seems to be necessary before grace is effective', is a plausible evocation of a kind of negative theology: she posits God as absence, in the cruelty and hopelessness of her narratives, where only the humiliation of proud individuals can open up the possibility of redemption.

By contrast, it was suggested above that 'evil' in Joyce's fiction operates, not as a radical condition, but as the result of suffocating social or historical constraints. Though the word 'paralysis': '…sounded to me like the name of some maleficient and sinful being,' (Joyce, 2015: 3), its 'deadly work' in Dubliners and in Joyce's other work does not call especially for any metaphysical investigation. On the contrary, it is a force that can be evaded —by fleeing to Paris, for example. At first glance, O'Connor is attempting, one might say, a more fundamental examination of the human situation. She and Joyce operate —perhaps— on different levels of theological intensity: René Girard's distinction again, between the 'romantic' writer, who describes and decries the suffocating external conditions which stifle the human spirit, and the 'novelistic' writer, who

---

3. See the classic works of Franz Fanon, *The Wretched of the Earth* (1961), and *Black Skin White Mask* (1952).

engages on a deeper anthropological (or indeed theological-anthropological) level.

From the examples we have discussed, both O'Connor and Joyce qualify for inclusion in Girard's 'canon': each is 'obsessed with violence as the subtle eroder of the differential it seeks to inflate'. Curiously, however, there has not been a great deal of Girardian scholarship on Flannery O'Connor, even though she and Girard would appear to have more in common, in terms of their shared ethical and faith commitments. By contrast, Girard has engaged with Joyce, devoting an important chapter of *A Theatre of Envy* to a mimetic reading of the lecture on Hamlet, given by Stephen Dedalus in the National Library.[4] This curious lecture, together with its discussion, is an extravagant speculation on whether Shakespeare 'is really' Hamlet senior or Hamlet junior. Its significance lies in how we are to situate the themes of fraternal betrayal, adultery and usurpation which are to be found throughout Shakespeare's work (and which qualify Shakespeare as one of Girard's 'obsessive' writers).

Girard's point with reference to Joyce is that the Irish writer, in the Hamlet lecture, reveals himself and Shakespeare to be on the same mimetic track. The speculation about Shakespeare's anguished erotic life gives us a key to understanding Bloom's own 'French triangle' with his wife Molly and her lover, 'Blazes' Boylan. More generally, it recapitulates the mutual search of father and son which is such an important structuring principle of *Ulysses*. Important theological resonances are never far away. The doctrine of the Trinity, which is the Christian account of reconciliation between father and son, is both expounded and lampooned in *Ulysses*. A strictly orthodox account would insist on the formal distinctions between the three Persons of the godhead, but the shift of the centre of gravity in Joyce's fiction, from rebellious son to loving and

---

4. The lecture occurs in the 'Scylla and Charybdis' chapter of Ulysses, and is analyzed by Girard in an essay entitled 'Do you believe your own theory?'; see also Johnsen (2003), for a Girardian reading of Joyce and other modernist writers.

saving father, requires such a blurring of the categories. Father and son are ultimately reconciled, because Joyce 'is' both.

III. 'Strategies of Grace'

Girard's distinction between romantic and novelistic fiction is fruitful, though in this instance I would distrust its neatness, and suggest that it is inadequate, if it is used to imply in Joyce a lack of ultimate seriousness. We are not, in other words, to read too much of Joyce into his 'satanic' hero, Stephen Dedalus. Alongside and throughout the parody and blasphemy, Joyce deploys an acute theological sensitivity.

Stephen is the self-dramatized spirit of denial: '—You behold in me, Stephen said with grim displeasure, a horrible example of free thought' (Joyce, 2015: 403). His refusal to pray before his mother on her death-bed is given pointed focus in Ulysses; more generally, Stephen's posturing looks not unlike the atheist rebellion of Hazel Motes in Wise Blood. In each case, the peculiarity of their dress compromises the rebellious posture: Motes is persistently mistaken for a preacher because of his hat, while Stephen's mourning suit, as Mulligan sarcastically points out, betrays the limits of his nonconformism. Hazel Motes wishes to establish 'the Church without Christ', while Stephen, seeking a definitive emancipation from the Church, is nevertheless dramatized as a martyr and Christ-figure, as well as a rebel.

In any case, the 'cursed Jesuit strain' is at work in him, even if it has been injected 'the wrong way'. Harold Levin summarizes some of the religious and theological influences which inflected Joyce's spiritual rebellion. He mentions the 'stigmata of aesthetic martyrdom', as Joyce felt himself bound 'to the cross of his own cruel fiction' (1946: 1). The modulation from flight to creator, from fledgling son to the father-image, is a modulation in Joyce's own attitudes. 'Language, religion, and nationality' were the nets impeding the flight of the young artist; but the artist in maturity, now sure of his powers, created his monumental achievement out of the same substances, of nationality, religion, and language. Joyce's imaginative constructions are 'grounded on the rock of his buried religious experience':

> His literary technique is richly colored by ecclesiastical symbolism; a series of notes on the liturgy of Holy Week, for example, accompanies the manuscript of Stephen Hero. There too he explains his conception of art as an 'epiphany,' a sudden illumination if not a divine revelation, a slight but definite insight into other lives, a fragmentary clue to the meaning of life as a whole. ...God is manifest, Stephen now believes, as 'a noise in the street' (Levin, 1946: 3).

Valentine Cunningham takes his cue from the observation of Cranley, Stephen's friend and confidante in *Portrait*, that Stephen's mind is supersaturated with the religion he is rejecting:

> Supersaturation: the excessive adding of an element to a liquid, going further than is strictly necessary, a severely overdone baptism. Joyce's texts come soaked in religion, supersaturated indeed in the specifically Christian, the Roman Catholic, the Irish Roman Catholic— an awesomeness of detailing, all the more obsessive as these writings' bulk expanded in an almost overwhelming exuberance of Catholicized baroque (Cunningham, 2007: 499).

Cunningham makes much of Joyce's rebellion in the form of sexual transgression and accompanying blasphemies (recorded extensively in *Portrait of the Artist* and *Ulysses*). More pertinent, I suggest, is his acknowledgement of the 'Hamlet' discussion and its theological implications. Stephen's wrestling with the problematic of father and son, here and elsewhere, is modelled on classical heresies regarding the persons of the Trinity. For example, the third century heretic Sabellius is singled out, for his belief that there was no essential difference between Father and Son. The father's usurpation by the son, and the metamorphosis by which they change places —Dedalus the father falling and drowning, son Icarus flying on— is the mythological heart of Joyce's fiction.

O'Connor's is of course a more positive and orthodox religious view; which does not mean that she always manages to render this effectively or convincingly (i.e. without overt preaching). This can be shown by comparing the climactic passage of O'Connor's 'The Artificial Nigger', and the final two stories from *Dubliners*, 'Grace' and 'The Dead'. In O'Connor's story, the relationship between an elderly man, Mr. Head, and his grandson, Nelson, has undergone a traumatic rupture. These country people are visiting the city: Mr. Head is trying to cure the grandson of his curiosity about urban life (and in the process to reinforce in him a 'poor white' sense of racial superiority). But they have become hopelessly lost. In an altercation with some of the locals, Mr. Head panics, and ends up denying all knowledge of the boy. This shocking incident shatters their relationship. They carry on walking through the strange city, shocked into silent estrangement, until they happen upon a garden ornament, a plaster representation of a smiling black man. This is the 'artificial nigger' of the story's title. Part of its face has been chipped away, and instead of grinning cheerfully, it is a face of agony. The vision mysteriously transfixes them both, and becomes an epiphany of reconciliation.

> The two of them stood there with their necks forward at almost the same angle and they shoulders curved in almost exactly the same way and their hands trembling identically in their pockets. Mr. Head looked like an ancient child and Nelson like a miniature old man. They stood gazing at the artificial Negro as if they were faced with some great mystery, some monument to another's victory that brought them together in their common defeat. They could both feel it dissolving their differences like an action of mercy. Mr. Head had never known before what mercy felt like because he had been to God to deserve any, but he felt he knew now (O'Connor, 1990: 268-9).

Importantly, this reconciliation nevertheless requires that the hierarchy be quietly restored: the elder recognizes the grandson's continued need for reassurance and guidance, even if his bitter resentment at being betrayed has been overcome.

The episode is striking, though theologically hardly understated. The grandfather's denial of the child in front of an angry group of bystanders, and the unexpected reconciling 'great mystery' of the plaster image of the black servant, signposts O'Connor's Christian intention. It is spelt out directly when we are told of Mr. Head's new religious understanding, of the relation between agony and mercy, as he judges himself 'with the thoroughness of God'. And yet, 'since God loved in proportion as He forgave, he felt ready at that instant to enter Paradise' (O'Connor, 1990: 269-70).

Compare this with the treatment of grace in the final two stories of *Dubliners*. In the story entitled 'Grace', Joyce depicts a parody of religious transcendence, in which a group of respectable middle-class Dublin men attend a retreat for businessmen. The Jesuit preacher offers them a vision of "salvation" which mirrors their own respectability: it is a matter of honest book-keeping, of keeping spiritual accounts, and humbly asking for forgiveness when the figures do not tally. Joyce is gentle in his satire, but what is on offer is the cheap grace of 'bourgeois Christianity', rather than a way out of the paralysis.

The finest and best-known story of the collection, 'The Dead', concludes with the famous description of snow, falling upon the living and dead— and upon the grave of Michael Furey, the childhood sweetheart who many years later still obsesses Greta, to the shocked anguish of her husband Gabriel. This moment of excruciating separation is comparable to the distance that opens up between Mr. Head and his grandson. It is similarly resolved, for Gabriel, by an intimation of reconciling love:

> Generous tears filled Gabriel's eyes. He had never felt like that himself towards any woman, but he knew that such a feeling must be love. The tears gathered more thickly in his eyes and in the partial darkness he imagined he saw the form of a young man standing under a dripping tree. Other forms were near. His soul had approached that region where dwell the vast hosts of the dead. He was conscious of, but could not apprehend, their wayward and flickering existence. His

own identify was fading out into a grey impalpable world: the solid world itself, which these dead had one time reared and lived in, was dissolving and dwindling (Joyce, 2015: 174).

The dissolution is more Shakespearean than directly Christian; no more does the image of the snow, which 'was general all over Ireland', promise transcendence or resurrection— and yet Christ is cited: in the 'dripping tree' under which the young man stands, in the 'crooked crosses and headstones, on the spears of the little gate, on the barren thorns'.[5] Ironically, this is a more authentic rendition of 'grace' than the bourgeois consolation preached to the retreatants in the preceding story— which has 'Grace' as its title.

On the evidence of the two examples cited here —'The Artificial Nigger' and 'The Dead'— O'Connor appears to be the most vulnerable to the charge of didacticism. Peter Hawkins notes this occasional lapse in O'Connor, as well as in Walker Percy and Iris Murdoch: a tendency to omniscient narrator and contrivance of 'predestined' plot (2004: 11). And yet all three writers are aware of the need for a 'strategy' which will enable each to communicate metaphysical truths to an uncomprehending readership. O'Connor writes dismissively of a generation of readers whose moral sense has been bred out of them; a generation of 'wingless chickens', unable to name accurately the things of God. All three writers are trying to conduct transactions with defaced or devalued coinage. For Hawkins, what unites the fictional writing of all three is the reworking of a basic pattern of conversion:

> a person forced by extraordinary circumstances to transcend the self-centred demands of the ego, who comes to see another person as real and full and who can finally see that person without the distortions

---

5. The image of snow falling on 'the lonely churchyard', where Michael Furey is buried, in fact takes us back to Tarantino: the opening shot of *The Hateful Eight* is a snow-covered crucifix in a graveyard. This is the only religious reference in the entire film: does its incongruent transcendence subtlety undermine the movie's cynical narrative of post Civil-War score-settling; or merely reinforce it?

of fantasy or ulterior motive; who can, that is, love someone else (Hawkins, 2004: 3).

The definition matches almost exactly the principle of conversion identified by Girard in Deceit, Desire and the Novel, though for Girard the 'circumstances' which catalyze the conversion are not 'extraordinary', rather they are the quotidian condition and tensions of mimetic interaction.

With regard to Joyce, Stephen's grandiloquent aim of 'forging the uncreated conscience of my race' (Joyce 2005: 385) echoes O'Connor's lament for the truncated moral sensitivity of her readership. Similarly, the pattern of conversion outlined above serves as a useful precis of the drama of *Ulysses*, the mutual discovery of father and son as Bloom and Stephen find their way to one another; perhaps especially in the case of the prodigal Stephen, of whom we are told early in the novel: 'Pain, that was not yet the pain of love, fretted his heart' (Joyce 2015: 389).

IV. Conclusion

I have drawn on Girard's mimetic theory, and its linkage of 'the sacred' and violence, to shed light on aspects of O'Connor and Joyce, with a view to illuminating both contrasts and convergence. My initial thought was that Joyce presents a kind of 'cultural criticism', while O'Connor's is a more fundamental critique of the human condition. Such a view would correspond to René Girard's distinction between 'romantic' and 'novelistic' fiction, a distinction which echoes Marx's famous dismissal of philosophers, who have only described the world, while the real challenge is to change it. In this way, Girard differentiates between literature which merely describes the mechanism of dysfunctional desire, and literature which exposes it and reveals the grace by which it can be overcome.

On further reflection, this contrast —which would credit O'Connor with a more 'serious' moral purpose than Joyce, because more religious or metaphysical— looks less tenable. It would be wrong to consider Joyce's rejection of the Church and the Catholic faith as anything but definitive; and yet Joyce was too good a theologian not to appreciate that any act of rebellion against God is self-defeating. Not every commentator is as strident as Lernout in stressing Joyce's break with religious faith: according to Harry Levin, for example, 'the problem of *Ulysses* is the age-old attempt to put Christian precept into practice'; (Levin 1946: 3) He regards *Ulysses* and *Finnegans Wake* as both eucharistic parody *and* celebration, in which 'the writer, expatriate and excommunicate, reasserts his sense of community and communion.' (*ibid*) If this judgement goes too far in the other direction from Lernout, at least it indicates that the issue of Joyce's religiosity is not at all clear-cut.

The exile's reassertion of community returns us to the question raised at the beginning of this essay, about O'Connor's 'Southern Gothic' vision and its 'translatability'. Is it so closely tied to its post-war Georgian setting —put bluntly, are her characters and situations so weird— that it becomes less accessible to a general readership? As noted above, the contemporary political tensions within the United States might cause us to look with fresh eyes at Flannery O'Connor. She herself caused disquiet, because of her ambiguous loyalty to her Southern white culture, and therefore to its racial limitations. Notable here is her refusal to meet James Baldwin, the writer and Civil Rights activist, in Georgia, because '[i]t would cause the greatest trouble and disturbance and disunion .... I observe the traditions of the society I feed on— it's only fair'[6].

It is hard not to read this as an indication of timidity and bad faith; but it is the utterance of a theological rather than sociological thinker. O'Connor's own fiction, thankfully, is more creative and expansive in exploring both the challenge and the possibility of transformation, including racial relations. But she writes from 'within the fray': not as a liberal, deploring the backwardness of southern culture, but as its child and product. And as a convinced Christian, she knows that the only

---

6. Flannery O'Connor, in a letter to Maryat Lee (O'Connor, 1979: 329).

true 'Other' to humanity is God, and that all other lines of demarcation are 'artificial'. In Christ, there is neither Greek not Jew, slave nor free.

O'Connor's acquiescence in the 'traditions of the society I feed on' could not be in starker contrast to the intentions of the cosmopolitan Joyce, who distances himself from his homeland and its religious and cultural mores, in order to 'forge the uncreated conscience of my race'. It is a violent uncoupling, though the instances of physical violence are few: the 'proto-martyr' Stephen is beaten by a priest and by school colleagues in *A Portrait*, and by drunken soldiers in *Ulysses*; and we have noted the thrashing of the young child by his father in 'Counterparts'. There is plenty of shocking material in Joyce's work, as the history of its censorship shows, but acts of physical violence are not among the offending matter. In Bloom there is, aside from the transgressive parodies and blasphemies, a 'Christic' readiness to absorb aggression and insults, rather than vent suffering on others. Stephen is determined not to suffer the fate of other Irish heroes betrayed and destroyed by the mob (Parnell is the great figure here, but the fate of Oscar Wilde had a considerable impact on Joyce). But he too, has a horror of violence and cannot retain vengeful feelings for long. This passivity is perhaps one of the few things Bloom and Stephen have in common; it can surely be understood as the force which draws them together across the Dublin landscape, battle-weary, to their mutual homecoming.

And if as Stephen declares in his Shakespeare lecture, reconciliation presumes a sundering, the sundering itself is for the sake of reconciliation. The pattern of exitus et reditus is thoroughly theological, and the fleeting but 'epiphanic' encounter of Bloom and Stephen echoes other such instances of 'all but union'. Levin comments on the significance of such encounters for Joyce's 'strategy of grace':

> By dwelling upon that interrupted nuance, that unconsummated moment, that unrealized possibility, Joyce renews our apprehension of reality, strengthens our sympathy with our fellow creatures, and leaves us in awe before the mystery of created things (Levin, 1946: 5)

Bibliography

Attridge, Derek (2004). *The Cambridge Companion to James Joyce* [2nd edition]. Cambridge: Cambridge University Press.

Cunningham, Valentine (2007). James Joyce. In Andrew W. Haas, David Jasper and Elisabeth Jay (Eds.), *The Oxford Handbook of English Literature and Theology*. Oxford: Oxford University Press, pp. 499-522.

Girard, René (1961). *Deceit, Desire and the Novel: Self and Other in Literary Structure*. Baltimore, MD: Johns Hopkins University Press.

Hawkins, Peter S. (2004). *Strategies of Grace: Flannery O'Connor, Walker Percy and Iris Murdoch*. New York, NY: Seabury Classics.

Johnsen, William A. (2003). *Violence and Modernism: Ibsen, Joyce, and Woolf*. Gainsville, FL: University Press of Florida.

Joyce, James (2015). *The Dover Reader* [Selected Works]. Mineaola, NY: Dover Publications.

--- (2000). *Occasional, Critical and Political Writing*. Oxford World's Classics. Oxford: Oxford University Press.

Lernout, Geert (2010). *Help My Unbelief: James Joyce and Religion*. New York, NY: Continuum.

Levin, Harry (1946). 'James Joyce', *The Atlantic Monthly Online*, December 1946, https://www.theatlantic.com/past/docs/issues/95sep/links/levi.htm. Accesed 10th December, 2018.

O'Connor, Flannery (1961 [1957]), *Mystery and Manners: Occasional Prose*. New York, NY: Farrar, Straus and Giroux.

--- (1979). *The Habit of Being. Letters of Flannery O'Connor*, edited by Sally Fitzgerald. New York, NY: Farrar, Straus and Giroux.

--- (2008). *Wise Blood*. London: Faber and Faber.

--- (1990). *Complete Stories*. London: Faber and Faber.

Death's Personal Call: The Aesthetics of Catholic Eschatology in Flannery O'Connor's "A Good Man is Hard to Find" and Muriel Spark's *Memento Mori*

Anabel Altemir-Giral
Ismael Ibáñez-Rosales

Flannery O'Connor (1925-1964) and Muriel Spark (1918-2006) never met, but they admired each other's work. In several letters, O'Connor refers to her reading of Spark's novels, including "a very lively one called *Memento Mori*" that she was reading in 1959 when she wrote to Maryat Lee (O'Connor, 1979: 331). Elsewhere, replying to Jane McKane in 1963, O'Connor remarked "I've got all of Muriel Spark" (O'Connor, 1979: 525). On 21 March 1964, writing to Father John McCown, a Catholic priest who had asked her about writers who shared their faith, she wrote: "The English are Waugh & Greene and Spark (Muriel)" (O'Connor, 1979: 570). On 15 May 1964, O'Connor thanks McKane for sending via mail "*The Girls of Slender Means*, which came at 12 o'clock noon and I finished before I went to bed. I really did like it, better than the others. Some of hers settle in the middle, but that one humps right along" (O'Connor, 1979: 577).

Muriel Spark, for her part, was frequently asked about O'Connor's works in interviews, for critics often noted affinities between her and O'Connor as Catholic writers. Kimball, for instance, states that "[Spark's] work recalls the Gothic realism of the American novelist and master of the short story Flannery O'Connor" (1993: 9). Haddox adds that "[b]oth writers avow a religious dimension in their work, both have a marked hatred for sentimentality and both are known for violence and shock" (2009: 43). Yet any comparison between the two writers reveals different critical responses to their respective writing careers. The reception of their work often provokes an asymmetry caused to a large extent by their references and statements about their faith and religious issues: "while references to Catholicism abound in Spark's novels (in this her work is far more overtly "Catholic" than O'Connor's), their significance is more obscure, lacking the portentous intrusions of the divine into everyday life that characterize O'Connor's fiction" (Haddox, 2009: 44). Keeping this in mind, one can fruitfully compare their approaches to the experience of death, for each writer employs a Catholic eschatological vision. In Muriel Spark's novel *Memento Mori* (1959) and Flannery O'Connor's short story "A Good Man is Hard to Find" (1953), one can find a sacramental imagination at work.

During an interview granted to *Jubilee Magazine*, Flannery O'Connor was asked about how her writing has been influenced by the idea that the creative action of the Christian's life is to prepare for his death in Christ. O'Connor replied, "I'm a born Catholic and death has always been brother to my imagination. I can't imagine a story that doesn't properly end in it or in its foreshadowings" (Magee, 1987: 107). Indeed, twelve of her twenty published stories end in the protagonist's death and, of her two novels, one begins with death and the other ends in it, with each featuring a murder. Death, or its foreshadowing, is the theme underlying most of O'Connor's fiction which, in Christian eschatology is the first of "the four last things to be ever remembered by a Christian —the others being Judgement, Hell and Heaven" (Spark, 1991: 1).

This quotation from the Penny Catechism is precisely one of the three epigraphs of Muriel Spark's novel *Memento Mori*. The Latin phrase means "remember that you must die" and has traditionally been used to refer to an emblem of mortality such as a skull, serving as a reminder that death awaits us all. Spark, however, replaces the skull by several voices heard over the telephone. Most of the characters in the novel are old, and many of them receive telephone calls reminding them that they must die. Although the message is always the same, the caller's identity and gender seems to vary. These calls are soon dismissed as auditory hallucinations since they are sometimes heard by those for whom they are not intended. Some receive the calls repeatedly. In the opening lines of the novel, Dame Lettie Colston receives her ninth such anonymous and macabre message. Unnerved by the calls, the old woman contacts the police, but they cannot identify the caller. Lettie's brother, Godfrey, is too preoccupied with his own problems to be sympathetic. He is exasperated by the mental deterioration his wife, Charmian, has suffered after her stroke. All members of Dame Lettie's circle end up receiving the same message. Each character responds to the telephone calls in ways that reflect their individual perspective toward death. The novel advances by narrating a series of mixed stories between the characters mentioned above and the elderly residents of a Medical Ward. The twelve occupants of the ward are collectively known as the Grannies and form, according to Page, "a kind of chorus, grotesque and pathetic, to the main action" (1990: 25). In fact, they are all united by scorn, resentment and boredom which seems to mask their awareness of impending death. Spark shows the different responses that people give when forced to face the idea of their own death. This is emphasized by the way some characters die: in a grim twist on the part of the author, those characters who do not take death seriously experience a violent death.

On receiving the messages, Dame Lettie, OBE, seventy-nine and pioneer penal reformer, like her brother Godfrey, blusters and complains: they treat it as a social nuisance and a personal affront to their social class. Thinking this a criminal act, they resort to calling the police and send a letter to the editor of the *The Times* calling for a consideration of this affront as a parliamentary "question in the House". Dame Lettie, Godfrey and nearly all of the characters who get the same sort of phone call appear as hollow figures driven by their human appetites and believe that the message of death is criminal. Because they deny the reality of death, each character becomes consumed by his or her personal obsessions to repress it from their consciousness. Lettie Colston enjoys bullying others, Godfrey lives in lust, Lisa Brooke languishes in vanity, Mannering exploits his egomania and Alec Warner, an elderly gerontologist, is dispassionate and rationalistic. Since they refuse a spiritual explanation behind the telephone calls, they deny the truth and inevitability of death and rationalize the "Hoax-caller" as "mass hysteria" (Spark, 1991: 152). By refusing to face their own mortality, each must follow their egotistical obsessions. It is as if Spark is alluding to Chesterton's words in Father Brown's "The Miracle of Moon Crescent": "You hard-shelled materialists were all balanced on the very edge of belief —of belief in almost anything" (Chesterton, 2001: 99). Yet unlike Dame Lettie and most of her set, Godfrey's wife Charmian, a former popular novelist who is near senility in the early part of the story but regains a grip of life as it progresses, is a Catholic who shows a calm acceptance of the inevitable. She reacts differently when she receives the first call:

> "Remember", he said, "you must die".
> "Oh, as to that", she said, "for the past thirty years and more I have thought of it from time to time. My memory is failing in certain respects. I am gone eighty-six. But somehow I do not forget my death, whenever that will be" (Spark, 1991: 127).

In a parallel plot that is relatively untouched by the drama of the outside world, the residents of the Maud Long Medical Ward are dealing with their own crises. No one is menaced by a mysterious caller, but by an overworked ward sister. Death on the floor is not a vague threat or an obituary in the newspaper, it is happening in a bed a few feet away. The "will-games," affairs, and intrigue of the upper-class elderly seem like amusements compared to the stark reality of life in the Maud Long Ward, where the patients live in fear of being thrown out into the streets when winter comes. In the ward, we find Jean Taylor, former servant and companion to Charmian, who followed her employer into the Catholic church long ago just to be nice, but acquired from it a spirit of resignation which stands her in good stead as she is bedridden and in constant pain because of arthritis. Together with Charmian Colston, she is the other character in the novel who attribute a spiritual significance to the telephone calls. It is Jean Taylor who most fully embodies wisdom and an understanding of the meaning of these events. Hearing of the telephone calls only from other characters who visit her in hospital, she arrives at an awareness of their significance. Early in the novel she tries in vain to explain to Dame Lettie the real nature of the calls: "Perhaps you might obey it (…) you might try to remember you must die" (Spark, 1991: 38). Later she offers the most explicit interpretation of its meaning: "In my belief (…) the author of the anonymous telephone calls is Death himself, as you might say. I don't see, Dame Lettie, what you can do about it. If you don't remember death, death reminds you to do so" (1991: 175). Jean Taylor seems to represent the authorial voice in the work. She stands for dignity and fortitude and possesses a faith undiminished by suffering. Her truth, nevertheless, is not to be believed by those around her as they are imprisoned in their own worldly personalities and lack any path to transcendence.

One of the most prominent examples in the novel is Lettie Colston, who builds a paranoid fantasy that the telephone caller is a member of a criminal gang determined to murder her. She ignores Jane Taylor's wise advice and continues searching for the culprit, unconsciously trying to punish the crime of death itself. In an ironic twist, her fantasy comes true. While she is in bed at night, two thieves break into her house. She hears in horror every movement they make. Once they have finished, they walk into her bedroom. After a while, they decide to leave the house. Just when they reach the bedroom door, one of them hesitates, goes back into her bedroom, picks up her stick and batters her to death. Dame Lettie's end is arbitrary and absurd. Spark uses her usual coarseness to stress the idea that death may come unexpectedly, and we should be prepared.

Spark's parodic use of the conventional detective story reinforces and illustrates the eschatological themes of *Memento Mori*. A popular genre of the late 19th and early 20th century that emerged at a time of rapidly declining religious faith, the detective genre takes for granted the primacy of human existence in a universe at the mercy of the laws of logic. Classic detective fiction sets itself the task of finding a solution on the assumption that all questions have answers. Indeed, humans are able to solve by themselves any mystery, helped only by the circumstantial phenomena of the material world, whether that be bloodstains, footprints, tobacco ash, profiles, and the like. Deductive reasoning and scientific methods and deductions presuppose that reason is what rules the universe. In Muriel Spark's novel, on the other hand, there is something mysterious that resists easy solution, but no solution, according to the official files. The subversive element that the author deploys makes clear the lack of values and faith in characters like Dame Lettie or Godfrey, who put death out of their minds by hiring a detective, Henry Mortimer. Significantly, Mortimer's family name comes from the Latin word for death, *mors, mortis* and is the one character, together with Jean Taylor, who accepts that Death itself is the author of the telephone calls. The "solution" is offered in a scene in chapter eleven suggesting a parody of the familiar "clearing up" scene in the classic detective story. Here the characters are assembled to hear the detective's deductions by which he has identified the criminal. Detective Mortimer explains:

> If I had my life over again I should form the habit of nightly composing myself to thoughts of death. I would practise, as it were, the remembrance of death. There is no other practice which so intensifies life. Death, when it approaches, ought not to take one by surprise. It should be part of the full expectancy of life. Without an ever-present sense of death life is insipid. You might as well live on the whites of eggs" (Spark, 1991: 150).

This view of death as "part of the full expectancy of life" suggests that the detective is, together with Jane Taylor, a spokesman for the authorial point of view. The author makes sure of that at the end of this same chapter, when we first learn that Mortimer has been receiving calls too. After answering the call, he says: "How strange (...) that mine is always a woman. Everyone else gets a man on the line to them, but mine is always this woman, gentle-spoken and respectful" (Spark, 1991: 153). This move on the part of the author, breaking the narrative levels, reassures her strategy and exposes her anagogical vision, which permeates the whole narrative. The "clearing up" scene ends with the detective's last deduction: "One factor is constant in all your reports. The words, "Remember you must die." It is, you know, an excellent thing to remember this, for it is nothing more than the truth. To remember one's death is, in short, a way of life" (Spark, 1991: 151). When Mortimer gets home again his wife tells him: "How I wish (...) you could have told them outright, "Death is the culprit". And I should like to have seen their faces" (153). The detective then answers: "The trouble with these people [is] they think that the C.I.D. are God, understanding all mysteries and all knowledge. Whereas we are only policemen" (153). In other words, Mortimer's solution does not satisfy most of the characters since a supernatural explanation is not enough for them. The author's intention is to subvert the natural and supernatural plots in her attempt to prove the importance of being aware of our own death. What we may call the worldly plot is complex, with its secrets and coincidences, humour and miseries, and its reliance on action, including crime. But the effect of this is almost parodic. The other plot, the supernatural or providential plot of the mysterious telephone calls and their significance, has an impressive simplicity. Spark invites the reader to consider our inevitable end as a real thing to have in mind, and consider our daily concerns less important, because the latter belong to this world, but our death and the way we face it may be our door to transcend our earthly limitations: what one must see as normal and simple in our own lives is that supernatural or eschatological announcement of the telephone calls.

The final words of the novel reveal this transition through a subtle parody of the classical ending and show an excellent exercise in eschatology. Jean Taylor, the first to solve the puzzle, is the last to be named at the end of a novel preoccupied with endings. Instead of the satisfactory, if not happy, endings that put an end to traditional fiction, the novel closes with a catalogue of deaths. As once critic rightly suggests, we are not offered a happy ever after but "an exchange of time for eternity" (Page, 1990: 27). The last page begins with the cold vocabulary of a death certificate (fractures of the skull, hypostatic pneumonia, uraemia, carcinoma of the cervix...) and ends with a shift to the spiritual world of Jean Taylor who spends her last days "employing her pain to magnify the Lord, and meditating sometimes confidingly upon Death, the first of the four last things to be ever remembered" (Spark, 1991: 219).

Similarly, O'Connor makes spectacular use of violent death to highlight this eschatological theme in her short story "A Good Man is Hard to Find." The story is about a family of six who, on their way to vacation from Georgia to Florida, are murdered by a trio of psychopaths when their car overturns. The Misfit, a former convict, dispassionately orders the murders of the whole family —from the baby to the grandmother— because the Grandmother foolishly recognizes and names him. The story is focalized on the Grandmother and every episode she is involved in, or responsible for, means an ironic foreshadowing of what happens later. She manipulates her family and controls every move in the story. However, her actions eventually turn out to be portents of death within O'Connor's aesthetics. Everything the Grandmother does or says anticipates their deaths. In the beginning of the story, the Grandmother tries to convince her son, Bailey, to take the family to east Tennessee for vacation instead of Florida by warning them about a newspaper article about the Misfit, an escaped convict heading toward Florida, and persuading him it might be dangerous. On the day of the trip, knowing her son would not allow it, the Grandmother hides her cat, Pitty Sing, in a basket in the car. Later, the cat will provoke the accident that leaves the family in the hands of the murderers. She also wears a dress and hat with flowers on it. This way, "[i]n case of an accident, anyone seeing her dead on the highway would know at once that she was a lady" (O'Connor, 1988: 138).

The Grandmother points out details along the highway which help the reader conceive an idea of her personality and thoughts. When she comments on a black child wearing no pants, standing in a shack doorway, and tells June Star that he is not wearing any pants because he probably does not have any, the grandmother simply paints a picture of the boy rather than try to understand the boy's situation. In the eyes of the woman, the boy belongs to the landscape instead of being someone whom she should feel connected, a fellow human being like one of her own children. The Grandmother's religious convictions are superficial, closer to a culture of good manners and self righteousness than belief. She continuously exposes traces of her shallowness and hypocrisy. In some sense, she "narrates" the story trying to usurp the author's role: in the opening scene, the first words seem directed to the readers: "Now look here, see here, read this" (O'Connor, 1988: 117). The Grandmother then tells her son Bailey what the Misfit did to some people foreshadowing their own tragic fate. O'Connor creates a lugubrious parody, but also an actual reflection, of the horrible murder of an ordinary family as it may be reflected in any local tabloid any day. Reading such macabre and morbid news is an uncanny feeling that most of us have experienced. As Frederick Asals observes:

> Surely an important part of the story's effectiveness, of the pleasure we are able to take in what, outlined, would seem merely grim tabloid material, comes from such stylization, from the ironic comedy which distances the reader from this family and particularly from its chief member, the grandmother. Nevertheless, she is "the chief member" only because the story has so presented her, priviledging her point of view over that of the others. Within the family itself, she is clearly a marginal figure. (1993: 18)

Anthony Di Renzo explains that the main objection many critics originally had to "A Good Man is Hard to Find" was precisely "O'Connor's extravagantly comic depiction of the grandmother and her family [which makes] it impossible for us to sympathize with them, even when they are being butchered by the Misfit" (1995: 141). Di Renzo refers to John Updike's opinion of O'Connor's writing as "cartooning" with "cruelty", reducing "all perspectives [to] the pintpoint tunnel of Jesus" (1983: 291). Martha Stephens argues that O'Connor's cartooning leads to an abrupt change in tone that breaks the story in two unsuccessfully from the comedy of the first half to the grim painfulness of the latter part as a sort of vengeance caused by O'Connor's doctrinal concerns simply "to wipe the grin off our faces" (1973: 17). William S. Doxey finds the story seriously flawed by a change not in tone, but in point of view, a swift he thinks is caused by O'Connor's idea of making the Misfit the agent of Grace: "The point of view shifts from the grandmother to the Misfit and the reader is suddenly left holding the bag... without a focus of narration" (1993: 96). According to her detractors, O'Connor's grotesque depiction of the family and her comic technique that ends abruptly in an outburst of violence turn these hopeless characters into human cartoons. These theories cause a perspective imbalance when critics approach O'Connor's story as a realistic fiction.

Mark Bosco seems more inspired when he creates an analogy between O'Connor's art and seventeenth-century Catholic Baroque aesthetics. Bosco draws a parallel between O'Connor's love for the grotesque and violent revelations with Caravaggio's "violent or melodramatic tableaus that bow to realism while at the same time allowing for anagogical interpretation" (2017: 183). In O'Connor's aesthetics, the human and the divine do not simply converge, they collide. For the skeptic or secular eye, however, this clash is camouflaged by the distortion of its violence that directs our attention beyond the canvas or the page. Bosco explains:

> The aesthetic strategies of the Catholic Baroque —an accessible experience of God through the lens of realism, an excessively dramatic action that leads to a superfluity of meaning, and the violent crash of a transcendent moment falling upon characters— provide a fascinating way to understand O'Connor's context within the larger artistic responses to Catholic faith. (2017: 186)

O'Connor's poetics is mainly based on the theological conviction that the reality of our world is given by a direct contact with God, that touch of Grace that helps us transcend death. Images and occasions of impending death mirroring that act of transition, a truly exercise of conversion, mark the climax of O'Connor's aesthetics. When the Grandmother convinces her son to take a detour to see a plantation, a series of shifts in the perspective of the scene highlights O'Connor's remarkable ability to combine realism, distortion, and symbolism into a unified image in perfect Baroque technique:

> They turned on to the dirt road and the car raced roughly along in a swirl of pink dust. (…) The dirt road was hilly and there were sudden washes in it and sharp curves on dangerous embankments. All at once they would be on a hill, looking down over the blue tops of trees for miles around, then the next minute, they would be in a red depression with the dust-coated trees looking down on them. (1988: 144)

First, the family look down "over the blue tops of trees for miles around," but the precise moment they drive down the place where they are meeting death, "a red depression," the trees are "looking down on them." This setting foreshadows the moment when they are taken into the woods to be killed, but also the transcendent moment when Grace will fall upon them. O'Connor, explaining the ending of her 1957 short story "A View of the Woods," comments on the meaning of the woods and trees as a recurring symbol in her fiction:

> The woods, if anything, are the Christ symbol. They walk across the water, they are bathed in a red light, and they in the end escape the old man's vision and march off over the hills. The name of the story is a view of the woods and the woods alone are pure enough to be a Christ symbol if anything is… (1979: 190)

In "A Good Man is Hard to Find," except the Grandmother, the rest of the family are taken to the woods to face death, on their way to Christ. When the Misfit orders his subordinate killers to take Bailey to the woods, the Grandmother "reached up to adjust her hat brim as if she were going to the woods with him but it came off her hand. She stood staring at it and after a second she let it fall on the ground" (O'Connor, 1988: 148). She is unable to enter the woods; she is not prepared. She just stands and stares as "[t]hey went off toward the woods and just as they reached the dark edge, Bailey turned and supporting himself against a gray naked pine trunk, he shouted, 'I'll be back in a minute, Mamma, wait on me!'"

(O'Connor, 1988: 148). The aesthetics of O'Connor's writing, her own art of fiction, is an art of anagogical vision. As one critic notes, "for O'Connor the logic of anagogy implies that the visible realities of this world only take on a fullness of meaning —indeed they only become truly *visible*— when seen in the paradoxical light of the unseen" (author's emphasis) (Candler, 2010: 12). The anagogical sense, he adds, is "the final of the four senses of scripture according to Christian tradition [and] refers to a text's figurative signification in relation to eternal glory or eschatological reality" (Candler, 2010: 12). This anagogical sensibility, a sacramental imagination, is often represented in O'Connor's work by the use of recurring images. The woods or the trees seem to represent Christ, as the writer explained, the source of salvation through the Tree of Life. An analogy may be established with the emaciated body of Christ on the Cross and its transformation into the symbol of salvation and resurrection. This sacramental imagination and the eschatological impulse of the narrative may be seen in O'Connor's description of the scenes: the innocent victims in "A Good Man is Hard to Find" wait for their destiny the moment before and after they meet the three psychopaths: "Behind the ditch, they were sitting in there were more woods, tall and dark and deep" (O'Connor, 1988: 145) and "Behind them the line of woods gaped like a dark open mouth" (146).

Peter Candler observes that O'Connor's anagogical imagination is represented "by the recurring image of the sun at the close of many of her stories" (2010: 12). When the Misfit first observes the six members of the family, he seems to be embarrassed and looking up at the sky he says: "Don't see no sun but don't see no cloud neither" (O'Connor, 1988: 147). Later, after the rest of the members of the family have been taken into the woods to be killed, the Grandmother is alone with the Misfit and she notices that she has lost her voice:

> There was not a cloud in the sky nor any sun. There was nothing around her but woods. She wanted to tell him that he must pray. She opened and closed her mouth several times before anything came out. Finally, she found herself saying, "Jesus, Jesus," meaning, Jesus

will help you, but the way she was saying it, it sounded as if she might be cursing. (O'Connor, 1988: 151)

The scene pictures an inversion of Christ's words on the Cross in Matthew 27:46, "Father, Father, why hast thou forsaken me?," just before giving up His spirit. In the short story, the Grandmother provokes a response on the Misfit, a kind of confession:

> 'Jesus *thown* everything off balance. It was the same case with Him as with me except He hadn't committed any crime and they could prove I had committed one because they had the papers on me. Of course,' he said, 'they never shown me my papers (...) Jesus was the only One that ever raised the dead,' the Misfit continued, 'and He shouldn't have done it. He *thown* everything off balance. If He did what He said, then it's nothing for you to do but *thow* a way everything and follow Him, and if He didn't, then it's nothing for you to do but enjoy the few minutes you got left the best way you can —by killing somebody or burning down his house or doing some other meanness to him. No pleasure but meanness' (O'Connor, 1988: 151-152).

The Misfit cannot discern whether or not Christ really came back from the dead. He says that if he were there at the time of Christ, he would have known for sure. The fact is that he has got an answer and seems to be more honest and insightful than the Grandmother when he tries to justify his crimes. That first inversion in which the Grandmother has her epiphany causes the Misfit's violent reaction. O'Connor displays this action of Grace as a kind of Eucharist inversion, "her violated body becomes the means whereby she is mysteriously united with Christ's grace as she repeats his suffering" (Sykes, 2009: 142). In O'Connor's sacramental imagination, violence becomes the way through which the sinner achieves Grace. Therefore, violence acquires a sacramental meaning: "Hiram and Bobby Lee return from the woods and stood over the ditch, looking down at the grandmother who half sat and half lay in a puddle of blood with her legs crossed under her like a child's and her face smiling up at the cloudless sky" (O'Connor, 1988: 152).

Every detail in the story seems to be a game of signs and symbols that leads the reader to foreshadow the fatal end. The manipulative Grandmother's mistakes become portents of doom that the author uses to confront the old woman with her own death. The Misfit, who drives the "big black battered hearse-like automobile" (O'Connor, 1988: 145), personifies death in the same way that Spark does in her novel *Memento Mori* with the mysterious telephone caller who remembers the elderly people that they must die. In O'Connor's story, the Misfit becomes the most attractive character in the story. He may be a cold-blooded, murderous psychopath, but he is also dignified and capable of existential suffering. The Misfit is described and defined aesthetically as the personification of Death. O'Connor's story begins with the Grandmother calling our attention to read through the paper the Misfit's looming menace while Spark's novel attracts our interest with the telephone message remembering that we must die. In the manner of the *memento mori* tradition, both writers remind us that preparation for death is the purpose of life. John Sykes remarks that, "Violence is here connected to eschatology, for the threat of death immediately places one in the context of last things, vaulting us into the realm of the anagogical" (2007: 45). Both works disclose the action of God's saving grace in the natural world by the terrible idea of death. In Spark's work, it is a case of remembering that death awaits us all and that suffering is a way to magnify the Lord. In fact, she wrote several works of both fiction and non-fiction on the Book of Job. One of the principles of O'Connor's work, Sykes rightly observes, "is that suffering is good, not evil, as long as that suffering is identified with the redemptive suffering of Christ." (2007: 42).

Despite Christ's declaration that we will survive death, mortality terrifies us. Spark and O'Connor offer a way to transcend death precisely through the terror that the very thought of death and suffering provokes. Both writers use shocking and sarcastic stories to show the characters' unavoidable meeting with death. Focusing the readers' attention on the moment of death —something that everyone must experience— both authors emphasize the transcendental meaning of life. The Scottish writer, in her work *My Conversion*, explained that fiction for her is "a kind of parable" (1961: 62). We must not forget that Spark started to write soon after her conversion to Catholicism as a way to help her cope with her new faith. Two years after writing this novel, the author declared: "I think there is a connection between my writing and my conversion, but I don't want to be too dogmatic about it. Certainly, all my best work has come since then" (1961: 59). She admits that her religion has provided her with a type of groundwork from which to write. *Memento Mori* is a good example since the novel seems, on the one hand, to warn us against the risks of not taking death seriously and, on the other hand, to let us know about the benefits of accepting our end as a necessary fact of life. Seen through the lens of a Catholic, death should be considered as a natural stage in life and not as a denial of it. Having death in mind help us give life a meaning. Thus, we are free to lead our lives in a way that, when they come to an end, everything can keep some sort of harmony.

According to O'Connor's words in *Mystery and Manners*, in "A Good Man is Hard to Find" we must not focus our attention on the dead bodies, but on "the action of grace in the Grandmother's soul" (1970: 113). In this sense, the Grandmother involuntarily acts as a vehicle for grace in her constant insistence on the idea of death. She drives symbolically the family's car toward their encounter with death, personified in the Misfit and his three shots on the old woman's chest opening her way to eternity with a sign of the Cross. As in *Memento Mori* the elderly residents of the asylum are meant to receive the phone calls, in "A Good Man is Hard to Find" the Grandmother is meant to meet the Misfit. Both works can be seen as a reminder for readers to consider death as a necessary ingredient of life and its "presence" as an occasion to transcend the earthly limitations of humans and leading their lives through higher levels of spirituality. Spark and O'Connor convey the action of Grace through their aesthetics in the form of eschatological fictions, which helps us "look forward to the resurrection of the body." This "looking forward" to the resurrection, O'Connor reminds us, is "the habit of art" (O'Connor, 1979: 100). It is her fiction, Spark explains, "out of which a kind of truth emerges" (Kermode, 1977: 133). If in our lives, as in the works analysed here, Death must be numbered among the characters, we should not forget that our personal call might be the next one.

Bibliography

Asals, Frederick (1993). Introduction. In Frederick Asals (Ed.), *A Good Man is Hard to Find*. New Jersey, NJ: Rutgers University Press, pp. 3-24.

Bosco, Mark, S.J. (2017). Flannery O'Connor as a Baroque Artist: Theological and Literary Strategies. In Henry T. Edmonson III (Ed.), *A Political Companion to Flannery O'Connor*. Lexington, KY: University Press of Kentucky, pp. 176-195.

Candler, Peter M. (2010). "The Anagogical Imagination of Flannery O'Connor," in *Christianity and Literature*, 60, 1: 11-33.

Chesterton, Gilbert K. (2001). *The Incredulity of Father Brown*. Cornwall: Stratus Books Ltd.

Doxey, William S. (1993). A Dissenting Opinion of Flannery O'Connor's 'A Good Man is Hard to Find.' In Frederick Asals (Ed.) *A Good Man is Hard to Find*. New Brunkswik, NJ: Rutgers University Press, pp. 95-100.

Haddox, Thomas F. (2009). "Religion for 'Really Intelligent People': The Rhetoric of Muriel Spark's Reality and Dreams," in *Religion & Literature*, 41, 3: 43-66.

Kermode, Frank (1977). "The House of Fiction." In Malcolm Bradbury (Ed.), *The Novel Today: Contemporary Writers on Modern Fiction*. Oxford: Alden Press, pp. 111-135

Kimball, Roger (1993). "The First Half of Muriel Spark," in *The New Criterion*, 11, 8: 9-16.

Magee, Rosemary M. (Ed.) (1987). *Conversations with Flannery O'Connor*. Jackson, MS: University Press of Mississippi.

O'Connor, Flannery (1971). *Mystery and Manners: Occasional Prose*. Edited by Sally and Robert Fitzgerald. New York, NY: Farrar, Straus and Giroux.

--- (1979). *The Habit of Being*. Edited by Sally Fitzgerald. New York, NY: Farrar, Straus and Giroux.

--- (1988). *Collected Works*. Notes by Sally Fitzgerald. Distributed by the Penguin Group. New York, NY: The Library of America.

Page, Norman (1990). *Muriel Spark*. London: Macmillan Education Ltd.

Spark, Muriel (1991). *Memento Mori*. Harmondsworth, UK: Penguin Books.

--- (1961). "My Conversion," in *Twentieth Century*, CLXX: 58-63.

Stephens, Martha (1973). *The Question of Flannery O'Connor*. Baton Rouge, LA: Louisiana State University Press.

Sykes, John D. (2007). *Flannery O'Connor, Walker Percy, and the Aesthetics of Revelation*. Columbia, MO: University of Missouri Press.

--- (2009). O'Connor and the Body: Incarnation, Redemptive Suffering, and Evil. In Harold Bloom (Ed.) *Flannery O'Connor*. New York, NY: Bloom's Literary Criticism - Infobase Publishing, pp. 139-166.

Updike, John (1983). *Hugging the Shore: Essays and Criticisms*. New York, NY: Knopf.

Quixotism and Modernism:
The Conversion of Hazel Motes

Brent Little

Quixotism often conjures up notions of an impractical idealism sometimes rooted in a rigid certainty. As is well known, the term stems from the title character of Cervantes's *Don Quixote*, often considered as Western literature's first novel. But Flannery O'Connor's Hazel Motes in *Wise Blood* suffers from his own unique quixotism. His determined attempts to begin a "Church without Christ" are grounded in an idealism marked with an intense certainty. But what is the nature of Hazel's quixotism? In the following, I argue that an investigation of this question informs a long-running debate amongst O'Connor scholars regarding the end of *Wise Blood*, a debate that centers on whether Hazel's self-imposed blindness manifests a healthy and legitimate Christianity. By examining Hazel's conversion in the light of his peculiar quixotism, his stunted, incomplete conversion comes into greater clarity. A dialogue with Charles Taylor's *A Secular Age* reveals that Hazel's quixotism is a distinctly modern variety, for it exalts autonomy and insists that the self should construct its own meaning and morality apart from the influence of a religious past.

When Hazel turns from his atheism after the destruction of his car, he retains one aspect of secular modernity: he continues to manifest an extreme form of modernity's autonomous, self-ordering individual; that is, if a hallmark of the modern self is one who creates meaning via their own construction, Hazel likewise attempts to achieve his own salvation autonomously. Fundamentally, Hazel's conversion lacks true community, that is, a community founded on mutual charity for others. Some readers regard Mrs. Flood, Hazel's landlady, as his community; from this perspective, Hazel witnesses to his new faith in his interactions with her. But such readings exaggerate the actual dynamics between Mrs. Flood and Hazel, and fail to consider Hazel's consistent pattern of behavior over the course of the novel, a pattern that indicates Hazel's lack of desire for authentic, mutually self-giving relationships, either before or after his conversion. At best, Hazel's and Mrs. Flood's relationship is forced community. At the root of this behavior lies an unconverted dimension of Hazel's character —a dimension that continues to operate with the anthropology of modernism: his desire to remain an autonomous individual not responsible for, or dependent upon, others beyond the barest necessary requirements.

THE QUIXOTIC HAZEL MOTES

My description of Hazel as quixotic refers to his unbending atheistic idealism. Before his conversion, Hazel relentlessly pursues the consequences of his belief that there is no sin and hence, no need for redemption: "I'm going to preach there was no Fall because there was nothing to fall from and no Redemption because there was no Fall and no Judgment because there wasn't the first two. Nothing matters but that Jesus was a liar," he proclaims atop his unreliable Essex (O'Connor, 1988: 59). In Hazel's view, there is no sin (29), and hence no need for a redeemer. Religiosity must be replaced by a hillbilly Nietzscheism that each person should create their own truth. As Susan Srigley observes, "Motes wants to create an alternative order of reality and become his own measure for truth" (Srigley, 2004: 62, 63).

O'Connor portrays Hazel's quixotism throughout the novel. Upon his arrival in Taulkinham, Hazel wastes no time in enacting his self-created philosophy, declaring "I don't believe in anything," shortly before he visits the local prostitute, Mrs. Watts (O'Connor, 1988: 17). Indeed, Hazel's expressions of his sexuality are conditioned by his determination to live out his nihilism as faithfully as possible. His visit with Mrs. Watts is less to do with sexual desire and more with proving that no sin is involved in his actions, because, without Jesus, there is no foundation for sin. Likewise, Hazel's interest in the underage Sabbath Lily Hawks is not primarily motivated by sexual attraction; instead, he wishes to demonstrate his unqualified commitment to his Church without Christ to her father, Asa Hawks, a preacher masquerading as a blind man.

Hazel's idealism is thus consistent but rigid, sincere but uncharitable. When Enoch steals a mummy from a local museum, Hazel destroys it as soon as he sees it. Enoch originally regarded the mummy as a sacred object. But Hazel will not tolerate replacing one form of religiosity with another. "I don't want nothing but the truth!" he declares to an irate Sabbath (O'Connor, 1988: 106; 107). In hindsight, it is fascinating that one of our first glimpses into Hazel's character is his desire that his trunk bed on the train bound for Taulkinham be "all dark, he didn't want it diluted" (O'Connor, 1988: 9). Hazel's distaste for anything "diluted" captures his quixotism.

Interestingly, Hazel's insistent atheism does not encounter much resistance from the population of Taulkinham. Besides the preacher Asa Hawks, no one engages him with serious disagreement. At the same time, his preaching of his new "Church" generates more curiosity than enthusiasm among Hazel's listeners, aside from the greedy Onnie Jay Holy who simply seeks financial gain (O'Connor, 1988: 83-85). "Taulkinham," Michial Farmer observes, "is O'Connor's iconic representation of the modern world —a world that is not so much hostile to Christian faith as it is utterly indifferent to it" (Farmer, 2015: 89). Such indifference would no doubt be at odds with Hazel's aggressiveness. One imagines that most citizens of Taulkinham would respond similarly to his fellow rail passenger to whom he insists that he would not believe in Jesus even if Jesus was on the train at the same time: she promptly retorts, "Who said you had to?" (O'Connor, 1988: 7). It is not Hazel's atheism that is remarkable amidst a secular city, but his fevered passion.

But Hazel's quixotism extends deeper than simply a sincere and consistent idealism. Unlike Cervantes's Quixote, who chases after windmills, dreaming of medieval chivalry, Hazel's quixotism is distinctly modern. By this I mean that the core tenet of Hazel's idealism is his insistence that he is in control and free from obligations towards others. His actions thereby are justified because they assert or maintain this independence from communal responsibilities. This dimension of Hazel's character —his insistence upon his autonomy— manifests an extreme dimension of secular modernism. In fact, Hazel's disdain for community is so deeply embedded in his self-understanding that it remains unchanged even after his conversion.

Hazel's Quixotic Modernism

Hazel's conception of self, a self who constructs meaning apart from community, aligns with a modern understanding of human agency in Western culture, as described by Charles Taylor in *A Secular Age*. Indeed, for Taylor, Western secular modernity is defined by a new conception of the human person, one that emerges in Western culture beginning in the medieval period. This modern trust in human agency provides the primary reason for the decline of religion in the West, and not commonly ascribed theories such as the rise of science; fundamentally, the deterioration of Western religiosity comes from the emergence of a new definition of the individual (Taylor, 2007: 25-28).

Taylor traces the rise of the modern person in medieval developments concerning nature. Specifically, nature comes to be viewed as self-sufficient, without a need for God (apart from the initial act of creation) or the supernatural. Taylor locates this development with the Aristotelian revival of the Middle Ages, paradigmatically found in the thought of Thomas Aquinas, in which creation begins to be viewed as ordered towards its own perfection. Later thinkers, such as William of Ockham, acerbate this trend even while rebelling against Thomistic scholasticism. Ockham's nominalism rejects the notion that a conception of the good can be grounded in the supposed ends of nature since this limits God's sovereignty, but nominalism's emphasis on God's transcendence over the world further divides the natural from the supernatural (Taylor, 2007: 91; 284; 773). "The great invention of the West," argues Taylor, "was that of an immanent order in Nature, whose working could be systematically understood and explained on its own terms" (Taylor, 2007: 15).

Against this backdrop, the medieval "porous" self morphs into the modern, "buffered" self. The "porous" self, the premodern self, lived in a world with no clear boundary between the self and the enchanted world. In an enchanted world, there is a "whole gamut of forces" which impose meaning on us, from demons to "charged" objects (such as sacramentals) to the cosmos. Time is experienced as both horizontal —the normal sequence of everyday experience— and vertical, in the sense of being oriented towards God. Further, the past, particularly the sacred past, continues to be a source of meaning for the porous person. In other words, there is both secular and sacred time. Additionally, the porous self believes that the entire cosmos is enchanted and as such points in some fashion to God. Thus, the porous self seeks meaning from what is external to its own mind, and this source of meaning is found in the past. The celebration of past sacred events (such as Good Friday) is one example of the past and present as inseparable for the pre-modern person (Taylor, 2007: 25-26; 32-35; 55-60). In addition, the enchanted world was not simply a world of good spiritual forces (such as the sacraments or God's angels), but also a world where demons and malicious magic could exert an influence. An ecclesial power, such as the Church and its sacred objects and rituals, protected us from such malevolent spiritual influences, and this protection was gained by living as a member of a cohesive society. Autonomy, in the modern sense of the word, would have been dangerous. In other words, as Taylor notes, "living in the enchanted, porous world of our ancestors was inherently living socially" (Taylor, 2007: 42).

In contrast, the modern self is a "buffered" self. Taylor argues that the definitive, secular turn occurs with the development of an exclusive humanism, one that postulates the "buffered self" as the source of meaning capable of ordering the world around it. It is this exclusive humanism —with the buffered self at the center— that gives the greatest impetus to the rise of modern unbelief. We move from a more communal conception of society, based on a religious heritage, to one centered on the individual. The buffered self does not live in fear of demons or magic, but sees itself as sufficient to achieve human flourishing. This includes a new moral ordering in which "civilization" is ordered for the mutual benefit of individuals. This moral ordering includes the interactions of one buffered self with another, as well as the discipline of the self's own instinctual, physical desires (Taylor, 2007: 21-22; 27-28). Above all, meaning for the buffered self is of one's own creation—one can detach one's mind from external forces. In other words, there is a clear separation between the individual and the surrounding world. The buffered self, Taylor notes, "can form the ambition of disengaging from whatever is beyond the boundary, and of giving its own autonomous order to its life" (Taylor, 2007: 38-39).

The buffered self thus moves in a disenchanted world. Nature is not a source of meaning, nor does it reveal a supernatural presence. Instead, nature is to be used to perfect the human person; likewise, societies' purposes are fulfilled according to the materials of nature (i.e. technology), and made possible due to a rational, instrumental knowledge of nature. Further, the individual lives aware that this ordering, and indeed meaning in general, originates and resides in the human mind. Unlike the porous self who seeks meaning externally, the buffered self creates its own criteria by which one is to live, and is not dependent on divine revelation. The buffered self now believes that order is defined solely to assist human flourishing, not necessarily to lead us to God, and that

Quixotism and Modernism: The Conversion of Hazel Motes

the power for this social ordering comes from our own capacity and not from any divine origins. Finally, if the porous, medieval person envisioned the self as moving amidst sacred, supernaturally directed time, the buffered, modern self fashions meaning from a secular, linear timeline. Consequently, the modern, buffered person is not as beholden to the past as the pre-modern, porous person (Taylor, 2007: 84; 90; 135; 142; 157; 294-295).

Taylor's categories of the "porous" self and the "buffered" self harmonize with O'Connor's portrayals of Hazel and Enoch. When they first meet, Enoch informs Hazel that he has no interest in "Jesus business," but surprisingly Hazel never shows a desire to make Enoch a disciple; in fact, he consistently rejects Enoch's attempts at friendship. Perhaps the answer lies in Enoch's obvious need for companionship; O'Connor even describes him with the appearance of "a friendly hound dog," a description that Enoch unwittingly takes upon himself with the exclamation at seeing Hazel again, "Well, I'll be dog" (O'Connor, 1988: 23, 46). If Hazel manifests the hallmarks of a buffered self—one who constructs his own meaning as distinct from community as possible— Enoch still desires community. Seen in the light of Taylor's thought, Enoch emerges as a person torn asunder. On one hand, he has no desire for conventional Christian community. But on the other hand, he still desires Hazel's friendship. In other words, like the porous self, Enoch is one who derives meaning from sources external to him. Even his misguided attempts to both meet the famous, movie "gorilla," and dress up in the gorilla suit himself are comical, albeit tragic, attempts to find community (O'Connor, 1988: 102, 112).

More prominently, Enoch manifests Taylor's porous self in his attraction to the mummy from the city's museum. Enoch may reject Christianity, but he still possesses the impulses to seek out meaning apart from his own autonomy, with an openness to mystery and the supernatural. Further, this meaning is rooted in the past. Above, I briefly alluded to Hazel's destruction of Enoch's mummy, but this was not Hazel's first rejection of Enoch's sacred object. When Enoch shows Hazel the mummy in the museum, he later collapses on the ground "with an exalted look," but Hazel violently rejects Enoch's supernatural mystery and throws a rock at him (O'Connor, 1988: 56-57). But Enoch is not yet deterred, for afterwards he still finds the man inside the glass case as "a mystery beyond his understanding" (O'Connor, 1988: 73).

Similarly, Enoch demonstrates his pre-modern belief in an enchanted world in his odd reverence for his washstand, the lower part of which has a "tabernacle-like cabinet" intended for a slop-jar, but that Enoch leaves empty out of a "certain reverence for the purpose of things and since he didn't have the right thing to put in it." The narrative even briefly describes this cabinet as reserved for "the treasure" (O'Connor, 1988: 74). Indeed, Enoch dreams and behaves around the washstand as if it was a sacred location:

> More than once after a big supper, he had dreamed of unlocking the cabinet and getting in it and then proceeding to certain rites and mysteries that he had a very vague idea about in the morning. In his cleaning up, his mind was on the washstand from the first, but as was usual with him, he began with the least important thing and worked around and in toward the center where the meaning was. (O'Connor, 1988: 75)

No wonder, then, that Enoch places his stolen mummy in the tabernacle, a sacred space for his sacred object —a space for mystery and ritual, and, as O'Connor notes, "where the meaning was." These are actions that exemplify Taylor's "porous," pre-modern person.

For Enoch, his impulses to seek out meaning in ancient sacred objects and rituals is a misguided, implicit desire for sacramentality that becomes idolatrous. He desires the presence of the sacred in creation, but he does not have a community to guide him. When he steals the mummy, dubbed in the narrative as the "new Jesus," he places him in the cabinet, which the narration ceases to describe as "tabernacle-like," and now describes simply as "the tabernacle." There the mummy explodes, and afterwards, Enoch's "expression had showed that a deep unpleasant knowledge was breaking on him slowly." (O'Connor, 1988: 98) It was the knowledge of his own foolishness, or, as he realizes afterwards, the knowledge that "one jesus was as bad as another" (O'Connor, 1988: 99). However, this does not mean he will pursue secular unbelief like Hazel, for, as his ill-conceived theft of the gorilla custom demonstrates, one aspect of the porous self remains —his desire for community.

Enoch's religious impulses help to clarify O'Connor's self-identification with Enoch in a letter to Betty Hester:

> I suppose what you work hardest on is what you know least, but listen, I never had a moment's thought over Enoch but I struggled over Haze. Everything Enoch said and did was as plain to me as my hand (O'Connor, 1979: 117).

Of course, O'Connor is not identifying herself with Enoch's idolatry, but rather with his intuition to look for sacredness in the physical world. Hazel, in stark contrast, strives to live as perfect a "buffered" self as possible in his rejection of sacred mysteries and rituals. He is the exact opposite of O'Connor herself; no wonder she found him the more difficult character to portray.

Hazel, unlike Enoch, desires to reject history as a source of meaning. If Enoch, as a porous self, seeks meaning originally in an ancient object, such as the mummy, Hazel claims that humans need to create their own meaning apart from the past. When Hazel preaches that "there was no Fall" and hence no need for Redemption (O'Connor, 1988: 59), he demonstrates his desire to achieve one of Taylor's characteristics of the autonomous, modern person, one "buffered" from outside influences, including his family's religious history. As John F. Desmond remarks, "Haze's quest is essentially about the meaning of the self in history. His early claims to nihilism and innocence are an attempt to escape history, the legacy of original sin transmitted to him as a human being and specified in the guilt he feels over the carnival sideshow visit" (1987: 55). But of course, his attempts to escape his past proves to be an impossibility, for his nihilism is defined against his family's Christianity. When he preaches "the church of truth without Jesus Christ Crucified" or "the Church Without Christ" (O'Connor, 1988: 31, 59), his language betrays that he remains haunted by his grandfather's Christianity, regardless of his protests otherwise. His nihilism depends on Christianity for its form and content —form, because Hazel imitates his grandfather by preaching atop a car— and content by constructing his beliefs as a rejection of his grandfather's southern, Protestant faith (O'Connor, 1988: 10-11). As Hazel insists, "Nothing matters but that Jesus don't exist," thereby unwittingly revealing that his entire construction of meaning is a reaction to Jesus (O'Connor, 1988: 29). In this sense, his sense of self remains trapped in a past, despite his claims and desires to the contrary.

Hazel's attempts to reject his past are intertwined with his insistence on his autonomy, again a characteristic of his "buffered" self. Curiously, this dimension of his character seems to predate his conversion to unbelief in the army (O'Connor, 1988: 13). Even as a child, and still in the thrall of his Grandfather's influence, Hazel believes that "the way to avoid Jesus was to avoid sin" (O'Connor, 1988: 11). This Pelagian impulse in Hazel's understanding of himself may give a clue to his conversion to unbelief. Indeed, what exactly causes Hazel's conversion to atheism?

Although much less scholarly attention has been given to Hazel's first conversion —since, logically, readers tend to focus on his Christian conversion as the climax of the story— O'Connor implies that his embrace of atheism is based not on intellectual reasoning, but upon his own desire for self-reliance. For example, when Hazel refers to his mother's Bible in the army so as to ward off the malicious influence of his army peers, they "told him that nobody was interested in his goddam soul" and that after all, "he didn't have any soul." At first, this implies Hazel's conversion to materialism may have been prompted by a desire to assimilate to the secularism around him, that is, to become a member of the community. O'Connor, however, makes the opposite clear. Instead, Hazel "took a long time to believe them because he wanted to believe them. All he wanted was to believe them and get rid of it once and for all, and he saw the opportunity here to get rid of it without corruption, to be converted to nothing instead of to evil." (O'Connor, 1988: 12) In other words, Hazel was already inclined towards disbelief, for he wished to cleanse himself of the ingrained religious impulses towards faith in Jesus from his family's history. Further, Hazel's rigid, self-centered quixotism shows through here, for he continues to maintain, just as he did as a child and as he will as a nihilistic preacher, that he can avoid evil without the help of divine grace. The army's assignments grant him time "to study his soul in and assure himself that it was not there. When he was thoroughly convinced, he saw that this was something that he had always known" (O'Connor, 1988: 12-13). One again notes Hazel's belief that he alone determines his own meaning. His insistence on his own autonomy and his reluctance to rely on others —the foundation of his modern, quixotic atheism— is already Hazel's formative desire prior to his conversion to atheism. Hazel does not come to unbelief in the army by reading Nietzsche or Heidegger, but because he wishes "to be converted to nothing."

O'Connor, however, indicates that Hazel is not in as much control as he believes. After all, his Christian past still haunts him. For example, his hat, remarks the narrator, gives him the appearance of "an elderly country preacher" (O'Connor, 1988: 3). Further, O'Connor consistently satirizes Hazel's faith in his own agency. On the train, Hazel is either ignored, controlled, or insulted by others around him, whether it is the porter, the steward, or Mrs. Hitchcok; at one point, the train even leaves without him (O'Connor, 1988: 8; 15). Little wonder that upon his arrival in Taulkinham, he seeks out a car so that he will never again be reliant upon public transportation.

This unreliable Essex comes to represent his "faith" (in the sense of trust) in his capacity to order and control his world. When Hazel declares to Sabbath and her father, Asa Hawks, his famous line, "Nobody with a good car needs to be justified" (O'Connor, 1988: 64), he is claiming that no one who can operate autonomously needs to rely on a God to save them. In addition, as Desmond points out, Hazel's car, as a "movable" object, symbolizes that his atheism is not rooted in "any concrete historical order" (1987: 55). In other words, the car indicates Hazel's desire to avoid community. He never has to stay trapped against his wishes. For example, when he threatens to abandon Sabbath and leave the city, he declares, "And I got a car to get there in" (O'Connor, 1988: 107). But even in this, Hazel's faith in modern technology is proven misguided. Hazel may hope the Essex is his path to independence, but he must rely on others to fix it. In fact, he never manages to travel very far from Taulkinham, and religious signs haunt him whenever he leaves town (O'Connor, 1988: 42; 65; 117).

Nonetheless, Hazel performs his most extreme manifestation of his quixotism via his car. As George A. Kilcourse observes, Hazel possesses a "ruthless honesty" that eventually leads him back to Christianity (Kilcourse, 2001: 55); indeed, Hazel's "ruthless honesty" prompts his murder of Solace Layfield. Layfield's crime is his imitation of Hazel's preaching, under Onnie Jay Holy's tutelage, for financial gain. In other words, he may have proclaimed the right creed, but he lacked authenticity and sincerity. "Two things I can't stand...a man that ain't true and one that mocks what is," declares Hazel shortly after he runs over Solace with his car (O'Connor, 1988: 115). Just as he rejected Enoch's mummy, Hazel rejects anyone who twists his atheist quixotism for less than idealistic ends.

Yet, Hazel's desire to live out the consequences of his philosophy catch up with him when a policeman, prompted by Hazel's lack of a license, pushes Hazel's car over an embankment, where it crashes irreparably (O'Connor, 1988: 118). Hazel experiences the outcome of his own belief that sin does not exist and that everyone can create their own truth. He stands defenseless before a police officer who harasses him, not because he was speeding, but because "I just don't like your face" (O'Connor, 1988: 117); in other words, the officer sees no need to justify his illegal devastation of Hazel's car other than a personal desire.

Quixotism and Modernism: The Conversion of Hazel Motes

It is tempting to see the Essex's demise as the end of Hazel's modern quixotism, but the text implies a more nuanced, qualified conversion. On one hand, Hazel's vision has shifted after his car's destruction: "His face seemed to reflect the entire distance across the clearing and on beyond, the entire distance that extended from his eyes to the blank gray sky that went on, depth after depth, into space" (O'Connor, 1988: 118). Hazel's perspective shifts from the materialism of his early modern atheism to a vision of the infinite, "depth after depth, into space." His vision opens to a new horizon beyond the mere physical world. In this sense, he no longer puts faith in his disenchanted worldview — the material world is no longer the sole reality. But on the other hand, Hazel remains true to form— he still clings to his self-reliance. Hazel refuses the police officer's offer to give him a ride. On a literal level, this is understandable, since how could he trust the police officer who just destroyed his car? But seen against the pattern of autonomy throughout his life, Hazel's decision to walk the three hours back to town by himself —with no attempt to hitchhike— is also consistent with his character. Upon arrival at his landlady's house, he promptly does what the fake preacher Hawks only pretends to do: He blinds himself with quicklime (O'Connor, 1988: 119).

Thus, Hazel remains a character of extremes. He remains quixotic —if he is going to convert, he will leave little room for a lukewarm, qualified faith. Instead, his conversion will be marked by an action that symbolizes unreservedly his turn from his previous atheistic worldview. Nonetheless, as will become clearer by the novel's end, Hazel's conversion is not completely to Taylor's "porous" self of the pre-modern world. His disenchanted materialism has crumbled, but he remains a modern, buffered self in both his rejection of community and his insistence on his own efficacy. Hazel's conversion stands in sharp contrast to young Tarwater at the end of O'Connor's second novel, *The Violent Bear It Away*. Tarwater's conversion involves a vision of a community of saints, including his uncle, being fed "from a single basket." Shortly thereafter, he receives the prophetic command: "GO WARN THE CHILDREN OF GOD OF THE TERRIBLE SPEED OF MERCY." Young Tarwater's response is to head "toward the dark city, where the children of God lay sleeping" (O'Connor, 1988: 477-79; Bold in the original).[1] Hazel, however, takes up no similar public mission, nor is there any indication that he envisions himself as a member of a mystical community. Instead, he retreats from society to ponder his conversion in private. Thus, Hazel becomes a mixture of Taylor's descriptions of the pre-modern, porous self and the modern, buffered self. Of the former, he recognizes his own sin and need for atonement before God, characteristics that align with the porous self in that this is an affirmation of meaning based on a religious past; but on the other hand, he retains his desire for independence and self-reliance characteristic of the modern, buffered person. If he must be a Christian, he will live out his Christianity according to his own desires, and as separate from responsibilities or charity for others as possible.

Hazel's Modern Faith

My hope in this section is that an analysis of Hazel in dialogue with Taylor's description of modernity (as described above) informs the frequent debate over Hazel's conversion. In brief, the question is whether readers interpret Hazel's self-imposed blindness as justifiable or morally problematic. One frequent topic of this debate is whether Hazel becomes an efficacious disciple of Christ. Some readers, such as Ralph Wood and Richard Giannone, argue that Hazel witnesses to Christ in his relationship with Mrs. Flood. For example, Giannone believes that Hazel's and Mrs. Flood's relationship is a kind of friendship, a friendship that opens Mrs. Flood to her own conversion by the time of Hazel's death (Giannone, 2015: -183-85). As Giannone rightly observes, "we are saved in community" (2015: 185). I remain, however, skeptical that Hazel himself recognizes or agrees with this insight.

---

1. For a discussion of the issue of community in *The Violent Bear It Away*, see Srigley, *Flannery O'Connor's Sacramental Art*, 132-33.

Quixotism and Modernism: The Conversion of Hazel Motes

Any evaluation of Hazel's conversion must consider the overall pattern of his behavior from the novel's beginning in order to recognize what has or has not changed in Hazel's character. Seen against this background, Hazel's quixotism has developed into a problematic form of Christian faith. Although Hazel now recognizes his sinfulness before God, he still desires to live as apart from authentic human community as possible. In other words, a hallmark of his quixotism, whether pre- or post-conversion, is autonomy, a defining characteristic of secular modernity, as highlighted above. Hazel spurs any attempt to build relationships of mutuality and friendship, whether with Sabbath or Enoch before his conversion, or with Mrs. Flood after his conversion. No wonder too, as few of us could match his intense principled consistency, whether about atheism or Christianity. If anything, his conversion seems to aggravate his disregard for community. If his atheism led him to preach from atop his dilapidated car in public to gain converts to his cause, his conversion prompts him to withdraw further from society, blind and taciturn with only Mrs. Flood as company, and she only out of necessity.

One justification for Hazel's blindness may be that it is Hazel's attempt to resist the temptation to sin. Hazel's act would then be a form of discipline. In Wood's reading, Hazel's self-blindness is Hazel's attempt to live out Paul's instructions in his letters to mortify the flesh (2009: 88-90). Hazel's rejection of physical sight, then, manifests his rejection of worldly values, and focuses his "vision" on his faith. No doubt there is some truth in this argument, but this does not mean that Hazel's actions represent an authentic, biblical Christianity. As Brian Ingraffia observes, Wood's argument does not take into account the fact that Paul's sufferings are inflected by others; they are not self-imposed, even if Paul's proclamation of the Gospel provokes others to persecute him (2009: 83). Paul's suffering is for, with, and due to others. Hazel, meanwhile, imposes his own sufferings on himself, and only out of concern for himself.

Further, how aware is Hazel of his own biblical tradition? Susan Srigley casts doubt on Hazel's familiarity with the Bible since, as a young man, he reads it, and only occasionally, with his mother's glasses, which blur and fatigue his eyesight (Srigley, 2009: 98).[2] Hazel's self-blinding affirms Srigley's observation. Hazel's act is the "sign" of his conversion, and I purposely use sacramental language here, for Hazel's mixture of quicklime and water serves as a perverted baptism in that it is an outward sign of a conversion to the Christian faith. As J. Ramsey Michaels argues, Hazel has made his body "the visible sacrament of his redemption" (2013: 37). But Hazel's self-mutilation misses a central dimension of Baptism: nowhere in the New Testament does one baptize one's self. A person is always baptized by another, whether it is Paul (Acts 9:18) or Jesus at the hands of John the Baptist. Meanwhile, Hazel, in contrast to his own biblical tradition, desires to live out his faith as autonomously as possible from the very beginning of his conversion. He creates and administers the sign of his conversion.

In addition, Hazel's behavior as Mrs. Flood's tenant indicates his indifference towards others. Haze makes no effort to apology for his murder to the victim's family, much less report it to the police. In other words, he will atone for his sin on his own terms. Other tenants ignore him, and he displays no willingness to engage with them. His act of discarding unneeded money from the government is certainly an ascetical act, a sign of his disdain for the world's priorities, but his action is not morally perfect. Mrs. Flood, of course, selfishly wants this money for herself, but her claim that Hazel could use that money to help the poor and needy, however insincere, nonetheless remains valid. Hazel *could* donate it to help others. True, he does then offer the excess money to Mrs. Flood, who recoils at the thought of charity, but the text gives no indication whether we are to regard this offer as a genuine act of generosity and friendship, or an indication that he makes the offer to end an unwanted conversation as soon as possible. Regardless, he provides no explanation of his behavior (O'Connor, 1988: 124).

---

2. Srigley also notes that Hazel at best seems to have a truncated understanding of Christianity, one that stresses humanity's debt to Jesus at the exclusion of God's love.

Quixotism and Modernism: The Conversion of Hazel Motes

Hazel, in fact, is consistently reluctant to speak about his conversion, thereby calling into question claims that his blindness helps him become a witness for his faith. When Mrs. Flood asks why he walks on rocks in his shoes, a reiteration of his self-imposed childhood penalty (O'Connor, 1988: 36), he responds: "To pay". After Mrs. Flood presses him on what he is paying for, Hazel responds "It don't make any difference for what...I'm paying;" he then retorts to her, "Mind your business...You can't see." (O'Connor, 1988: 125) Wood considers Hazel's extreme ascetical behavior —from the stones in his shoes to the barbed-wire under his shirt— as a form of mortification of the body, penance, and an example of the Calvinistic notion of "vivification"; in Wood's reading, Hazel's actions are not works-righteousness (2009: 89; 90). I remain unconvinced as "to pay" is *primarily* transactional language, language of debt and recompense, not necessarily language of discipline. But in either case, the crucial point is to note Hazel's complete refusal to engage Mrs. Flood's question. At the very least, Hazel certainly fails the admonition of 1 Peter 3:15 for believers to be able to give an account of one's hope to another. "Mind your own business," he tells her instead. In other words, his salvation does not concern her.

Thus, even if Hazel does participate in some meager form of community with Mrs. Flood, he is reluctant at best. Giannone argues that Hazel's and Mrs. Flood's relationship turns into a friendship; as they sit on the porch together, "a rapport is taking hold. On this patch of common ground, light and air lift the dark suffocation smothering their forlorn lives. One solitude is opening out to another. Need meets need" (2015: 178). Although friendship, as Giannone points out, can be a stage on one's journey towards God, authentic friendship also conventionally implies a mutual, reciprocated desire for the good of the other, such as in Aristotle's classical definition of a perfect friendship (Giannone, 2015: 185; Aristotle, 2009: 145-146). Alas, the text does not indicate that Hazel wants a relationship with Mrs. Flood beyond the bare necessities of food and shelter. If anything, Hazel seems to regard her as a necessary nuisance. Far from a rapport blossoming between landlady and tenant on the porch, Hazel barely acknowledges her existence: "…she could never tell if he knew she was there or not. Even when he answered her, she couldn't tell if he knew it was she. She herself. Mrs. Flood, the landlady. Not just anybody. They would sit, he only sit, and she sit rocking, for half an afternoon and not two words seemed to pass between them, though she might talk at length." (O'Connor, 1988: 122) In addition, as Mrs. Flood's personal interest in Hazel increases, she begins to make him more delicious dishes; he in turn eats the food quickly without gratitude "as if all his attention were directed elsewhere and this was an interruption he had to suffer" (O'Connor, 1988: 126). One notes that the initiative in both scenes belongs entirely to Mrs. Flood; she alone is interested at building a relationship with Hazel. Hazel's actions may be a sign of his conversion, since, after all, his attention is presumably focused on his repentance, but it does not manifest any desire for true friendship based on mutual concern and enjoyment of the other's company.

Regardless of Mrs. Flood's growing affection for Hazel, Hazel himself remains disengaged from human relationships. O'Connor once remarked in a letter that Hazel is "in no state to practice charity" after his conversion (O'Connor, 1979: 335). Indeed, this is true up until the very end. When Mrs. Flood unwisely proposes marriage to him, justifying it on the grounds that "there's nobody to help us," Hazel's response is to create as much distance between her and himself as possible; Hazel walks by her silent and "expressionless," out into the winter air (O'Connor, 1988: 128-129). There is no indication he desires friendship in this action. Instead, his behavior manifests a desire to escape as quickly as possible. When the police officers find him near death, his insists, "I want to go on where I'm going…" (O'Connor, 1988: 131). Again, this is not the response of one witnessing to his faith to others, for the police officers, clueless to his ambiguous meaning, hit him over the head; nor does it demonstrate concern for Mrs. Flood's salvation. Instead, Hazel's only concern is for his salvation: "*I* want to go on where *I'm* going." And, of course, he most assuredly does not want to go back to Mrs. Flood.

Quixotism and Modernism: The Conversion of Hazel Motes

Hazel's actions, therefore, demonstrate that he is a most reluctant, self-centered Christian disciple.[3] As Debra L. Cumberland notes, "Even at the end of the novel, there is not a single moment of human connection, genuine kindness, or an expression of love" (Cumberland, 2011: 7). There is no hint that he cares for anyone's salvation but himself. As O'Connor writes in a letter regarding the religiosity of Hazel and his family:

> Wise blood has to be these people's means of grace —they have no sacraments. The religion of the South is a do-it-yourself religion [...] It's full of unconscious pride that lands them in all sorts of ridiculous religious predicaments. They have nothing to correct their practical heresies and so they work them out dramatically (O'Connnor, 1979: 350).

Hazel's "do-it-yourself" religious culture combined with his inflexible idealistic temperament means that his conversion manifests itself as a self-reliant conversion, not in regards to God's grace necessarily, but in regards to his human relationships. It is, in other words, an autonomous conversion, unconcerned with community. His desire for self-ordering and control remains even if he acknowledges the existence of sin and the necessity of Jesus. His faith then is greatly deformed and severely truncated at best; his existential beliefs may have changed from atheism to Christianity, but his pattern of behavior remains thoroughly modern.

That said, Wood and Giannone, along with others, are correct that Hazel's behavior does change Mrs. Flood. She regards herself as "clear-sighted," and with little need for religion (O'Connor, 1988: 119; 123; 125), until, that is, she becomes more acquainted with Hazel. She intuits that the blind Hazel "had the look of seeing something" (O'Connor, 1988: 120). Gradually, she senses the presence of a greater reality perceived by Hazel, but one obscure to her vision: "Every now and then she would have an intimation of something hidden near her but out of

---

3. In contrast, Wood claims that Motes is not "selfishly concerned only about his own salvation, as if he cared nothing for the world that lies in ruin so long as he himself can be snatched like a brand from the cosmic bonfire." (2009: 90)

her reach." (O'Connor, 1988: 125). Her growing perception tracks with her increasing affection for Hazel —she moves from her conviction that he is somehow cheating her from money (O'Connor, 1988: 122) to her ill-begotten plan to marry him. But I would caution that whatever effect Hazel has on Mrs. Flood is ambiguous at best. As O'Connor describes at the novel's end:

> She shut her eyes and saw the pin point of light but so far away that she could not hold it steady in her mind. She felt as if she were blocked at the entrance of something. She sat staring with her eyes shut, into his eyes, and felt as if she had finally got to the beginning of something she couldn't begin, and she saw him moving farther and farther away, farther and farther into the darkness until he was the pin point of light (O'Connor, 1988: 131).

Why does Mrs. Flood believe she is "blocked at the entrance of something"? Can she not hold this vision steady in her mind or begin this journey by herself because it requires God's grace, or is she unwilling herself to accept this grace? If the latter, then we should call into question the efficacy of Hazel's discipleship. As Cumberland notes, Mrs. Flood may receive only "a niggling awareness of divine mystery" as she stares into Hazel's dead eyes (2011: 18). If Hazel does prompt Mrs. Flood's conversion, it is in spite of Hazel's disregard of her overtures for friendship.

As Srigley asks, "Why do we assume that when O'Connor describes Hazel Motes as a Christian despite himself it means that he understands Christianity well?" (2009: 99) Indeed, there is a certain impoverishment with Hazel's conversion. He may no longer accept Western secularity's disenchanted view of reality, but his anthropology is still very much modern: he insists on living out his ill-formed faith as an autonomous individual, unwilling to build relationships of community with others. Thus, the text indicates that we should focus less on justifying Hazel's motivations and instead wonder, wonder that God's grace can have any impact on the selfishness of Mrs. Flood when it is working through the selfishness of Hazel. So focused is his attention upon restitution that he fails to consider how grace may operate in the world either in others or in himself. His self-blindness and flight from Mrs. Flood indicate his desire to eliminate possibilities to be an active disciple in the world. If Hazel does succeed as a witness to Mrs. Flood, it is not through his conscious intentions, but through God's grace working in a fallen world, grace that converts despite human beings' efforts to the contrary.

Bibliography

Aristotle (2009). *The Nicomachean Ethics*. Translated by David Ross, revised Lesley Brown. New York, NY: Oxford University Press.

Cumberland, Debra L. (2011). Flannery O'Connor and the Question of the Christian Novel. In John J. Han (Ed.), *Wise Blood: A Re-Consideration*. Amsterdam: Rodopi, pp. 3-23.

Desmond, John F. (1987). *Risen Sons: Flannery O'Connor's Vision of History*. Athens, GA: University of Georgia Press.

Farmer, Michial (2015). "'Never the Right Food': The Physical and Spiritual Worlds in John Updike's *Rabbit, Run* and Flannery O'Connor's *Wise Blood*," in *Religion and the Arts*, 19, 1-2: 84-106.

Giannone, Richard (2015). "Flannery O'Connor's Theology of Friendship: Blasphemer and Pagan Landlady," in *The Conference on Christianity and Literature*, 64, 2: 171-86.

Ingraffia, Brian (2009). "'If Jesus Existed I Wouldn't Be Clean': Self-Torture in Flannery O'Connor's *Wise Blood*," in *Flannery O'Connor Review*, 7: 78-86.

Kilcourse, Jr., George A. (2001). *Flannery O'Connor's Religious Imagination: A World with Everything Off Balance*. Mahwah, NJ: Paulist Press.

Michaels, J. Ramsey (2013). *Passing by the Dragon: The Biblical Tales of Flannery O'Connor*. Eugene, OR: Cascade Books.

O'Connor, Flannery (1979). *The Habit of Being*. Edited by Sally Fitzgerald. New York, NY: Farrar, Straus, and Giroux.

--- (1988). *The Violent Bear It Away*. In Sally Fitzgerald (Ed.), *Collected Works*. New York, NY: Library of America, pp. 329-479.

--- (1988). *Wise Blood*. In Sally Fitzgerald (Ed.), *Collected Works*. New York, NY: Library of America, pp. 1-131.

Srigley, Susan (2004). *Flannery O'Connor's Sacramental Art*. Notre Dame, IN: University of Notre Dame Press.

--- (2009). "Penance and Love in *Wise Blood*: Seeing Redemption?," in *Flannery O'Connor Review*, 7: 94-100.

Taylor, Charles (2007). *A Secular Age*. Cambridge, MA: Belknap Press of Harvard University Press.

Wood, Ralph C. (2009). "Hazel Motes as a Flesh-Mortifying Saint in Flannery O'Connor's *Wise Blood*," in *Flannery O'Connor Review*, 7: 87-93.

A Christian *Malgré Lui*: Crisis, Transition, and the Quixotic Pursuit of the Ideal in Flannery O'Connor's Fiction

XIAMARA HOHMAN

> "What I call the tragic sense of life in men and peoples is at any rate our tragic sense of life, that of Spaniards and the Spanish people, as it is reflected in my consciousness, which is a Spanish consciousness, made in Spain. And this tragic sense of life is essentially the Catholic sense of it, for Catholicism, and above all popular Catholicism, is tragic."
>
> Miguel de Unamuno, *Tragic Sense of Life*

Since the 1952 publication of her first novel, *Wise Blood*, Flannery O'Connor and her fiction have been the subjects of a great deal of scholarship. While these literary and theological analyses certainly have a value, it seems to me that there is something more human, more concrete, more urgent in Flannery O'Connor's writing. In other words, we can only approach the central value of O'Connor's work if we are willing to ask the central question. Some critics, like George A. Kilcourse, Jr., have focused on O'Connor's "religious imagination" and the role that it plays in calling her readers to conversion and a greater awareness of mystery. Similarly, in *Flannery O'Connor: Hermit Novelist*, Richard Giannone examines the role of the ascetic tradition and the teachings of the Desert Fathers in O'Connor's fiction. In their work, Susan Srigley and Christina Bieber Lake have focused on the incarnational and aesthetic elements of

O'Connor's novels and short stories, positing that it is in the grotesque figures O'Connor draws that our own fragmentation is revealed, ultimately calling us to wholeness in Christ.

Still others, Sarah Gordon and Bieber Lake among them, have preferred to examine the religious implications of O'Connor's work through a feminist lens. In their scholarship, both Gordon and Bieber Lake adopt a Bakhtinian approach to O'Connor's work, but the two draw very different conclusions regarding whether or not her texts can be read as feminist. In *Flannery O'Connor: The Obedient Imagination*, Gordon questions the marginalization of women and African Americans in O'Connor's work, finally concluding that O'Connor was "obedient" to the patriarchal structures of both the Catholic Church and the historical period in which she lived. In *The Incarnational Art of Flannery O'Connor*, Bieber Lake pushes back against those critics of O'Connor, like Gordon, who are wont to read O'Connor's work as decidedly un-feminist, and, finally, makes a case for the continued relevance of O'Connor's work in the face of the latest iteration of "disembodied autonomy": posthumanism (2005: 240).

While much has been made of the religious aspects of O'Connor's fiction, very little has been said about the ways in which her characters attempt to deal with periods of transition and crisis. Here, I will make a case for why it might be useful to do so, drawing upon Mark Greif's *The Age of the Crisis of Man: Thought and Fiction in America* and comparing a sampling of O'Connor's characters to the literary figure who I believe best exemplifies a man who, unable to deal with the rapid changes of his time, abstracts himself from reality and enters into an enduring but ultimately misguided quest for the ideal: Don Quixote. In drawing this comparison, I hope to tease out some truth about the ways in which human beings deal with social and political change and the ways in which O'Connor calls us to transcend the moments of crisis in which we find ourselves. At a time of crisis, when Camus and others thought that the only response was despair, O'Connor proposes a sober hope that echoes that which is related in the figure of the dying Don Quixote.

Don Quixote and Flannery O'Connor

In his 1972 article, "Flannery's South: Don Quixote Rides Again," Ted R. Spivey writes that the South that Flannery O'Connor describes in her novels and short stories bears little resemblance to the South in which she lived: "From what I knew of her personally and from what I have read by others about her, I cannot find Flannery's South. Nor can I find it in the books and critical articles that are now appearing everywhere, most of them perceptive but none accounting for the strangeness of the world she created" (1972: 38). Seeking an answer in his own conversations with O'Connor and in his experiences teaching O'Connor's work to students, Spivey eventually concludes that "it is the spirit of the Spanish Catholicism of an earlier day, summed up for me, at least, in the figure of Don Quixote, that haunts much of her best work" (1972: 39). Though he admits that "in [his] conversations with her she often mentioned Irish Catholicism, French Catholicism, and of course American Catholicism, but never Spanish Catholicism" (1972: 39), Spivey goes on to draw some parallels between the characters in O'Connor's fiction and Don Quixote, claiming that both "[refuse] to live without those ideals that...make true community possible" (1972: 40), "see life essentially as comedy, and...are aware of the deep tragic nature of existence" (1972: 40), "make it plain... that their heroes apply the terms of books which possess their minds without comprehending the meaning of the terms to the world to which they are applied" (1972: 41), and "make it plain that even though the characters' hearts may be in the right place, they nevertheless are possessed by a fanatical madness" (1972: 41).

While there is a great deal of insight in Spivey's claims, his argument is primarily supported by his memories of O'Connor, his experience teaching her work, and his "own speculations" (1972: 39) about the origin of her South rather than by textual evidence. Further, it is somewhat surprising that in arguing that O'Connor is employing a particularly Spanish Catholicism, best exemplified in *Don Quixote*, Spivey does not make use of Miguel de Unamuno's 1921 work, *Tragic Sense of Life*, which was translated into English and available in the United States after

1954, or of Unamuno's 1905 work, *The Life of Don Quixote and Sancho*. Finally, while Spivey asserts that "it is clear to the careful reader that Flannery's great subject is the person of "wise blood," ... who is driven to seek God even while fleeing Him" and that "Flannery's South has at its center this person, who seems grotesque to those who have accepted our machine-dominated society in the belief that it is the only reality they can know" (1972: 42), he does not attend to the ways in which both Cervantes and O'Connor are products of their unique points in history or to the lessons that can be learned by modern readers who find themselves dealing with moments of crisis and transition.[1] It is this topic that I wish to take up in the following pages. Here, I will begin by discussing the socio-political landscape in which Cervantes thrust his tragicomic hero. I will then examine some of the ways in which *Don Quixote* functions as a text that is both unique to its time and that exemplifies the kind of Spanish Catholicism written about by Unamuno. Finally, I will examine the ways in which O'Connor's characters function as "quixotic" heroes of the period of crisis and transition that characterized the post-World War II United States before making some concluding remarks about the ways in which readers of the 21st century might make use of these works.

The Political and Social Landscape of Cervantes's Spain

In the fifteenth and sixteenth centuries, under the rule of King Ferdinand and Queen Isabel and later of their grandson, King Charles I of Spain, Spain went "from a collection of intermittently warring kingdoms to becoming an emerging nation state, and had then rapidly gone on to acquire a world-wide empire" (Ife, 2002: 12). During their rule, Ferdinand and Isabel ended the period of *convivencia* that Spain had previously

---

1. The latter of these two oversights seems particularly curious given that 1972, the year Spivey's article was published, has also been considered a time of social and political crisis in the United States, as the country was still embroiled in the widely-protested Vietnam War, and five men had been arrested in connection with what would later come to be known as the Watergate Scandal.

enjoyed, expelling the Jewish and Muslim residents of Spain;[2] limited the power of the Spanish nobles through the war against Granada; strengthened the power of the Catholic Church through the Inquisition and other policies; prioritized and made possible widespread education; and expanded their empire to include land in the New World (Ife, 2002: 12-18). After the death of Isabel in 1504 and then of Ferdinand in 1516, Charles I ascended the throne and, following in his grandparents' footsteps, continued to expand the empire.

Although Charles I was, by all accounts, "a skillful diplomat" (Ife, 2002: 19), his rule was not without difficulty. During the early years of his reign, Charles was forced to quell a number of revolts, and the sheer size of the Spanish empire made it difficult for him to remain in one place for long. Further, in response to Martin Luther's break with the Catholic Church, Charles entered Spain into a number of religiously-motivated wars, all of which put a great financial strain on the crown. In the 1550s, convinced "that his vast multinational conglomerate was too large to be manageable ... he split the empire into two parts, handed on the original Holy Roman Empire inherited from the Austrian Habsburgs to his brother Ferdinand, and left the Castilian, Aragonese, and Burgundian inheritances to his son Philip" (Ife, 2002: 21).

In 1556, Charles I's son, Philip II, came to power. Unlike his father, Philip "established a capital in Madrid, built a headquarters at the Escorial and ran the empire from a tiny office with the help of a small group of trusted advisors" (Ife, 2002: 21). He continued the work of his father and grandparents by "using a range of repressive measures [designed to strengthen the power of the Catholic Church in Spain]—the Inquisition and the *auto de fe*, the index of prohibited books and a ban on Spaniards studying abroad" (Ife, 2002: 21). Further, both his foreign policy and his

---

2. *Convivencia*, or "coexistence" was a remarkable period in Spanish history in which the Jewish, Muslim, and Christian residents of Spain lived in relative peace with one another. For a more in-depth discussion of *convivencia*, its implications, and both the skirmishes and agreements that informed this time period, see B.W. Ife's "The Social and Political Context," which appears in *The Cambridge Companion to Cervantes*.

work to crush the rebellions of the *moriscos*[3] in Spain and of the Protestants and separatists in the Netherlands proved just as costly as the military undertakings of Charles I. His military troubles were further complicated when the Spanish Armada, previously thought "invincible," failed to defeat the British navy (Ife, 2002: 22-23). Neither Philip nor Spain recovered from this blow, "and when he died in 1598, the crown was in debt for eight times its annual revenue" (Ife, 2002: 23).

Don Quixote: A Man in Transition

It was in this turbulent period that, in 1605, Miguel de Cervantes Saavedra published Part I of what came to be his best-known work, *Don Quixote*. In this now classic story, Cervantes tells of a delusional *hidalgo*,[4] who, after reading a number of chivalric romances, declares himself a knight and rides out into the world seeking quest after misguided quest to prove his worth. In Part I, Don Quixote, accompanied by his faithful squire Sancho Panza[5] and trusty steed, Rocinante, tilts at windmills, as-

---

3. Spanish Muslims who were forced to convert to Christianity.

4. According to Ife, the role and status of the *hidalgo* in the early seventeenth century Spain was quite complicated. During the latter half of the sixteenth century, a number of formerly poor Spaniards made their fortunes through farming and in the New World, thus shifting the power dynamics in Spain. In an effort to regain their foothold, "the old Christian ruling classes closed the ranks and hit back with the one thing money cannot buy: blood" (Ife 2002: 27). As a result, a number of laws were made to protect the status of the blue bloods, especially those who could prove "pure Christian origin," from being overtaken by the newly rich (Ife 2002: 27). This then created a series of conflicts between the (often impoverished) hidalgos and the far wealthier "self-made man (*hijo de sus obras*)"; these tensions can be seen throughout Don Quixote (Ife, 2002: 27).

5. It should be noted that Sancho, who is described as a "good man...but without much in the way of brains" is largely swayed by Don Quixote's promise that "it might happen one day that he would have an adventure that would gain him, in the blink of an eye, an ínsula, and he would make him its governor" (Cervantes, 2003: 55), a promise that Sancho hopes for throughout the novel. This is not, however, to diminish Sancho's care for Don Quixote, who would surely be lost without his squire.

saults a friar, slaughters a group of sheep that he believes to be an enemy army, releases (and is attacked by) criminals bound for the galleys, and generally causes chaos wherever he goes. This is done all in the name of chivalry and of Dulcinea, the name that Don Quixote gives to Aldonza Lorenzo, a peasant girl from a village near his own who has no idea of his oath to her or of his deeds.

Here, I would like to suggest that *Don Quixote* can be read as the story of a man who, unable to deal with the rapid changes taking place around him, abstracts himself from reality. According to Frederick De Armas, author of *Don Quixote among the Saracens: A Clash of Civilizations and Literary Genres*, it seems fitting that the story of a misguided knight might appear in the early seventeenth century: "Although Philip [II] reigned for about half a century, his final days were plagued with 'disaster and defeat'...Like his father, the glories of empire proved elusive in the end —his Quixotic quest, although in many ways triumphant, was a partial failure. It is no wonder that Cervantes penned his novel not long after Philip's demise" (2011: 3). Although Part I of Don Quixote is quite humorous, the story is tinged with the sense of sadness that accompanied the end of the reign of Philip II. In the novel, Don Quixote, the somewhat impoverished[6] *hidalgo*, becomes disenchanted with the real world and longs for a return to the Golden Age of Spain, a time when chivalry was upheld and men of his status were well-respected knights:

---

6. In the novel, Don Quixote's finances are described as follows: "Somewhere in La Mancha, in a place whose name I do not care to remember, a gentleman lived not long ago, one of those who has a lance and ancient shield on a shelf and keeps a skinny nag and a greyhound for racing. An occasional stew, beef more often than lamb, has most nights, eggs and abstinence on Saturdays, lentils on Fridays, sometimes squab as a treat on Sundays —these consumed three-fourths of his income. The rest went for a light woolen tunic and velvet breeches and hose of the same material for feast days, while weekdays were honored with dun-colored coarse cloth. He had a housekeeper past forty, a niece not yet twenty, and a man-of-all-work who did everything from saddling the horse to pruning the trees" (Cervantes, 2003: 19). Here, while it is clear that Don Quixote will not starve to death in the streets, it is also clear from his meager fare and few servants that his is not a rich house, although the lance and ancient shield suggest the former nobility of his family.

"His fantasy filled with everything he had read in his books, enchantments as well as combats, battles, challenges, wounds, courtings, loves, torments, and other impossible foolishness, and he became so convinced in his imagination of the truth of all the countless grandiloquent and false inventions he read that for him no history in the world was truer" (Cervantes 2003: 21). Indeed, throughout his misadventures, it soon becomes apparent that Don Quixote has very little understanding of the reality of those knights that he attempts to imitate, as can be seen in his refusal to sleep,[7] to eat,[8] and to pay for his lodgings.[9] As these banal actions are not recorded in the romances he read, Don Quixote views them as beneath the knight errant, who must practice a sort of asceticism or self-denial in order to prove his commitment to the code of chivalry.

In Part II, published in 1615, Cervantes takes his misguided hero in a more tragic direction. He becomes, as De Armas suggests, "A ghost of power. ... rather than retiring from the world, he enters the world and seeks power through melancholy visions. The emptiness of this pursuit... makes him into a ghost of all power" (2011: 10). It is this emptiness that is highlighted in Part II and that reveals the sorrowful trajectory of a man

---

7. Cervantes writes, "Don Quixote did not sleep at all that night but thought of his lady Dulcinea, in order to conform to what he had read in his books of knights spending many sleepless nights in groves and meadows, turning all their thoughts to memories of their ladies" (2003: 61).

8. In response to Sancho's offer to share his bread, cheese, and onion while they are on the road, Don Quixote replies, "I shall tell you, Sancho, that it is a question of honor for knights errant not to eat for a month, and when they do eat, it is whatever they find near at hand, and you would know the truth of this if you had read as many histories as I; although there are many of them, in none have I found it written that knights errant ever ate, unless perhaps at some sumptuous banquet offered in their honor; the rest of the time they all but fasted" (Cervantes, 2003: 74).

9. Upon being asked to pay for his room in a nearby inn, Don Quixote replies, "What you can do now is forgive the debt, for I cannot contravene the order of knights errant, about whom I know it is true, not having read anything to the contrary, that they never paid for their lodging or anything else in any inn where they stayed" (Cervantes, 2003: 121).

who, unable to deal with the world in which he lives, descends further into madness. Before departing on his third sally, Don Quixote once again expresses his desire to return to the Golden Age of Spain and his displeasure with his own time:

> I only devote myself to making the world understand its error in not restoring that happiest of times when the order of knight errantry was in flower. But our decadent age does not deserve to enjoy the good that was enjoyed in the days when knights errant took it as their responsibility to bear on their own shoulders the defense of kingdoms, the protection of damsels, the safeguarding of orphans and wards, the punishment of the proud, and the rewarding of the humble. (Cervantes, 2003: 465).

In this passage, it is clear that Don Quixote is still pursuing the ideal, despite the fact that he is aware that the Golden Age of knight errantry has ended, and this nostalgia for a time gone by further reveals Don Quixote's inability and unwillingness to deal with the changes happening around him. Shortly after, Don Quixote rouses Sancho Panza and goes forth, but this time, his niece, housekeeper, and neighbors conspire against him in an ultimately successful ploy to force him to retire honorably from knight errantry.

As is made clear to the reader, Don Quixote's refusal to remain grounded in reality once again makes him the object of scorn. After a number of further misadventures, including an attack on a puppet show, Don Quixote's vanquishing of the Knight of the Wood, and a period of time spent with a duke and duchess who seek to exploit Don Quixote's madness and Sancho's foolishness for their own amusement, Don Quixote's journey comes to an end. Bachelor Sansón Carrasco, this time disguised as the Knight of the White Moon, challenges Don Quixote to combat, once again over Dulcinea, and this time, Don Quixote is defeated. The Knight of the White Moon, after affirming that Dulcinea is, in fact, very beautiful, sets forth the terms of his victory: "The satisfaction I ask is that the great Don Quixote retire to his village for a year, or for as long as I shall determine, as we agreed before entering into this battle" (Cervantes, 2003: 887). Don Quixote agrees and returns home, where he has a few more minor adventures, but the shock of his defeat finally proves too great for the knight to overcome. On his death bed, Don Quixote repents of his earlier follies and reclaims his true identity:

> "Good news, Señores! I am no longer Don Quixote of La Mancha but Alonso Quixano, once called *the Good* because of my virtuous life. Now I am the enemy of Amadís of Gaul[10] and all the infinite horde of his lineage; now all the profane histories of knight errantry are hateful to me; now I recognize my foolishness and the danger I was in because I read them; now, by God's mercy, I have learned from my experience and I despise them." (Cervantes, 2003: 936).

So saying, Alonso Quixano asks for a priest to hear his confession and makes out his final will and testament, rewarding his niece, housekeeper, and Sancho for their loyalty to him and swearing that his niece will be disinherited if she marries a man who reads books of chivalry (Cervantes, 2003: 937-38).

In his reading of *Don Quixote*, first published in 1905 under the title *The Life of Don Quixote and Sancho*, Miguel de Unamuno provides us with further insight into how the character of Don Quixote might be taken by a Spanish reader. In a foreword to the 1914 edition of the text, Unamuno states that he is "more Quixotist than Cervantist" and writes of his hope "to free Don Quixote from Cervantes himself" (1967: 4). In freeing Don Quixote from Cervantes —and from the "university graduates, curates, barbers, dukes, and canons" (1967: 11)— Unamuno proposes that we view Don Quixote not as a raving madman who can't be trusted but as a man who, in giving himself over to his madness, becomes a holy figure who shares the "same temperament…[as] that cavalier of Christ, Iñigo de Loyola… who… was very warm in constitution and

---

10. One of the knights whom Don Quixote idolizes early in the novel.

very choleric" (1967: 26).¹¹ Thus, Unamuno comes to view Don Quixote's madness as Christlike, writing that the hidalgo "made the greatest sacrifice on the altar of his people: he sacrificed his wits" (1967: 28).

For Unamuno, Don Quixote is a paradoxical figure. He is baptized into his ministry by "two whores turned into maidens by Don Quixote" (1967: 36), driven by "self-love" (1967: 54) and yet "one of the purest examples of true humility" (1967: 55-56), and, finally, both deeply rooted in his own time and its accompanying poverty (1967: 24) and able to transcend his own time as a result of that rootedness (1967: 79-80). Perhaps most importantly, Don Quixote "knows who he is, [and] he need fear no one except God, who made him what he is" (1967: 49). It is this knowledge of himself and his ability to give himself over to the will of God that allows Don Quixote to resist what Unamuno calls "Sanchopanzism, now called positivism, now naturalism, now empiricism… [which] mocks the quixotic ideal" (1967: 95) and keeps one from being open to any kind of understanding reached through faith or the imagination. Ultimately, although Don Quixote repents of his madness, thus giving up his access to this type of understanding, Unamuno rejoices in the fact that quixotism is kept alive in the figure of Sancho Panza: "It is Sancho, your faithful Sancho, Sancho the Good, who went mad when you were cured of madness on your deathbed, Sancho it is who will establish quixotism upon the earth forever" (1967: 314).

In his later work, *Tragic Sense of Life*, Unamuno extends his disapproval of Cervantism, and thus, Sanchopanzism, in order to illustrate his understanding of the folly of Spanish Catholicism, which he refers to as the "tragic sense of life." The tragic sense of life, according to Unamuno, derives from the fact that the human being is a "man of flesh and bone; the man who is born, suffers, and dies—above all who dies" (1954: 1). It

---

11. Throughout *The Life of Don Quixote and Sancho*, Unamuno draws a number of parallels between Don Quixote and St. Ignatius of Loyola, based, in part, on his observation that "*Life of the Blessed Father Ignatius of Loyola*, a work which appeared in the Castilian tongue in 1583…was in the library of Don Quixote, who consequently read it" (1967: 32).

is this consciousness of death, Unamuno says that drives human beings to seek ways in which he or she can become immortal: "This means that your essence, reader, mine, that of the man Spinoza, that of the man Butler, of the man Kant, and of every man who is a man, is nothing but the endeavor, the effort, which he makes to continue to be a man, not to die" (1954: 7). Unamuno then proposes that it is out of this drive that philosophy, human feelings, and religious traditions are born. The tragedy of Catholicism, and of Spanish Catholicism in particular, is thus that it cannot abandon its foolish "longing for the immortality of the soul, for the permanence, in some form or another, of our personal and individual consciousness, [which] is as much of the essence of religion as is the longing that there may be a God" (1954: 221). It is this quiet hope, however, which Unamuno locates in the figure of the dying Don Quixote, that is embodied in O'Connor's fiction and that makes plausible Spivey's claim that "it is the spirit of the Spanish Catholicism of an earlier day, summed up…in the figure of Don Quixote, that haunts much of her best work" (1954: 39).

THE UNITED STATES IN TRANSITION: THE AGE OF CRISIS

The story of *Don Quixote* has been repeated in many iterations since its publication,[12] but here, I wish to focus primarily on the ways in which the title character's inability to adjust to social and political changes are mirrored in the work of Flannery O'Connor. In order to do so, it is useful to discuss the sense of danger felt by writers of the mid-twentieth century.

In his book-length study, Mark Greif proposes that the twentieth century be considered the "Age of the Crisis of Man," a period characterized by the upheavals following both world wars, the shock of Hitler's rise to power and of the atrocities committed in his name, and the chaos

---

12. In her book, *The Southern Inheritors of Don Quixote*, Monserrat Ginés (2000) writes that quixotic elements can be read in the fiction of Mark Twain, James Branch Cabell, William Faulkner, Eudora Welty, and Walker Percy.

of the 1960s. During this time, writers and intellectuals attempted to deal with the sense that "they were living in a unique and uniquely bad time" (Greif, 2015: 5), and, therefore, their writing became preoccupied with questions of the nature and existence of man. As Reinhold Niebuhr wrote, "Man has always been his most vexing problem. How shall he think of himself? Every affirmation which he may make about his stature, virtue, or place in the cosmos becomes involved in contradictions when fully analysed" (qtd. in Greif, 2015: 4). It was in this period, about which O'Connor wrote, "Right now the whole world seems to be going through a dark night of the soul" (1988: 100), that Flannery O'Connor came of age.

THE QUIXOTIC MAN IN FLANNERY O'CONNOR'S FICTION

In her essay, "Some Aspects of the Grotesque in Southern Fiction," O'Connor warns against the tendency of the modern reader to misread "characters who are forced out to meet evil and grace and who act on a trust beyond themselves...[as] typical Don Quixotes, tilting at what is not there" (1969: 42).[13] While this certainly appears to be a very good reason *not* to draw a comparison between our impoverished *hidalgo* and O'Connor's characters, I would argue that in various ways, Flannery O'Connor's characters can be read as articulating a number of the complexities of Don Quixote that Unamuno brings to light, particularly Don Quixote's deep and inexplicable attraction to God even in moments of crisis and despair. It is in dealing with the sense of crisis articulated by Greif, as well as their ability to alert O'Connor's readers to a hope sprung from grace, that they embody the Quixotic. Like Don Quixote, the characters of O'Connor's fiction are characterized by a nostalgia for the past, and in chasing after this age gone by, they become at once comic and tragic. According to Monserrat Ginés, author of *The Southern Inheritors of Don*

---

13. Interesting, although we do know from Arthur F. Kinney's book, *Flannery O'Connor's Library: Resources of Being* that she owned a 1954 edition of *Don Quixote*, this appears to be O'Connor's only direct reference to Cervantes's novel.

Quixote, "Certain southern writers have been particularly sensitive to the fundamental themes of Cervantes' novel: the insoluble discord between the real and the ideal and the attempt, at once grotesque and dignified, to affirm one's individuality in complete disregard of common sense and against all the demands of historical reality" (2000: 3). It is in light of this sensitivity that I wish to examine the ways in which Hazel Motes of *Wise Blood*, Mr. Shiflet of "The Life You Save May Be Your Own," and Julian of "Everything that Rises Must Converge" function as Quixotic men, preoccupied by their quests, albeit perverse, for truth, morality, and a return to the innocence of the past.

WISE BLOOD

In Flannery O'Connor's debut novel, *Wise Blood*, which she characterized in her "Author's Note to the Second Edition," as "a comic novel about a Christian *malgré lui*, and as such, very serious, for all comic novels that are any good must be about matters of life and death," in other words, the tragic sense of life, the main character, Hazel "Haze" Motes, can be read as searching for meaning and purpose after returning from World War II, in which it soon becomes apparent that he has been both bodily and spiritually injured. Haze embarks on a journey to "do some things [he's] never done before" (1952: 7). Once he arrives in Taulkingham, Haze meets Enoch Emery, who in his biography of O'Connor Brad Gooch characterizes as, "Playing Sancho Panza to Haze's Don Quixote" (204) and begins his quest to "preach a new church—the church of truth without Jesus Christ Crucified" (1952: 51). While it is true that Hazel is, at least consciously, attempting to break with his past as a follower of Christianity, it becomes clear to the reader that much of this attempt stems from the trauma he suffered throughout his childhood and while he was fighting in World War II. This is made clear following Haze's attempts to maintain his moral superiority over his fellow soldiers:

> They told him he didn't have any soul and left for their brothel. He took a long time to believe them because he wanted to believe them. All he wanted was to believe them and get rid of it once and for all, and he saw the opportunity here to get rid of it without corruption, to be converted to nothing instead of to evil. The army sent him halfway around the world and forgot him. He was wounded and they remembered him long enough to take the shrapnel out of his chest...and then they sent him to another desert and forgot him again. (1952: 18)

It is in this Quixotic quest for nothing rather than the "wild ragged figure" of Christ "[moving] from tree to tree in the back of his mind" (1952: 16) that Haze enters into his tragicomic—and often foolish—pursuit.

Just as Unamuno tells us is true of Don Quixote, Haze is consumed with the battle to "purify himself" of his "self-love" (1967: 54), although it cannot be said that Haze appears to "[love] all humanity" (1967: 54) as Don Quixote does. In the chapters that follow, we see Haze attempt, unsuccessfully, to spread the "Good News" of his newly formed church after being baptized into his ministry by a "whore" of his own, Mrs. Watts;[14] become entangled with Sabbath Hawks and her father, the supposedly blind preacher Asa Hawks; kill a false prophet in a move that echoes Don Quixote's assaults on those who he views as either enchanted or unchivalrous;[15] and finally, blind himself in an attempt to see truth. While, unlike Don Quixote, the question of Haze's eventual redemption remains unresolved,[16] it is clear that Haze's efforts stem from

---

14. It is perhaps worth noting that unlike Don Quixote, who, as we have already seen, "turn[s his 'whores'] into maidens" (1967: 36), Haze does, in fact, give in to the "charms" of Mrs. Watts.

15. This is supported by Olivia McGuire who, in her article, "'Incarnational Art': Thing Theory and Flannery O'Connor's Wise Blood," writes, "In this case, the murder is a physical manifestation of Hazel's total contempt for blasphemy, though he does not want to recognize it as such" (2013: 520).

16. The question of Hazel's redemption has been taken up by a number of scholars. Some, like Jonathan Witt and Ralph C. Wood, argue that he has been saved; both

his sense of displacement in the modern world. His dress, mannerisms, and adherence to outdated modes of asceticism[17] place him squarely in a world that no longer exists. Indeed, Haze is first described as having "a stiff black broad-rimmed hat on his lap, a hat that an elderly country preacher would wear" (1952: 4). Like Quixote's ancient armor, this hat becomes the object of much ridicule and the symbol of Haze's ties to the past throughout the novel, and, like Quixote, it is because he ultimately clings to his sense of a warped truth, rather than to a hope for New Life in Christ, that Hazel Motes meets his end.

"THE LIFE YOU SAVE MAY BE YOUR OWN"

In Flannery O'Connor's short story, "The Life You Save May Be Your Own," the Quixotic spirit is once again embodied in the character of Mr. Shiftlet. When he arrives at the farm of the Lucynell Craters, Mister Shiflet, upon being told that the car is broken, states, "Nothing is like it used to be, lady... The world is almost rotten" (1971:146). From this statement,

---

draw upon O'Connor's own writing to make the argument that Hazel is a saint who is "grotesquely participating in Christ's own suffering" (Wood 87). Others, like Brian Ingraffia and Susan Srigley, argue that Hazel does not achieve salvation and that even if he is seeking redemption, that redemption is not apparent to the reader. Srigley goes on to say that "O'Connor is criticizing this blindness by illustrating penance not as irrelevant or primitive, and not as an attempt to earn salvation, but as destructive and meaningless when performed in the absence of love and responsibility for others" (2004: 94). For Srigley, then, it as a result of Hazel's lack of care for others that we can conclude that he does not achieve salvation.

17. In addition to blinding himself, Hazel's ascetic practices are detailed at numerous points throughout the novel. After seeing a wriggling woman in a coffin at the carnival, Hazel is described as putting rocks in his shoes and walking a mile and a half in them as penance (1952: 56-60). After Hazel has blinded himself, Mrs. Flood discovers that Haze has strapped barbed wire to his chest and tells him, "Well, it's not normal. It's like one of them gory stories, it's something that people have quit doing —like boiling in oil or being a saint or walling up cats" (1952: 228). Once again, this points to Hazel's tendency to follow long-discarded practices in an attempt to purify himself and pursue his perverted notion of the truth.

it can be ascertained that, like Hazel, Mr. Shiflet has experienced some kind of disillusionment with the modern world, likely as a result of the loss of his arm.[18] While it is not clear how Mr. Shiflet became injured, his statements, although surely false, connote a desire to return to an age-of-innocence chivalry. This is revealed in his exchanges with the older Mrs. Lucynell Crater, to whom he says, "Lady…where would you find you an innocent woman today? I wouldn't have any of this trash I could just pick up" (1971: 149). Like Don Quixote, Mr. Shiflet appears to be privileging an innocence that is long gone, although it should be noted that in his later marriage to and abandonment of the very innocent but mentally handicapped young Lucynell Carter, he reveals himself as caring only about monetary gain.

Furthermore, the chivalric views he falsely espouses lead to both the older Mrs. Lucynell Carter and, finally, himself, being duped. Upon being asked whether or not he would like to marry the younger Lucynell, Mr. Shiflet states, "Some people'll do anything anyhow these days, but the way I think, I wouldn't marry no woman that I couldn't take on a trip like she was somebody" (1971: 152). While he does, eventually, take Mrs. Carter's money and leave Lucynell at a diner, the language that Mr. Shiflet uses in this passage seems to uphold an old code of honor that no longer seems to be of any value in the modern world. This is made clearer in an exchange with Mrs. Carter in which Mr. Shiflet expresses a longing for things past in a manner that echoes both Don Quixote and Hazel Motes:

> "I told you you could hang around and work for food," she said, "if you don't mind sleeping in that car yonder."
> "Why listen, lady," he said with a grin of delight, "the monks of old slept in their coffins!"
> "They wasn't as advanced as we are," the old woman said. (1971: 149)

---

18. When Mrs. Lucynell Carter first beholds Mr. Shiflet, she notices that "his left coat sleeve was folded up to show there was only half an arm in it" (1971: 145).

Here, Mrs. Carter's response seems to echo that of Mrs. Flood,[19] calling Mr. Shiflet back to the modern world whose attitudes he eventually embraces and uses to harm others.

At the end of the story, Mr. Shiflet is finally called to a recognition of his failures. After picking up a hitchhiker, Mr. Shiflet reaches a moment of clarity in which his own mother's love and goodness is revealed to him: "My mother was a angel of Gawd...He took her from heaven and giver to me and I left her" (1971: 156) As Mr. Shiflet has just abandoned his new bride at a roadside diner, aptly named "The Hot Spot" (1971: 154-55), this realization seems especially timely, and for a moment, it appears as if Mr. Shiflet will finally be called to the consciousness of his misdeeds that Don Quixote experiences at the end of his own journey. The moment, however, is short lived. After being told to "go to the devil!" by the hitchhiker, Mr. Shiflet once again turns into himself before racing on to the next town: "Mr. Shiflet felt that the rottenness of the world was about to engulf him. He raised his arm and let if fall again to his breast. 'Oh Lord!' he prayed. 'Break forth and wash the slime from this earth!" (1971: 156). Thus, the brief period of Mr. Shiflet's conversion is ended, and he remains alienated from the modern world, a Quixotic man without the final peace of God.

"Everything that Rises Must Converge"

While Mr. Shiflet's dislocation, like that of Hazel Motes's, seems to be linked to his body, that of the main character in "Everything that Rises Must Converge," Julian, seems to be rooted in an intellectual understanding of the world. Julian, an out-of-work college graduate living with his mother, finds himself both disgusted with her inability to adjust to the changes of the modern world and unaware of his own. This disgust is revealed in a statement Julian makes to his mother that follows shortly after his own dreams of grandeur: "Knowing who you are is good for

---

19. See note 15.

one generation only. You haven't the foggiest idea where you stand now or who you are" (1971: 407). While here, Julian is responding to his mother's delusions of the former prosperity of their family —built on slave labor, it soon becomes clear to the reader that he is more tied to his mother and to his family than he thinks.

These tensions become magnified when Julian and his mother take a ride on the newly desegregated city bus. The differences in supposed attitudes between Julian and his overtly racist mother come to bear in the story that follows. Both characters feel a sense of moral superiority towards others: Julian feels that as a modern man who has accepted desegregation and, in yet another perversion of Christ's commandment, "loves all humanity" (1967: 54), he is superior to his mother, and his mother feels that she is superior to the black characters in the story and superior to her son as *qua* mother. While this tension is not a new one in southern literature, it does create a situation in which each is driven to uphold his or her own notion of honor. As Ginés points out, "The institution of slavery…[and] the patriarchal foundations of southern society and the emphasis it gave to the notions of honor, chivalry, and the importance of lineage over work and money" are elements of the "root of the myth of the Lost Cause" that southern characters pursue (1967: 3).

Thus, much like Don Quixote who seeks to restore honor and chivalry in seventeenth century Spain by correcting the actions of perceived oppressors, Julian endeavors to correct his mother's behavior and expose to her the error of her ways in the twentieth century. As Julian is unable to see the mote in his own eye, however, this story, like so many of O'Connor's, comes to a tragic end. Julian and his mother board the city bus so she can go to her class at the Y, and Julian is quickly caught up in dreams of teaching his mother a lesson. He is soon "tilted out of his fantasy again as the bus stop[s]" (1971: 415), and an African American woman and her child board. Seeing an opportunity for his dreams to come true, Julian hopes that the woman will sit next to his mother. Instead, the little boy sits next to his mother, and the woman sits next to Julian (1971: 415). It is in this scene that Julian's own myopic view of race becomes clear. Although he is the one who claims to uphold racial equality, his desire to use the African American woman and her child to teach his mother a lesson reveals his own tendency to other and objectify the African Americans that he comes across. Conversely, his mother's interaction with the woman, to whom she exclaims, "Isn't he cute?" (1971: 417) is far more natural. Thus, it becomes clear that for Julian, the African-American characters are merely pedagogical tools at best and instruments of revenge at worst, revealing his own inability to transition smoothly into the new reality in which he lives.

The story comes to a tragic end when, after attempting to give the child a penny, Julian's mother is assaulted by the African American woman, who shouts, "He don't take nobody's pennies!" (1971: 418). While it is true that Julian's mother is somewhat patronizing here, we know that this is the way that Julian's mother treats all children, not just black children (1971: 415-17). After her assault, Julian demonstrates once again that he has prioritized his quest for honor and morality over those who love him. After yelling that he told her not to give the boy a penny, Julian callously tells his mother, "Now get up" (1971: 418) and forces her to begin walking. Upset by the woman's actions and her son's response, Julian's mother then swoons in what the reader can only assume is a fatal heart attack. Like Don Quixote, Julian is then left only with the realization that he has mistreated those he loved in his pursuit of the ideal and an "entry into the world of guilt and sorrow" (1971: 420).

IMPLICATIONS FOR THE PRESENT

Now, at the beginning of the twenty-first century, the world has, again, become a place of great social and political change. Growing inequality in the distribution of wealth, technological advances, the rise of "post" theory and "post-truth," and the success of far-right leaders in global political movements have left many feeling displaced, regardless of social class or political affiliation. In such circumstances, many are struck with the desire to turn, like Don Quixote, to an idealized past, as we have seen from the success of slogans like "Make America Great Again" and "Make Britain Great Again" and of the proliferation of "listicles" titled "37 things only 80s/90s/2000s kids will know" that can be found throughout the internet. Although Cervantes wrote in the early seventeenth century and O'Connor in the mid-twentieth century, it is thus clear that their message, that we are called to be radically present to one another and to the time in which we live, is both relevant and of the utmost importance.

As is clear in the stories of Don Quixote, Hazel Motes, Mr. Shiflet, and Julian, those who are unable to adjust to change are doomed to foolish pursuits of the unattainable ideal and, ultimately, to tragic endings. For both Cervantes and O'Connor, however, there is a way out: despite themselves, both O'Connor's characters and Don Quixote seem to be searching for a wholeness that both authors posit can only be found in Christ. As Kilcourse reminds us, "[O'Connor's] stories of conversion summon us time and again to contemplate the mystery of the Christ who throws off balance every status quo that threatens to seduce and paralyze us with its tempting illusion" (2001: 13). Therefore, it is only by unchaining ourselves from our past misconceptions and confessing the ways in which our misdeeds have harmed those we loved, as Don Quixote does from his death bed, that we might truly become free. These stories call us to radical renegotiation of our selves and our ideas as the world changes around us. Thus, as Miguel de Unamuno writes in *Tragic Sense of Life*, we must remember to "attack wisely and cautiously. Reason must be our weapon. It is the weapon even of the fool" (1954: 305) —indeed, a fool: for Christ's sake.

Bibliography

Bieber Lake, Christina (2005). *The Incarnational Art of Flannery O'Connor*. Macon, GA: Mercer University Press.

Cervantes Saavedra, Miguel de (2003). *Don Quixote*. Translated by Edith Grossman. New York, NY: Ecco.

De Armas, Frederick A. (2011). Pillars of Genre/Ghosts of Empire: An Introduction. In *Don Quixote among the Saracens: A Clash of Civilizations and Literary Genres*. Toronto: University of Toronto Press, pp. 1-24.

Giannone, Richard (2000). *Flannery O'Connor: Hermit Novelist*. Urbana, IL: University of Illinois Press.

Ginés, Montserrat (2000). *The Southern Inheritors of Don Quixote*. Baton Rouge, LA: Louisiana State University Press.

Gordon, Sarah (2000). *Flannery O'Connor: The Obedient Imagination*. Athens, GA: The University of Georgia Press.

Greif, Mark (2015). *The Age of the Crisis of Man: Thought and Fiction in America, 1933-1973*. Princeton, NJ: Princeton University Press.

Ingraffia, Brian (2009). "'If Jesus Existed, I Wouldn't be Clean: Self Torture in Flannery O'Connor's Wise Blood," in *Flannery O'Connor Review*, 7: 78-86.

Ife, B.W. (2001). The Historical and Social Context. In Anthony J Cascardi (Ed.), *The Cambridge Companion to Cervantes*. Cambridge: Cambridge University Press, pp. 11-31.

Kilcourse, George A., Jr. (2001). *Flannery O'Connor's Religious Imagination: A World with Everything off Balance*. New York, NY: Paulist Press.

Kinney, Arthur F. (1985) *Flannery O'Connor's Library: Resources of Being*. Athens, GA: The University of Georgia Press.

McGuire, Olivia (2013). "'Incarnational Art': Thing Theory and Flannery O'Connor's Wise Blood," in *Religion and the Arts*, 17, 5: 507-22.

O'Connor, Flannery (1971). *The Complete Stories of Flannery O'Connor*. New York, NY: Farrar, Straus and Giroux.

--- (1969). Some Aspects of the Grotesque in Southern Fiction. In Sally and Robert Fitzgerald (Eds.), *Mystery and Manners*. New York, NY: Farrar, Straus and Giroux, pp. 36-50.

--- (1988). *The Habit of Being*. Edited by Sally Fitzgerald. New York, NY: Farrar, Straus and Giroux.

--- (2007). *Wise Blood*. New York, NY: Farrar, Straus and Giroux.

Spivey, Ted R. (1972) "Flannery's South: Don Quixote Rides again," in *Flannery O'Connor Bulletin*, 1: 37-43.

Srigley, Susan (2004). *Flannery O'Connor's Sacramental Art*. Notre Dame, IN: University of Notre Dame.

--- (2009). "Penance and Love in Wise Blood?: Seeing Redemption," in *Flannery O'Connor Review*, 7: 94-100.

Unamuno, Miguel de (1967). *Our Lord Don Quixote: The Life of Don Quixote and Sancho with Related Essays*. Translated by Anthony Kerrigan, Edited by Anthony Kerrigan et al, vol. 3. Princeton, NJ: Princeton University Press.

---. *Tragic Sense of Life* (1954). Translated by J.E. Crawford Flitch. New York, NY: Dover Publications.

Witt, Jonathan (1993). "Wise Blood and the Irony of Redemption," in *The Flannery O'Connor Bulletin*, 22: 12-24.

THE OTHER AS ANGELS:
O'CONNOR'S CASE FOR RADICAL HOSPITALITY

MICHAEL BRUNER

"Do not neglect to show hospitality to strangers, for by this some have entertained angels without knowing it." (Hebrews 13:2)

The inhospitable tenor of our historical moment, which has been marked by a return (some would say regression) to more nativist impulses —political, cultural, and religious— gives O'Connor's depiction of radical hospitality a more compelling urgency. From Madrid to Berlin, Rome to Paris, Toronto to Los Angeles the influx of refugees from the south to the north by the tens of millions has forced the issue regarding the nature and limits of hospitality. For this reason, no period in recent history is more ripe for examining new ways of conceiving what true hospitality looks like. The role of the church in this conversation, as both the repository and manifestation of the *locus classicus* of hospitality found in Scripture, is crucial if it is to continue to embody Christ's radical call to welcome and embrace the Other.[1] Flannery O'Connor's fiction can serve

---

1. In his book, *Poetic Theology: God and the Poetics of Everyday Life* (2011), William Dyrness contends that the church must be involved in justice-making as the ultimate form of *koinonea*, which gives symbolic forms their eschatological character. There is, in other words, an element of aesthetics involved in questions of radical hospitality,

as a guide for such a call, providing not only a picture of what radical hospitality might look like but also a winsome yet withering critiques of hospitality as it is practiced in much of contemporary culture.

This chapter will examine Flannery O'Connor's use of the motif of *home* as a code or device in her fiction to show how Christian hospitality functions over and against other forms of hospitality and, specifically, so-called "Southern hospitality." In such an inversion, the "Other" becomes the angelic visitor, the immigrant becomes the friend, the stranger becomes the brother or sister. In this sense, O'Connor's depiction of Christian hospitality serves as an indictment of its southern cousin, where the biblical mandate to care for the poor and dispossessed, to shoulder the burdens of the orphan and widow, and to clothe the naked stands in stark contrast to conventional notions of hospitality, which, essentially, amount to manners without mystery. Manners alone were not, for O'Connor, a moral category. Manners were made up of, and even contained, "the texture of existence that surrounds you," while mystery was an anagogical reality that gave rise to, and served as a conduit for, God's severe mercies (O'Connor, 1969: 103). In O'Connor's fiction, radical hospitality is depicted as the province of divine action and, as such, serves as a controlling metaphor for the Kingdom of Heaven. O'Connor's vision of hospitality parallels the biblical injunctions to take care of the 'least of these.'[2]

---

which preferences, it seems to me, artistic portrayals of hospitality, such as those found in O'Connor's fiction. If creation, as both nature and culture, is the theater for God's glory, as Dyrness argues, one of the chief places this glory is manifest is in the human image. If we are to attend to such forms of glory, then, we do so most effectively by caring for the image in the other. Beauty and justice are thus linked together by hospitality, so that the mandate that "man does not live by bread alone" becomes, from an aesthetic perspective, a call for a banquet, a heavenly feast. Such a call to radical hospitality means that we don't merely provide people shelter, but that we turn our houses into homes (see *esp.* chapter nine in Dyrness).

2. Hans Schenk explicates what the biblical injunctions surrounding hospitality amount to, which, to the modern ear, seem not only mysterious but impractical:

The Other as Angels: O'Connor's Case for Radical Hospitality

Radical, or Christian, hospitality is distinguished from, but is also an expression of, Christian charity. But whereas Christian charity is a love one shows for the friend as well as the enemy in any circumstance, radical hospitality is defined, quite simply and more specifically, as the *taking in* of the Other —often the marginalized and outcast— as one's own. It is the expression of love explicitly illustrated in the parables of the Good Samaritan and Prodigal Son. In the case of the Prodigal Son, of course, the play is on the notion of the Other. It is, quite literally, the son who is taken back in, but it is also, and in fact, NOT the son who is taken back in by the father, as the son renounces his inheritance, and thus his legal status as son, at the beginning of the story. He is no longer an inheritor. He gives voice to this in his prepared confession: "I am no longer worthy to be called your son. Take me in as on your hired servants." Technically, he is correct. But God is not concerned with technicalities in situations involving the Other.

Given this definition of hospitality as a very specific form of love in which the Other is taken in as one's own, the Incarnation, then, can be defined as the ultimate expression of Christian hospitality, where the Son does not consider equality with the Father as something to be assumed but empties himself and becomes one of us —the Other— precisely that he might usher us, his brothers and sisters, into the realm of divine and eternal hospitality.

The hospitality of the Global South —typified by the Spanish phrase "Mi casa es su casa"— is a closer approximation of the biblical vision

> In both Old and New Testaments, there is an emphasis on caring for those in need which not only include the poor, orphan, and widow, but also the sojourner and stranger in the land. Jesus communicates that caring for those in need (which includes the stranger) is caring for Jesus himself... God's people in the Old Testament are frequently refugees and immigrants themselves... These immigrations, especially the stay in Egypt, are God's basis for commanding the Israelites to care for those who are aliens, strangers, and sojourners in their own land. God specifically tells them that "You shall treat the stranger who sojourns with you as the native among you, and you shall love him as yourself, for you were strangers in the land of Egypt..." (2008: 5-7; unpublished manuscript).

of radical hospitality than any notion of hospitality associated with the Global North, for example, but even the South's tradition of manners, when separated from the mystery that gives it substance, falls far short of the biblical vision of an eschatological community of justice and mercy. "Traditional manners," O'Connor once wrote, "are better than no manners at all," (1969: 200) but this statement serves merely to illustrate the point that, for O'Connor, traditional manners are the minimum threshold. They're better than nothing, but Christian manners —which are deliberately tied into the mystery of the Kingdom of God and God's radical grace— go far deeper into the human experience because they incorporate the radical claim of hospitality envisioned in the gospels.

In her introduction to *The Habit of Being*, Sally Fitzgerald gives a beautiful description of O'Connor's sense of hospitality, which was every bit as much a product of the biblical witness as it was of her southern gentility, though Fitzgerald does not make that explicit connection:

> What else, though, do the letters tell us of the storyteller herself? The overriding impression is of a *joie de vivre*, rooted in her talent and the possibilities of her work, which she correctly saw as compensating her fully for any deprivations she had to accept, and as offering her a scope for living that most of us never dream of encompassing. From this sensibility grew a wonderful appreciation of the world's details: the vagaries of human personality; the rich flow of the language she heard around her; the beauty of Andalusia, the family outside Milledgeville where the O'Connor's went to live after Flannery fell ill, and of the birds, homely or regal, with which she peopled it; [and] the hospitality she and her mother offered to friends and strangers alike; good food…; talk, books, and letters (Fitzgerald, 1979: xiii).

Fitzgerald adds that O'Connor "was as generous with her correspondents as she and her mother were in their hospitality" (Fitzgerald, 1979: xvi). I would add that O'Connor's generous and voluminous correspondence was, in fact, one of the major manifestations of her radical hospitality.

The Other as Angels: O'Connor's Case for Radical Hospitality

The conflicts in O'Connor's stories have been traditionally understood as arising from competing visions of truth. Though I believe this is true, what is too often lost in such a conclusion is the effect of such competing visions. I want to suggest that a vision for the subversive Kingdom of God, which O'Connor always had one eye trained on as she wrote her stories, invariably leads to the conflict in her stories as that vision runs up against competing visions of what counts for hospitality. *Am I my brother's keeper? How are we to treat the resident aliens among us? What does it mean to love my enemy? Who is the good Samaritan of our day?* These and other questions offer ways of understanding the true call of radical Christian hospitality that O'Connor envisioned —the kind of hospitality that Elizabeth Newman calls "at once abundant and terrifying" (Newman, 2005: 136).

It is instructive to note, at the outset, the etymological connection of "hospitality" to "hospital," something O'Connor grew increasingly familiar with as the claws of her lupus sank deeper into her body. In her short story "A Good Man is Hard to Find," it is the Grandmother's gesture of biblical hospitality —of welcoming the stranger as a child of one's own— that gets her heart blown to smithereens. Her newly transformed heart, of course, is the one thing that the Misfit simply could not abide. Why? Because it —the Grandmother's heart— had become the seat of radical biblical hospitality, so he had to annihilate the offending organ, as if shooting her in the chest three times —a bit excessive, if you ask me— would somehow remove the invitation to the cosmic reality she had just encountered and had then extended to the Misfit: that he was, in fact, one of her own babies, one of her own children! Exclamation point.

Is there a more radical testimony to loving one's enemy, which is the apex of true Christian hospitality, than that? And of course, as is O'Connor's wont, the Misfit's violent response to God's love actually allows the Grandmother to make good on her newly radicalized vision: no greater love has one than this, that one lays down one's life for another.

In one of her earliest stories, "The Turkey," the protagonist, Ruller, is taking the dead, 10lb. turkey he's just "captured" home to his —he hopes— proud father, like some long lost prodigal son coming home with a prize. In the midst of Ruller's chase after the turkey, the boy has had a conversion (of the O'Connor kind), and instead of cursing God, he is now praying to God. And what is his prayer? That God send him a beggar so that he can give the beggar his last and only dime, so that he can make good for the gift of the turkey that God sent to him. He prays and prays for a beggar, and one comes —only not in the form Ruller had been expecting. And they —these beggars, these tenants' children— don't want his dime. They want his turkey. And so they take it. And that's that. Ruller meets God's expectations for hospitality head on. It isn't some beggar who wants his dime who God sends, though Ruller meets her, too, and gives her his dime. No, God is interested in the kind of hospitality that turns us inside out —the Rich Young Ruler (read Ruller) kind of hospitality— where one sells everything one has, gives the proceeds to the poor, and then follows Christ. Of course, in this story, when the biblical injunction of radical hospitality is realized and the turkey is forfeited to the tenants' children, Ruller isn't following God. God is following him, chasing him, in fact, all the way Home:

> He turned toward home, almost creeping. He walked four blocks and then suddenly, noticing that it was dark, he began to run. He ran faster and faster, and as he turned up the road to his house, his heart was running as fast as his legs and he was certain that Something Awful was tearing behind him with its arms rigid and its fingers ready to clutch (O'Connor, 1988: 752).

That Something Awful with its fingers ready to clutch? This is the biblical God intent on grabbing him, and O'Connor's readers, by the throat to take us far beyond our comfort zone of well-mannered hospitality that we conveniently substitute for the radical hospitality we are actually called to. Ruller prayed, even begged, for a beggar to show up. And God, in his inimitable kindness, mercy, and dark humor, gives Ruller what he asks for. In exchange for forfeiting the turkey —everything, in other

The Other as Angels: O'Connor's Case for Radical Hospitality

words— the Poor Young Ruller gets God; or at least the hard hit in the chest that one experiences when meeting the God of Abraham, Isaac, and Jacob (renamed *Is-ra-el*, or one who contends with God). Welcome to biblical hospitality. We should note, too, that this is the same Ruller who, not incidentally, after his deep-in-the-woods conversion, considers twice in the story that he "might found a home for tenants' children" (O'Connor, 1988: 750). Hospitality in the abstract —if, indeed, there is such a thing— is always a more pleasant and innocuous thing than hospitality in its concrete and specific, incarnated form. Such an Incarnational hospitality, with its divine summons to love the Other, is the mystery behind the mere manners of its southern cousin.

Southern manners and southern hospitality go hand in hand, and O'Connor was familiar with both, though the former (manners) dictates the latter's (hospitality) limits. One is hospitable only to the degree that southern manners dictates. The hospitality connected to the mystery of God and to the Christ that embodies such radical hospitality, on the other hand, which O'Connor was far more acquainted with, stands over and against such patrician —even exclusive— notions of hospitality. This mysterious hospitality, which most of O'Connor's stories in one way or another point to, requires compassion, and compassion isn't compassion if pain isn't shared. Compassion (*com-passio*, or literally, to suffer alongside), is the radical biblical vision of hospitality that O'Connor was after in each of her stories. Indeed, it is that radical hospitality that her characters essentially suffer, and sometimes die, for. Witness, again, the Grandmother in "A Good Man is Hard to Find." In welcoming the Misfit as one of her own, she's effectively welcoming him home. Needless to say, he's not interested in coming home. At least not yet...

This notion of home plays a central role in Nelson's and his grandfather's sojourn into the city in O'Connor's story, "The Artificial Nigger." Mr. Head reminds his grandson that this strange city is where the boy was born —and therefore, presumably, where the boy is *from*: "This is your old home town," the Grandfather, who is all head and no heart, says. But Nelson's bites back: "I never said I wanted to come. I only said

I was born here and I never had anything to do with that. I want to go home" (O'Connor, 1988: 263).

But scarcely an hour later on their fitful journey to nowhere, the roles reverse. This time it's Mr. Head who wants to get home: "We're going to get home!" he cries breathlessly. But, O'Connor tells us, as far as Nelson is concerned, "Home was nothing to him" (O'Connor, 1988: 269). These are two souls wandering around looking for a home they can't find, or for that matter, define. They don't understand the connection between their basic and essential hostility —their lack of hospitality— and their homelessness. And what wakes them up from their stupor? The plaster statue of "a Negro sitting bent over on a low yellow brick fence that curved around a wide lawn." "An artificial nigger!" the Grandpa exclaims (O'Connor, 1988: 229). This figure, meant to be a lawn ornament with racist humor attached, becomes the means for Nelson and the Grandfather to find a connection with humanity, and specifically, with the Other. The figure looks miserable, all the more so because he was meant to look happy, "but the chipped eye and the angle he was cocked at gave him a wild look of misery instead" (O'Connor, 1988: 229). This is followed by one of the more memorable passages in all of O'Connor fiction:

> The two of them stood there with their necks forward at almost the same angle and their shoulders curved in almost exactly the same way and their hands identically in their pockets. Mr. Head looked like an ancient child and Nelson like a miniature old man. They stood gazing at the artificial Negro as if they were faced with some great mystery, some monument to another's victory that brought them together in their common defeat. They could both feel it dissolving their differences like an action of mercy. Mr. Head had never known before what mercy felt like because he had been too good to deserve any, but he felt he knew now. He looked at Nelson and understood that me must say something to the child to show that he was still wise and in the look the boy returned he saw a hungry need for that assurance. Nelson's eyes seemed to implore him to explain once and for all the mystery of existence.

> Mr. Head opened his lips to make a lofty statement and heard himself say, "They ain't got enough real ones here. They got to have an artificial one."
> After a second, the boy nodded with a strange shivering about his mouth, and said, "Let's go home before we get ourselves lost again (O'Connor, 1988: 229).

Recognizing one's lost-ness is, apparently, a prerequisite to finding one's true home (see the parable of The Prodigal Son). In like manner, feeling the Other's pain becomes not only the crucial element in radical hospitality but (or so it appears) the precursor to salvation ('When you did it to the least of these,' Jesus said, 'You did it to me'). It is the only thing, O'Connor tells us, that we can bring with us to God:

> Mr. Head stood very still and felt the action of mercy touch him again but this time he knew that there were no words in the world that could name it. He understood that it grew out of agony, which is not denied to any man and which is given in strange ways to children. He understood it was all a man could carry into death to give his Maker and he suddenly burned with shame that he had so little of it to take with him. He stood appalled, judging himself with the thoroughness of God, while the action of mercy covered his pride like a flame and consumed it. He had never thought himself a great sinner before but he saw now that his true depravity had been hidden from him lest it cause him despair. He realized that he was forgiven for sins from the beginning of time, when he had conceived in his own heart the sin of Adam, until the present, when he denied poor Nelson. He saw that no sin was too monstrous for him to claim as his own, and since God loved in proportion as He forgave, he felt ready at that instant to enter Paradise (O'Connor, 1988: 231).

For O'Connor's characters, of course, homecomings are spiritual and not geographical sojourns. There is often a geographical element to these sojourns, but the way Home for a character in her stories is via the narrow path that leads to salvation, not a train back to one's house or some highway into a distant city. And the sojourns of her characters always and necessarily involve a journey through the pain of the Other. An O'Connor reader knows when one of her characters has truly been redeemed: when the radical summons of Christian hospitality confronts them like a sledgehammer and, crucially, they extend that hospitality to another. They suddenly experience an empathy for the world's suffering that they never could have before, and now they cannot help but extend it to someone else. It is precisely in the necessity of descending through the valley of the shadow of death, which, in O'Connor's world, often involved a literal death, that one is able to arrive at the banquet table of hospitality envisioned in Psalm 23, the biblical vision *par excellence* of radical hospitality. Every journey home for an O'Connor character is, in other words, a sacramental sojourn into the radical hospitality of the Kingdom of God, which is supremely communal and never individual.

In "The Comforts of Home," the only O'Connor story with the word "home" actually in the title, home functions as a waystation for the homeless, and the whole story is an extended meditation on true hospitality. It opens with the son, Thomas, staring down at the new house guest named Star Drake, the homeless "slut" from a local boarding house who his mother has invited to live with them, a mother who, from Thomas' perspective, is "about to wreck the peace of the house" because of her "daredevil charity," O'Connor's wonderful euphemism for the radical Christian hospitality that the mother shows to this young girl. And the peace of the house is indeed about to be wrecked, because that peace, a peace informed only by manners, is a peace exclusive and stifling, not inclusive and inviting; it is an electric blanket not too disimilar from an electric fence. But of course, the radical hospitality of God is not a blanket but a banquet, at a table large enough to fit the whole world, large enough, even, for a slut like Star Drake. Such radical hospitality accords with O'Connor's vision of home:

> Thomas, who had not got out of the car at all, or looked at her after the first revolted glance, said, "I'm telling you, once and for all, the place to take her is the jail."

The Other as Angels: O'Connor's Case for Radical Hospitality

> His mother, sitting on the back seat, holding the girl's hand, did not answer.
> "All right, take her to the hotel," he said.
> "I cannot take a drunk girl to a hotel, Thomas," she said." You know that."
> "Then take her to a hospital."
> "She doesn't need a jail or a hotel or a hospital," his mother said, "she needs a home" (O'Connor, 1988: 584).

Another of O'Connor's stories from her second collection, "The Enduring Chill," also examines the relationship between death and home and between "hospital" and "hospitality," as we see in the following exchange between the protagonist Asbury and his mother:

> ...with a sudden ferocity, she said, "You did well to come home where you can get a good doctor! I'll take you to Doctor Block this afternoon."
> "I am not," he said, trying to keep his voice from shaking, "going to Doctor Block. This afternoon or ever. Don't you think if I'd wanted to go to a doctor I'd have gone up there where they have good ones? Don't you know they have better doctors in New York?"
> "He would take a personal interest in you," she said. "None of those doctors up there would take a personal interest in you."
> "I don't want him taking a personal interest in me." Then after a minute, staring out across a blurred purple-looking field, me said, "What's wrong with me is way beyond Block," and his voice tailed off into a frayed sound, almost a sob (O'Connor, 1988: 549).

Of course, Asbury is right, because his is a spiritual dislocation, something that can only be cured by a radical hospitality that invites broken spirits like his into communion.[3] He needs a home, not in order to die, as is his wish, but in order to die and be reborn. And it's a home that even his mother cannot provide, which Asbury, to his credit, knows. Only the Church can provide such a home, even if it does come

---
3. See also the road to Emmaus story, where the risen Christ is recognized in the offering of hospitality and food, or communion.

in the form of a bumbling, half deaf priest from "Purrgatory" who only speaks in theological clichés. Asbury, like Ruller, got what he'd asked for but not what he'd expected. It was a visit —two visits, actually— offering him the kind of hospitality that would cure his sin-sick soul, one from the priest and the other from the Holy Spirit:

> He glanced across the room into the small oval-framed dresser mirror. The eyes that stared back at him were the same that had returned his gaze every day from that mirror but it seemed to him that they were paler. They looked shocked clean as if they had been prepared for some awful vision about to come down on him . . . The old life in him was exhausted. He awaited the coming of new (O'Connor, 1988: 572).

The "new" comes in the form of "the Holy Ghost, emblazoned in ice instead of fire..." But as biblical hospitality goes, this experience will prove to be, at least for the time being, a purifying terror. As those familiar with O'Connor know, redemption in the guise of God's love, grace, and mercy is often a terrible comeuppance for those who experience it. Asbury isn't prepared for the violence that such a radically new picture of home represents.

A final example of O'Connor's juxtaposition of southern vs. Christian hospitality, the latter serving as a thematic representation of God's Kingdom of radical inclusivity, comes from her short story "Revelation," which introduces two competing notions of hospitality, one beset by manners alone and the other infused with divine mystery.

The first, embodied in the protagonist, Ruby Turpin, one of the most insufferable of all O'Connor's characters, typifies for the reader the kind of manners without mystery that O'Connor so witheringly critiques. The opening scene sets us up for the central role that competing notions of hospitality will play in the story. It takes place in a hospital waiting room (of all places), which Turpin quickly sizes up with her beady little eyes and her beady little soul as soon as she walks in. She assesses the seating arrangement, pushes her husband Claud down in one the unoccupied chairs, then notices a couch for two occupied by a snot-nosed little boy whose mother is totally oblivious to the fact that a southern lady is standing, still needing a place to sit:

> [Ruby Turpin's] gaze settled agreeably on a well-dressed grey-haired lady whose eyes met hers and whose expression said: if that child belonged to me, he would have some manners and move over—there's plenty of room there for you and him too (O'Connor, 1988: 633).

Turpin continues to examine the furniture and the people in it, as if the placement of seats, the square footage of the room, and the social strata of its occupants somehow delineate the invisible rules of hospitality that govern such a place. And Turpin's own assessment of the people in the room shows her notions of proper etiquette precisely for the façade of kindness they represent. Not a person in the room is spared her totalizing rebuke and preening moral rectitude, all done with a friendly smile and good southern manners. We learn that Turpin occupies herself at night "naming the classes of people":

> On the bottom of the heap were most colored people...; then next to them —not above, just away from— were the white-trash; then above them were the homeowners, and above them the home-and-land owners, to which she and Claud belonged. Above she and Claud were people with a lot of money and much bigger houses and more land... Usually by the time she had fallen asleep all the classes of people were moiling and roiling around in her head, and she would dream they were all crammed together in a box car, being ridden off to be put in a gas oven (O'Connor, 1988: 636).

The glimpse O'Connor provides her reader of the state of Turpin's ghoulish soul tells us all we need to know about who she truly is: a white-washed sepulcher. This is the picture O'Connor has of manners bereft of mystery. And lest we hold up Christian virtues as sufficient unto themselves, O'Connor envisions a final homecoming and the kind of hospitality that greets all of us there —all of us Others— and it is not the homecoming Turpin expects.

As she and Claud return to their farm home after being hit over the head with a book by a young girl in the doctor's office, they crest the hill and Ruby Turpin, O'Connor tells us, looks out "suspiciously" on the scene:

> The land sloped gracefully down through a field dotted with lavender weeds and at the start of the rise their small yellow frame house, with its little flower beds spread out around it like fancy apron, sat primly in its accustomed place between two giant hickory trees (O'Connor, 1988: 647).

O'Connor might as well be describing a shire in Tolkien's *The Hobbit*. And yet, Ruby Turpin eyes it suspiciously. Why? Because a change is already taking place in her that she will have to contend with more directly in short order. The words of the prophet —that is, the teenage girl— are still ringing in her ears, and Ruby Turpin will come to slowly realize that the view of the world she has carefully crafted over a lifetime of clichés and prejudices, with its well-defined southern caste system of heaps and classes, is, quite literally, upside down. Turpin's world is about to be turned rightside up by a revelation of radical divine hospitality. "I am not," she says tearfully, "a wart hog from hell." "But the denial had no force," O'Connor tells us, and "the girl's eyes and her words, even the tone of her voice... brooked no repudiation." What Ruby Turpin cannot abide by —and the incredulity of the Misfit comes to mind when he blames Christ for turning everything upside down— is how a "respectable, hard-working, church-going woman" could simultaneously be a warthog from hell.

She experiences a momentary reprieve from this cosmic battle raging inside her when she meets up with the three black women and little boy who work her property and she gets the equivalent of a presidential cabinet meeting of sycophants:

The Other as Angels: O'Connor's Case for Radical Hospitality

> "You so sweet. You the sweetest lady I know."
> "She's pretty, too."
> "And stout... I never knowed no sweeter white lady."
> "That's the truth befo' Jesus... Amen! You des as sweet and pretty as you can be" (O'Connor, 1988: 650).

Of course, even Ruby Turpin isn't fooled by this flattery. She wants to hear the real truth, and so she takes up a conversation with God at the end of the story. *"How am I a hog and me both?"* she demands. *"How am I saved and from hell too?" "Why me?"* She then proceeds to rant and rage against God, and in the ranting and raging, again her true, hog-like nature is on full display:

> "Go on," she yelled, "call me a hog! Call me a hog again. From hell. Call me a wart hog from hell. Put that bottom rail on top. There'll still be a top and bottom!"
> A garbled echo returned to her.
> A final surge of fury shook her and she roared, "Who do you think you are?" (O'Connor, 1988: 653).

The answer comes in the form of a revelation to end all revelations, returning *"to her clearly like an answer from beyond the wood."* This time, however, she has no response, as her gaze turns to the hogs lying in the corner who are grunting softly *"with a secret life."* She lifts her eyes and raises her hands *"in a gesture hieratic and profound."* A benediction, in other words, and what she sees in this revelation is the divine economy of radical hospitality, one that upends and reverses the southern hospitality she had so closely guarded and depended upon:

> A vast horde of souls... rumbling toward heaven. There were whole companies of white-trash, clean for the first time in their lives, and bands of black niggers in white robes, and battalions of freaks and lunatics shouting and clapping and leaping like frogs. And bringing up the end of the procession was a tribe of people whom she recognized at once as those who, like herself and Claud, had always had a little of everything and the God-given wit to use it right. She

leaned forward to observe them closer. They were marching behind the others with great dignity, accountable as they had always been for good order and common sense and respectable behavior. They alone were on key. Yet she could see by their shocked and altered faces that even their virtues were being burned away (O'Connor, 1988: 654).

Such a view of radical hospitality, where the bottom rail is on top and the freaks and misfits are at the front of the line—and not just any line but the line Home and into eternal life—is the vision O'Connor again and again imparts to us, her readers, with all of our own closely-hugged manners and manifestations of cultural hospitality. And it is a vision that O'Connor deftly and repeatedly incarnates into her stories, whether in the form of a Grandmother about to be shot to death who offers eternal life in a gesture to a serial killer, or a group of tenant's children hell-bent on having their turkey, or the statue of a black lawn jockey, or a mother's "daredevil charity" towards a wayward slut, or a revelation of the redeemed on their way to heaven, including all the warthogs from hell whose virtues are being burned away. All of these serve as O'Connor's trumpet-blasting indictment of the world's well-manicured manners, bereft of any mystery, and thus bereft of any true or lasting hospitality.

O'Connor's blazing vision of radical hospitality upends and transforms her readers' theological notions of home (Heaven, the subversive, eschatological Kingdom of God) as being, not a place where everyone we love is, but a place where we love everyone; where we love the Other. The uncompromising hospitality of Heaven, in other words, determines —extends, redeems, explodes— the boundaries of well-considered Christian manners, and as such, Christian hospitality becomes the antithesis of southern hospitality, whose manners determine the reaches of its hospitality. In God's celestial economy, as in O'Connor's stories, the bottom rail always ends up on top, so that even the virtues of our well-considered hospitality —manners and all— are burned away in the mystery of divine charity. We are no longer showing hospitality to strangers. We are entertaining angels.

Bibliography

Dyrness, William (2011). *Poetic Theology. God and the Poetics of Everyday Life*. Grand Rapids, MI: Wm. B. Eerdman's Publishing Co.

Fitzgerald, Sally (Ed.) (1979). *The Habit of Being: Letters of Flannery O'Connor*. New York, NY: Farrar, Straus and Giroux.

Newman, Elizabeth (2005). "Flannery O'Connor and the Practice of Hospitality," in *Perspectives in Religious Studies*, 32, 2: 135-47.

O'Connor, Flannery (1969). *Mystery and Manners: Occasional Prose*. New York, NY: Farrar, Straus and Giroux.

--- (1988). *O'Connor: Collected Works*. New York, NY: Literary Classics of the United States, Inc.

Schenk, Hans. "A Christian Response to Immigration in the United States." (Unpublished manuscript).

The Holy Bible (1984). New International Version. Grand Rapids, MI: Zondervan House. Print.

"A Purifying Terror": Apocalypse, Apostasy and Alterity in Flannery O'Connor's "The Enduring Chill"

José Liste Noya

On the 16th of July, 1944, early morning in the New Mexico desert, the United States successfully tested its first atomic bomb, a prototype of the weapon that would later be used in a genocidal attack on Hiroshima on August 6, 1945. The test was code-named "Trinity" by the guiding spirit of the Los Alamos staff, Robert Oppenheimer, apparently drawing on submerged memories of the reading of the poetry of John Donne. Oppenheimer thus textually inaugurated the often paralyzing ambiguity with which the atomic bomb and atomic energy would be received in the following years, oscillating, as in Donne's poetry, between apocalyptic doomsday scenarios and transcendent visions of ultimate redemption for all mankind.[1] The "theme of a destruction that might also redeem"

---

1. According to Rhodes (1988: 571-572), the poem Oppenheimer initially had in mind was Donne's late "Hymn to God my God, in my Sickness" in which the poet imagines a deathbed preparation for his demise that converts death in conventional Christian fashion into the entrance into the "holy room" of eternal life: "So death doth touch the resurrection". But the unresolved ambivalence between destruction and redemption, the dichotomy that a trinitarian vision would hopefully surpass, is best expressed in Rhodes's view by Donne's sonnet nº 14 of his *Divine Meditations*, one of his "Holy Sonnets", that in a more personally anguished way faces this apparently indivisible duality. "Batter my heart, three-personed God" appeals abjectly the speaker, admitting the violence of the divine as the only passageway beyond this paralyzing

(Rhodes, 1988: 572), of a respectable theological lineage, allowed one to make ultimate sense —a sense of the ultimate— of that which threatened to make sense-making itself wholly spurious when there was nothing left to be made sense of.

Nevertheless, an ideologically-charged sense-making, a discursive polarization with its rhetorical ripples felt in all forms of textual production, would be the wake of that destructive event. The rhetorical fallout of that event, a sort of textual radioactivity with its lingering half-lives, remained as testimony to the implicit discursive presence of the weapon which set off the global reverberations that coalesced as the apparently fixed polarities of the Cold War face-off. Indeed, as historians of the Cold War and its governing nuclear threat have traced, the "Bomb" itself—first A-Bomb then H-Bomb as if in promise of a berserk alphabetical series— made sure, in paradoxical but threateningly uncertain manner, that the Cold War would remain "cold", congealed in the realpolitik doctrines eventually labelled *détente* and M.A.D., mutual assured destruction.[2] In this sense, without for a moment discounting the localized "hot" conflicts in mostly third-world countries or satellite states of the world superpowers that peppered the Cold War period, one could speak of

---

stasis of the mortal. The imagery employed sustains the effort required to vanquish the violence of death with the paradoxical counter-violence of the sacred: "o'erthrow me, and bend / Your force, to break, blow, burn, and make me new. [...] Take me to you, imprison me, for I / Except you enthral me, never shall be free, / Nor ever chaste, except you ravish me."

2. As John Lewis Gaddis restates in one of his many books on the Cold War, the atomic bomb and especially thermonuclear devices ensured that "an absolute weapon of war could become the means by which war remained an instrument of politics" (2005: 62) but this also meant that "there could be no rational use, in war, for a weapon of this size" (2005: 62-63). The illogic of developing such apocalyptic weaponry lead to the madness of Cold War rationality: such a war could only be avoided by frantically preparing for it. Rhodes quotes the always belligerent Winston Churchill on this paradoxical strategy: "[T]he new terror [...] brings a certain element of equality in annihilation. Strange as it may seem, it is to the universality of potential destruction that I think we may look with hope and even confidence" (1988: 65). This seems a strange echo of the self-destructive desire for immersion in the trinitarian divine.

the Cold War as a discursive conflict in which ideologically-inflected Newspeaks shared between them in often rhetorically-violent tension a public domain characterized as one of conformity, containment and enforced consensus. An enduring discursive chill pervaded all levels of public life and, accordingly, permeated the literary sphere in diverse forms, especially in the period before the showdown and backing down of the superpowers on the occasion of the Cuban crisis during John F. Kennedy's presidency.

This period also sees the production of Flannery O'Connor's brief but intense literary opus. Despite O'Connor's characteristically straightforward assertion that "the meaning of a piece of fiction only begins where everything psychological and sociological has been explained" (O'Connor, 1988: 300), she produced a body of narrative texts that manage to chart through their rhetorical excess the textual trace of discursive practices that effectively set the bounds of such domains as the psychological and sociological throughout the 1950s. One of these discourses is that of what we could call in Orwellian fashion *Atomspeak*, the ambivalent discourse of atomic threat and atomic promise, so useful throughout this period and recurrently thereafter as a prod and bolster to ideological conformity and imperialist acquiescence, as Paul Boyer has shown. The barely submerged death-wish inherent in such discourse, in both its dystopian and utopian varieties, reappears in the existentialist numbness of much postwar American writing. Indeed, its apocalyptic scenarios —"apocalypse" as both destruction of the corrupt old and revelation of the transcendent new— rehearse in only apparently paradoxical fashion a millennial vision in American culture, a history-annulling transcendence that can be traced back to the American Puritans but which is not exclusive to them.

In this case, however, the blatantly terminal nature of the apocalyptic redemption bred its own apostate responses, a refusal of the scenario either in political and moral terms or in a sort of religious retreat from annihilation that sidesteps it through a transcendent evasion. Asbury Fox, the protagonist of "The Enduring Chill" will be denied the death he vaingloriously, quite apocalyptically desires, but it will be replaced by the self-humbling, ferociously coercive experience of enforced redemption of his infantile apostasy. The threat of self-inflicted destruction is the path to a self-annulling abrogation of personal initiative. The destruction of self and other, the destruction of all, promised by the bomb easily and figuratively tilts over into an escape from the personally-experienced anomie of the postwar world or into the avowedly adversarial dissent of a Flannery O'Connor intent on opening the gates of what she called the "true country" of the sacred through her narratives of violent purgation of what she saw as the unavoidable but ultimately dispensable contingencies of the political and the personal.[3]

This is the tall order of her story about the "Holy Ghost" as she bluntly put it, "The Enduring Chill", a story she initially drafted in late 1957

---

3. John Lance Bacon makes the point that her fictions "project a religious alternative to the Cold War consensus" (1993: 85) but his insistence on seeing Flannery O'Connor as a Cold War dissenter lacks sufficient textual support as his analyses tend to rely on rather straightforward analogies established a bit too literally, unconcerned with the rhetorical work of the texts themselves (for example, seeing Asbury Fox as a Cold War intellectual – though Bacon does admit that a "viable role for the American intellectual is conspicuous by its absence from O'Connor's fiction", 1993: 51). Bacon argues for the dissenting value of O'Connor's fiction by suggesting that she forwards her critique through "political allegory", thus enabling her to both protest against containment and consensus but protect herself from ideological attack. No convincing textual analysis, however, is forthcoming to actually demonstrate this or to explore the theoretical bounds of O'Connor's use of allegory. Indeed, Bacon seems to side with conventional O'Connor criticism in seeing her religious viewpoint as providing a safely transcendent vantage from which to effect a critique that has no actual relevance for the quite immanent politics of the day. Such transcendental dissent banishes all political and social options to the status of empty tokens beside the "true country" supposedly beyond any political distinctions; capitalism and communism in the context of the Cold War become the same thing but the self-evident rightness of the capitalist polity is never doubted. Though O'Connor's aversion to cultural conformity can be aligned with political dissent, as Bacon suggests, it expresses itself in the manner of much reactionary response to the liberal consensus: it misidentifies, quite intentionally, the ideological target and ends up affirming the political status quo by disdaining it through transcendental oversight. Or, rather, the ideological critique is fundamentally accurate but the alternative sought ends up shoring up the ostensible enemy.

but which was published in July 1958 in *Harper's Bazaard*. Flannery O'Connor, like some of her critics, eventually expressed dissatisfaction with her story and for apparently the same reasons. In particular, she objected to the ending, a conclusion in which the top-heavy symbolism of the tale —"very obvious but the only thing possible" (O'Connor, 1988: 257)— takes on a literal weight that drowns out all nuance and ambiguity. As James Mellard has suggested, often "O'Connor simply tells her readers —either through narrative interventions or by extra-textual exhortations— how they are to interpret her work" (1989: 626).[4] In this very explicitness, however, as opposed to the New Critical doctrine of understated meaningfulness that O'Connor subscribed to, one may find an unexpectedly subversive literalness that disrupts the rhetorical (or allegorical) intentions of the figurative and the figural. The "ghost" of the real, the personal and political real, unavoidably reveals itself as "implacable" (O'Connor, 1980: 114) as the figurative Holy Ghost in her story through the very figurations that becloud it. The literalization of the figurative in the story, skewed narratorially towards O'Connor's fundamentalist Catholic concerns, also allows figurative shape to a prevailing public concern in this Cold War context, that is, the literal otherness of the material and discursive implementation of a device, the atomic bomb, that would do away with all all figurality, all phenomenality, all literality. Like O'Connor's authoritarian God, the atomic bomb functions as an absolute alterity that would annihilate all others, an Otherness that denies others terminally. O'Connor's story is not about the bomb but, like much fiction of the period, its rhetorical presence can be detected within O'Connor's own apocalyptic scenarios as she figures forth her divine Other. The virtual materialization of the figurative in her fiction does not shut down its rhetorical reach in line with authorial intentionality as expressed elsewhere but inevitably disseminates in other directions the rhetorical excess of her writing. O'Connor asserted in her letters

---

4. He does so, however, in an article which itself applies early Lacanian notions of the Other in a way which is reductive of hermeneutic plurality. His rather mechanical analogies ironically approximate the sort of "anagogical" readings that O'Connor sometimes proposed for her work in imitation of Biblical hermeneutics.

that in fiction writing "[e]verything has to operate first on the literal level" (O'Connor, 1988: 299) in order to bring to representational light the figurative, often figural, meaning she ultimately intended. To make *literal*, however, at least within a fictional representation, is to remain within the bounds of the *letter*, the text, and thus to open the text to the alterity of the rhetorical. The Other resists full rhetorical capture and, vice versa, rhetoric, the very *textuality* of a text, opens up its alterity.

This alterity, whether O'Connor's figurative anticipation of the sacred or the imminent but always postponed threat of nuclear cataclysm, can only be foreshadowed in rhetorical form and thus participates in the textual slipperiness of the rhetorical for better or worse. As Jacques Derrida asserted in a well-known essay on the phenomenon of the nuclear, the essential feature of the latter is that it is *"fabulously textual, through and through"*, in both the sense that the arming and delivery of nuclear weaponry relies on modern techniques of information and communication but also to the extent that it is still thankfully a *fable*: "for the moment, a nuclear war has not taken place: one can only talk and write about it" (Derrida, 2007: 393). As such, however, it remains a fiction, a rhetorical event and a material non-event given that it "has no precedent" (2007: 393) —and so partakes of the fictionality and rhetoricity of literature itself.[5] In this, it is similar to O'Connor's sacred, something always imminent, even rhetorically immanent in her fictional landscapes, but never fully representable because, akin to the effects of a nuclear strike, the advent of the divine is the banishment of the textual, the implosion of the distance between text and referential reality, the healing of the rift between the Word and the world. The revelatory apocalypse of this eschatology, however, is mirrored in rhetorical terms by the destructive

---

5. I borrow the term "rhetoricity" from Paul de Man who employed it to refer to a text's rhetorical mode or nature, not merely its powers of persuasion. Specifically, it refers to the figurative power of a text and to all textuality's reliance on figuration and how this endlessly defers any determinate referential closure. Hence, for de Man, "literary" describes "any text that implicitly or explicitly signifies its own rhetorical mode and prefigures its own misunderstanding as the correlative of its rhetorical nature; that is, of its 'rhetoricity'" (de Man, 1983: 136).

apocalypse of nuclear Armageddon. Precisely for this reason, Derrida makes clear, the "terrifying 'reality' of nuclear conflict can only be the signified referent, never the real referent (present or past) of a discourse or a text" (2007: 393). He takes this further, in ways which suggest the role of the rhetoric of the transcendent in O'Connor, by linking this supposedly revelatory destructiveness with the "archive", that body of textual representations which can only exist as such, otherwise named "literature", because the referent they appeal to is fictionally created by the very archive and its institutionalization. This rhetorically-invented but also material textuality would be obliterated by the atomic conflagration. Its very annihilation can only be imagined much as the blinding descent of the Godhead can only be imagined and figuratively represented given that the (non-)event of their actual coming implies the voiding of all representation. This "total and remainderless destruction of the archive" (Derrida, 2007: 400) reveals for Derrida the nature of what he calls "literature" (perhaps this is also the nature of "God"?). Literature's referent is created performatively, it is a rhetorical invention, and its connection to the "real" is enacted through that rhetorical performativity. The effacement of literature is thus intrinsic to its inscription, Derrida suggests, for that effacement is precisely what the inscription is there to ward off. Literature exists to defer "the encounter with the wholly other" (Derrida, 2007: 403), the unimaginable void before / beyond the textual or the deafening, blinding divine, while doing so by always figuring it forth in usually implicit fashion. The bomb would —we can only imagine, in literary fashion— materialize this encounter by utterly doing away with the material and the textual means of representing the material. Apocalypse can only be forthcoming, not actual, for its Revelation would also be the end of all revelation: "no apocalypse, not now", as Derrida titles his essay.

Perhaps this paradox, the literally transcendent destructiveness of the bomb conjoined at least figuratively —quite literally for some of the faithful— with the redemptive violence of the divine, also lies in the background of O'Connor's unease over her fictional resolution.

If so, it is a sentiment she shares with other cultural producers of the postwar period, high and low, themselves sharing in their own way in Derrida's theoretically dense reflections. A revealing example, as Paul Boyer points out (1994: 25), is country singer Fred Kirby's 1945 song, "Atomic Power", which brings together in plaintive fashion both the promise and the menace of nuclear energy while also connecting it with the ideologically-sanctioning purposes of a sometimes revengeful god. The "brimstone fire", an infernal substance unnervingly brought down from heaven itself, is a gift for the chosen nation, unnamed but understood in the song, "given by the mighty hand of God", a gift used justifiably against the "power of Japan", reduced now to penitence for their sins: "Hiroshima, Nagasaki / Paid a big price for their sins". The jingoism of the recent war effort may account for this frightening self-righteousness but the lyrics also contemplate the ambivalence in harnessing the divine for one's own mundane purposes. "Working with the power / Of God's own holy hand" is a hazardous mission, perhaps even a sinful appropriation of the exclusive rights of the transcendent godhead as the song's final stanza would seem to suggest. One could easily go from helper and favored child of the divine to devil's apprentice, a trajectory that the cultural imaginary of the period often projected onto the atomic scientists who participated in the making of the bomb. At the same time, the song's concluding judgement day vision, as, for example, in many a Puritan text, allays a sense of human responsibility and agency in the utter passivity with which destruction is undergone: "But on that day of Judgment / When comes a greater power / We will not know the minute / And we will not know the hour".

Asbury Fox, the protagonist of "The Enduring Chill", believes he knows the exact hour and even minute of his impending death, a fatuousness which immediately brands him as one of O'Connor's self-deluding characters, either pseudo-intellectuals normally tainted in the narrator's eyes by the progressivist ethos of Northern liberals or staunch Southerners, usually property-owning rural women like Asbury's mother, comfortably ensconced in social, moral, racial and religious stereotypes to which they only pay lip service but to which they also adhere self-defensively. Figuratively infantilized by the narrator's irony, Asbury is a flawed artist figure, unable in his equally imperceptive mother's eyes to do "real work, not writing" (O'Connor, 1980: 88). In quite unambiguous fashion, the narrator depicts the son's revolt against what he considers the mother's stifling, castrating presence as a displacement of his own unacknowledged failure in the aesthetic and ethical realms. Until forcefully submitted to a series of comic dialogues at cross-purposes in which his own projected self-image as tolerant, cultured martyr is shattered in the mirror of his own reflection in the face of the story's others, Asbury remains blind to his own repressed otherness, his dependence on the (m)other, and his annulment of others through racial and cultural stereotyping. All in all, Asbury remains his mother's son, an echo of her narcissistic blindness to various forms of otherness, the two a familial echo of the perceptual and moral entrapment experienced by the story's main characters.

Death and the "Negro", to use O'Connor's term, often figuratively associated in her fiction, are two modes of otherness, ontological and racial, deployed by the story. The figure of the black, indeed, acquires a symbolic presence in her fiction which is both an acknowledgment of the centrality of the black to the world she depicts, even if only an "artificial nigger", as in the title of one of her best stories, but also a domestication of the black's singularity as moral and cultural agent. The symbolic figuration, as Toni Morrison (1992) has shown, is a response to the racial other which quite easily slides over into a defensive projection that annuls that very otherness. This ambivalence in the use of the figure of the black in O'Connor's fiction, while reflecting the unstable congealment of racial politics in the 1950s, is routinely exploited by her to question the very racial and social consensus which it is supposed to buttress. Thus, in this story as in others, the figure of the black is recruited as a symbolic touchstone and triggering device for the protagonist's aborted revolt and self-deception. Asbury's self-deluding revolt against his mother and her unquestioned mores specifically takes the form of infringing the social and racial limits of Southern society. He recalls a previous attempt at "rapport" (O'Connor, 1980: 96) by smoking with the "Negro" hands in the dairy's barn. This ironic moment of "communion when the difference between black and white is absorbed into nothing" (O'Connor, 1980: 97), backfires when the milk is later returned as it has been tainted by the smell of smoke. The incident is both a parodic prefiguration of the desired apocalyptic moment given its risk of provoking a conflagration in the barn and a debunking reinstatement of the realism of "place", both Asbury's and the blacks'. Asbury's gesture is implicitly seen by them as a travesty of true communion, a farcical self-projection rather than a true, socially-impossible opening to the black other in this context. This is further compounded by Asbury's drinking of the unpasteurized milk that causes the undulant fever that he self-complacently identifies as sign of his impending, self-glorifying death. The blacks' unconscious insistence on "speaking to an invisible body located to the right or left of where he actually was" (O'Connor, 1980: 96) is also an unwitting awareness of the "invisible" codes and conventions that govern their world. The ostensible conservatism of the narrator's undermining presence here is, nevertheless, realistic in its vision of the white self's obliviousness to its own defining polarities as opposed to the blacks' historically painful awareness of the stereotyped otherness that that obliviousness consigns them to: "What he do is him,' Randall [one of the Negro hands] said. 'What I do is me" (O'Connor, 1980: 98).

Death is a greater symbolic presence in the story, if only because it colors all of Asbury's self-centered ruminations. But one should always keep in sight O'Connor's careful social and cultural placement of her admittedly transcendental concerns. The Otherness above is only ever experienced through the otherness below. Thus, the failure to respond to one determines, in her fictional world, the failure to respond to the other. A final attempt to achieve communion with the blacks by Asbury as he undergoes the savage self-denuding of the story's final passages—"preparing himself for the encounter as a religious man might prepare himself for the last sacrament" (O'Connor, 1980: 110) —ends in farce— "You sho do look well" repeat mechanically both hands in response to Asbury's demand for what he mistakenly believes is a deathbed scene of mutual self-recognition that flouts his mother's racial etiquette. Their rehearsed responses to his lame travesty of transracial brotherliness deny Asbury any sincere transgression of the conventions he himself blindly relies upon. Learning almost immediately from homely Dr. Block that he is only suffering from recurring bouts of undulant fever, ironically acquired in a previous episode of fraudulent communion with the black hands by drinking unpasteurized milk as an infantile gesture of revolt against his mother's barn rules, Asbury resigns himself to a lack of "significant experience" (O'Connor, 1980: 112). Appropriately, it is only now at the end, having been forced to surrender control over experience, that he is left helpless before experience in its undetermined otherness. An event takes place that remains undefined yet overdetermined in the symbolic explicitness that apparently troubled O'Connor itself. The water stain on the ceiling that had disturbed Asbury's youth becomes a literalization of the Pentecostal bird-imagery that has pervaded the narrative. The "Holy Ghost" makes its appearance as the literal figure or figurative literality of "a purifying terror", which "emblazoned in ice instead of fire, continued, implacable, to descend" (O'Connor, 1980: 114).

What is descending, of course, as my clumsy play with literalness and figuration is meant to suggest, is language itself, even down to the possible intertextual allusion to Robert Frost's poem, "Fire and Ice".[6] Within the logocentrism of a Christian perspective, this descent of language is not necessarily the evasion of the real but its fullest realization, the redemptive moment when the Word returns to the Flesh. But for an unbelieving reader, it is difficult to get away from the rhetorical after-effects of the literalization of the figurative. In this case, far from sealing off the excesses

---

6. Frost's almost aphoristic short poem toys with the possible modes of apocalyptic destruction, first favoring fire given the human speaker's experience of what he has "tasted of desire" in worldly life but then opts for the benumbing "destruction of ice" based upon his complementary experience of the human denial of passion, much as Asbury represses his true emotional dependency on what he disparages. In one of her comments on the story in her letters, O'Connor quipped in comic bleakness that she saw "no reason to limit the Holy Ghost to fire. He's full of surprises" (O'Connor, 1988: 293).

and extensions of the symbolic, the making explicit of the symbol may work to set off the processes of symbolization in other directions. The literal, after all, especially within the textual environment of a fiction, is merely another mode of the figurative, one whose figurative excess is considered to have been curtailed and, perhaps, fixed, congealed. In this light, the rhetoric of literality, rightly seen, can be considered a form of apostasy with respect to the figural or figurative apocalypse the text seeks, its revelatory transcendence of the textual. It retrenches on the promise of transcendence and returns us to the textual and discursive articulations that make up the language of transcendence. These articulations bring that transcendence down to earth, "implacably"; they historicize it as a situated rhetorics.[7]

This religiously charged language is intentionally used to focus attention not just on the thematics of O'Connor's text but also on its rhetoric and on that rhetoric's contamination by and entanglement with Cold War discourse, its own particular discursive context. The motif of death that throughout the tale provides the discursive nexus, in this case, for the death vaingloriously desired by Asbury and self-defensively denied by his mother, must be set within the context, suggested by the story's imagery, of the terminal death promised by (the officially denied but also indirectly threatened) atomic holocaust. From the moment he is

---

7. In an early study of O'Connor's fiction and specifically of their rhetorical intent, Carol Shloss makes the point that "any writer of religious sensibility is inevitably forced into the role of rhetorician" (1980: 7) given the need to surmount her secular audience's resistance or hostility. Though O'Connor herself insisted on close attention to the realistic as a pathway to the transcendent, Shloss suggests that the figurative play and rhetorical extremity she resorts to may "enrich the texture of realistic narration without usurping the realistic surface with abstract, revealed meanings" (1980: 80). Indeed, she believes that "minimal consideration of O'Connor's stories reveals that the author's analogies begin with the concrete world as theme, and the process of inference leads us not directly to spirit, but to an expanded sense of the physical environment" (1980: 3). This expanded sense, of course, would not do away with what O'Connor calls "spirit" or "mystery" but, as I suggest, align (perhaps malign) those concerns with the quite material context of the discursive and rhetorical environment constituted by language and history.

welcomed home in rather tasteless fashion by his sardonic sister —"The artist arrives at the gas chamber" (O'Connor, 1980: 90)—, the story undercuts Asbury's death-wish by subtly associating it with the numb mindset of the Cold War consensus at its height in the 1950s. What is seen on one level, then, as the protagonist's willful refusal to perceive the ravaging alterity that will consume him spiritually and psychologically, the seeds of which he already contains right from the start, is also a displacing response to or a misrecognition of a transpersonal atmosphere of impending doom that marked the period in general.

Asbury's frustrated transcendence-seeking visions of the beginning, framed by O'Connor's trademark "startling white-gold sun, like some strange potentate from the east" (O'Connor, 1980: 82), may prefigure the final arrival of the "god he didn't know" (O'Connor, 1980: 82). They also initiate the process of displacing self-projections that can be read along both religious and more threateningly mundane lines. Asbury's pathetic aestheticizing of spiritual and social commitment is, at the same time, a denial of others, a denial of the Other and an unacknowledged denial of a terminal alterity that conflates the two in an annihilating nothingness. To put this in other terms, the arrogance implicit in the desire for death and/or redemption on one's own terms rather than submitting to the Other, however we may want to qualify that Other, reveals, as is fitting in the case of this failed artist, the recklessness of the belief in the demiurgic control of the moment of apocalypse. Extrapolating this personal madness to the M.A.D.ness of geopolitical realities, one finds the same unfulfillable belief in the use of atomic weaponry as a strategy of military-political and socio-ideological containment. Hence, in both cases, the failure of the paradoxically death-denying, idealizing death-wish when faced with the literal realities of the domestic scene: "He had become entirely accustomed to the thought of death, but he had not become accustomed to the thought of death *here*" (O'Connor, 1980: 83). *Here* within the story, is the Southern rural setting of his mother's home, the place where Asbury will discover his "true condition". In O'Connor's work, however, the South is employed as a distorting mirror that reveals the truth of the nation at large precisely through its superficially grotesque deformations. Its admittedly failing ability to do so is due in part, as O'Connor herself admonished, to the fact that it is the only region of the United States to have undergone the experience of military defeat.

Its forgetting of this, the South's nostalgic sentimentalization of that defeat, is thus the social correlate of the attitudes of the likes of Asbury, not just of his mother. The desire for a controlled death, a death that paradoxically triumphs over death as in the South's idealization of its past defeats, projected in Asbury's visions of his own death and burial, are a means of domesticating what can never be a successful self-representation.[8] The analogy with the self-unravelling discourse of nuclear threat is suggested through Asbury's recalling early on his "friend Goetz" (a phonetic travesty of "God"?), for whom "death was nothing at all" (O'Connor, 1980: 85). Goetz, significantly, had recently returned from atomically-devastated "Japan", his face "purple-splotched with a million indignations" (O'Connor, 1980: 85) in visual echo of the nuclear victims of the East. Later on, faced with the deathly sterility of his social and cultural environment, Asbury dangerously misinterprets death as "a gift from life", "his greatest triumph" (O'Connor, 1980: 99). While another example of O'Connor's stock parody of the fashionable existentialist stance of self-glorifying resignation to a death-like angst or ennui, such assertions fit in menacingly with Cold War pride in America's atomic power and its apparent safeguarding of her military and moral invincibility; that is, the shockingly condescending absurdity of converting one's fearfully denied self-destruction into a triumph over total annihilation.

The comic literalism of Asbury's mother is another example of O'Connor's reiterated use in her stories of impercipient characters to undercut the unrecognized impercipience of their supposedly perceptually and intellectually superior protagonists. Her literalistic allusion to "*Gone*

---

8. In the context of Asbury's role as a travesty of the artist / writer, this is parodied by his mother's suggestion that he write "a book about down here [...] another good book like *Gone With the Wind*" (O'Connor, 1980: 99).

With the Wind" (O'Connor, 1980: 99) as a literary model for Asbury introduces a mass-cultural artifact that, both within the Southern context of rapidly failing historical memory and the national context of a voiding of the present and future as temporal sites for the creation of a historically-informed memory, can be read as a bleakly comic allegory of future nuclear holocaust (one recalls a popular comic version of nuclear annihilation, *When the Wind Blows*, published in 1982 during the Reagan years' heightening of Cold War tensions). His mother's suggestion to "Put the war in it" (O'Connor, 1980: 99), in this light, becomes a non-figurative allusion to the subtextual presence in O'Connor's fiction of the Cold War consensus, of the barely suppressed imaginary scenario of a truly memory-less present future, a world where the slate has been wiped clean for the first and only time, but a slate that will no longer be able to receive the impress of memory's writing.

It is appropriate, then, for a story which explores in indirect fashion the rhetorics of overlapping but contradictory discourses, that O'Connor should focus at times on the material literality of reading and writing to convey the ultimate purpose of her own textual literalizations. One literalism undercuts another as the story's own strategy of parodic literalization undermines the self-serving discourses of both characters and their socio-political context. Recalling my earlier reflections on the literal and the figurative, one could say that the narrator's figurative literalism debunks the literal figurations of the characters. Or perhaps vice versa, for there is no stopping such textual play. The mother's literalism, targeted by the son's revengeful Kafkaesque letter which he plans to leave her after his death, becomes the ironic reflection of Asbury's own failure to perceive the literal, including the literal otherness of his own self. This is reflected in his failure to deal with the textual literality of the figurative as shown in the very writing of that letter which he will ultimately fail to hand to his mother (and to the reader, for it will remain a sort of self-purloined letter): "If reading it would be painful to her, writing it had sometimes been unbearable to him —for in order to face her, he had had to face himself" (O'Connor, 1980: 91). Tellingly, it is the unread letter itself that is first associated with the phrase that makes up the story's title. Asbury ponders the "enduring chill" (O'Connor, 1980: 92) it will supposedly provoke in his mother, in part a consequence of its initial ambiguity or even incomprehensibility for such a literal-minded reader. As the story as a whole makes clear in literally textual manner, the source of the "chill" lies in the letter or the literal, in the insidiously pervasive discourses that the protagonists figure metaphorically in a self-defensive gesture evading a literal and textual reality. The "chill" of the Cold War was essentially discursive. Asbury, thus, egregiously misreads Yeats's apocalyptic lyric, "The Second Coming" (in ironic parallelism, perhaps, with Oppenheimer's ambivalent citing of Donne's lyric), as a paean to self-transcendence rather than the advent of some "rough beast" intent on terminating the "nightmare" of history. The narrator even highlights Asbury's textual sins by punningly foregrounding the textual materiality of his own name: the implicit connotations of the name come comically forward as "Azzberry" (O'Connor, 1980: 95) or "ass Bush" (O'Connor, 1980: 100), the latter expression being Asbury's own.

O'Connor is not averse to provide corrective readings in her story, along the lines that the comic deflation of the protagonist's name follows. This is a role she reserves for the likes of the Pentecostally-named Jesuit, "Ignatius Vogle" (from the German for "bird", *vogel*), and, more extensively, the blunt conclusiveness of "Father Finn", the evocatively-named furious catechizer and harbinger of the apocalyptic doom preordained for the likes of Asbury, whom he chastises as "a lazy ignorant conceited youth!" (O'Connor, 1980: 107). The priest, indeed, seems to enact the text's strategies of rhetorical literalization of language and he animates Asbury's own suppressed literalism that will lead to the ironic materialization of his childhood visions and metaphors in the figure of the water stain-come-Holy Ghost. The dogmatic literalism of the priest's ritualistic catechizing, a rude rebuke to Asbury's expectations of refined conversation, undercuts Asbury's metaphorical evasions of the literal: "Asbury moved his arms and legs helplessly as if he were pinned to the bed by the terrible eye" (O'Connor, 1980: 107), another Kafkaesque echo. Even here, though, the overbearing symbolism of these concluding passages, their literalization of the specifically Christian symbol, ruptures their referential purposes and returns us to the other Other permeating O'Connor's text.

It is not a question of choosing Others and establishing a hierarchy of relevance in the uses of alterity. What O'Connor's language manifests in her use of "the discourse of conditionality in the service of the holy unconditional" (Johansen, 1994: 77) are the power-inflections discourse takes as well as the contestation of those inflections through the very discourses that they shape. If "her reason for dissenting from the Cold War consensus was religious" (Bacon, 1993: 62), her religious thematics and fundamentalist rhetorics wavered uncertainly and unavoidably between conformity and conflict. This is the tension that some critics have formally located in her "as if" constructions, the bringing forth through unresolved similes of both a certified literal reality and a properly unnameable condition of the transcendentally "true". In the words of Edward Kessler, the "complex meanings evoked by O'Connor's *as if* center on power, an inexplicable energy acting on the mind and on or through external nature" (1986: 62). Named God or the Bomb, such denominations are merely labels for what resists representation in its full force. Yet the naming itself, within their respective discourses, is a discursive attempt to harness their discourse-annulling powers. In the Cold War period —but not only then— "the point of popular religion [was] not coherent wisdom or meaning so much as power" (Ellwood, 1997: 12), the self-transcending sense of surrender to power that inevitably and perhaps consciously played into the hands of the discourse of nuclear power. The discourse of power is tainted with a self-justifying religiosity just as religious discourse finds itself contaminated by self-righteous assumption of power. O'Connor's deliteralizing figurations and defiguring literalizations reveal this mutual imbrication while never imagining for a moment that the "enduring chill" of this discursive entrapment can be merely waved away. O'Connor combats it by succumbing to it but, in succumbing, her texts expose it, *literally*.

BIBLIOGRAPHY

Bacon, Jon Lance (1993). *Flannery O'Connor and Cold War Culture*. Cambridge: Cambridge University Press.

Boyer, Paul (1985). *By the Bomb's Early Light: American Thought and Culture at the Dawn of the Atomic Age*. Reprint, Chapel Hill, NC: University of North Carolina Press, 1994.

de Man, Paul (1983). *Blindness and Insight: Essays in the Rhetoric of Contemporary Criticism*. 2nd ed. London: Methuen.

Derrida, Jacques (2007). No Apocalypse, Not Now (Full Speed Ahead, Seven Missiles, Seven Missives). In Peggy Kamuf & Elizabeth Rottenberg (Eds.) *Psyché: Inventions of the Other, Volume I*. Stanford, CA: Stanford University Press, pp. 387-409.

Ellwood, Robert S. (1997). *The Fifties Spiritual Marketplace: American Religion in a Decade of Conflict*. New Brunswick, NJ: Rutgers University Press.

Gaddis, John Lewis (2005). *The Cold War: A New History*. New York, NY: Penguin.

Johansen, Ruthann Knechel (1994). *The Narrative Secret of Flannery O'Connor: The Trickster as Interpreter*. Tuscaloosa, AL: University of Alabama Press.

Kessler, Edward (1986). *Flannery O'Connor and the Language of Apocalypse*. Princeton, NJ: Princeton University Press.

Mellard, J. M. (1989) "Flannery O'Connor's Others: Freud, Lacan, and the Unconscious," in *American Literature*, 61, 4: 625–643.

Morrison, Toni (1992). *Playing in the Dark: Whiteness and the Literary Imagination*. Cambridge, MA: Harvard University Press.

O'Connor, Flannery (1980). *Everything That Rises Must Converge*. London: Faber & Faber.

--- (1988). *The Habit of Being: Letters of Flannery O'Connor*. Ed. Sally Fitzgerald. New York, NY: Noonday Press.

Rhodes, Richard (1988). *The Making of the Atomic Bomb*. London: Penguin, 1988.

Shloss, Carol (1980). *Flannery O'Connor's Dark Comedies: The Limits of Inference*. Baton Rouge, LA: Louisiana State University Press.

An Unpleasant Little Jolt:
Flannery O'Connor's *Creation ex Chaos*

Thomas Wetzel

In Flannery O'Connor's story, "Why Do the Heathen Rage?", yet another of O'Connor's exasperated maternal figures recognizes in a time of trouble that the world she inhabits is not quite what it seems. She had recently found a book about the early Church fathers that her ne'er-do-well son Walter had been reading, and in it she noticed a passage Walter had underlined:

> Listen! The battle trumpet blares from heaven and see how our General marches fully armed, coming amid the clouds to conquer the whole world. Out of the mouth of our King emerges a double-edged sword that cuts down everything in the way. Arising finally from your nap, do you come to the battlefield! Abandon the shade and seek the sun (O'Connor, 1971: 486).

Her revelation appears in the story's final paragraph: "That was the kind of thing he read —something that made no sense now. Then it came to her, with an unpleasant little jolt, that the General with the sword in his mouth, marching to do violence, was Jesus" (O'Connor, 1971: 487).

It is surprising how little attention has been paid to this story in the numerous discussions of the use and purpose of violence in O'Connor's fiction.[1] Not only does the story overtly express a connection between Jesus and military violence, but the narrative is one of the final stories published by O'Connor during her lifetime and was the opening section of a new novel on which she had planned to devote the next several years of her life. This particular vision of Jesus, in other words, likely reflects O'Connor's most mature thinking on the relationship between divine grace and violence, and "with [that] unpleasant little jolt," this story reminds the reader of the biblical description of Jesus as the Divine Warrior. Perhaps the single most consistent and recurring image of God offered throughout both the Hebrew Bible and the New Testament, the Divine Warrior imagery describes violence and creation —as well as violence and re-creation— as necessarily connected in the divine plan of cosmic restoration. This unpleasant little jolt opens a wide new window for viewing the violence that occurs within O'Connor's fictional world.

As many readers likely already know from the story itself, Walter's mother has stumbled upon not just a quotation from a letter written by St. Jerome, but more specifically, a reference to the New Testament book of Revelation, written ca. 100 CE. There, Jesus appears in an

---

1. Although many scholars have written on the portrayals (and use) of violence in O'Connor's stories, almost none have written any sustained reflection on "Why Do the Heathen Rage?", and even fewer have used the story as a meaningful source to make sense of O'Connor's connection between violence and the divine presence in her stories. This is especially true among those scholars who rely on René Girard's understanding of religious violence. One of the very few to discuss this story is Marian Burns in her "O'Connor's Unfinished Novel" (from *Critical Essays on Flannery O'Connor*. Ed. Melvin J. Friedman and Beverly Lyon Clark. G.K. Hall and Co. 1985. 169–80).

For examples of more typical readings of the violence portrayed in O'Connor's stories, see John F. Desmond (1997), "Violence and the Christian Mystery," in *Literature and Belief* 17, 1 & 2: 129–47; Doreen Fowler (2011), "Flannery O'Connor's Productive Violence," in *Arizona Quarterly: A Journal of American Literature, Culture, and Theory* 67, 2: 127–54; Thelma J. Shinn (1968), "Flannery O'Connor and the Violence of Grace," in *Contemporary Literature* 9, 1: 58–73; Susan Srigley (2007), "The Violence of Love: Reflections on Self-Sacrifice through Flannery O'Connor and René Girard," in *Religion and Literature* 39, 3: 31–45; and in particular, the collected essays found in the 2010 volume edited by Avis Hewitt and Robert Donahoo: *Flannery O'Connor in the Age of Terrorism: Essays on Violence and Grace*, Knoxville: University of Tennessee Press.

apocalyptic vision as the Rider on a white horse, and John of Patmos describes him in this way:

> He judges and wages war in righteousness. His eyes were a fiery flame, and on his head were many diadems.[...] He wore a cloak that had been dipped in blood, and his name was called the Word of God. The armies of heaven followed him, mounted on white horses and wearing clean white linen. Out of his mouth came a sharp sword to strike the nations. He will rule them with an iron rod, and he himself will tread out in the wine press the wine of the fury and wrath of God the almighty. He has a name written on his cloak and on his thighs, "King of kings and Lord of lords" (Rev. 19:11b–16).[2]

At the same time, many readers might not know that the imagery in this passage comes directly from a much earlier biblical text, Isaiah 63, likely composed by an anonymous author in the fifth or sixth century BCE as an addition to the original eighth century prophecies received by the prophet Isaiah. This passage offers a conversation between the prophet and the LORD,[3] the God of Israel. "Why is your clothing so

---

2. Quotations from the New Testament and the deuterocanonical texts of the Roman Catholic Scriptures will come from the *New American Bible* (Revised Edition). Citations from the Hebrew Bible (often referred to as the "Old Testament" in Christian usage) will come from the most recent revised translation of the *Tanakh* by the Jewish Publication Society. Although each translation is found in numerous standard editions, specific bibliographic data for an easily accessible version of each appears in the "Works Cited" list at the end of the essay.

3. As many readers are likely aware, most English translations of the Hebrew Bible use the term "the LORD" (rendered in capitals) to indicate the presence of the divine name YHWH in the original Hebrew. Because this name of the God of Israel is not pronounced by some branches of observant Judaism, I have chosen to retain the translation tradition of using "the LORD" to indicate the name's presence, except in certain cases where I wish to emphasize that the quotation is referring to the God of Israel by name. (In many, but far from all, of the cases where English translations use *God*, the divine name present in the original Hebrew is *Elohim*.) These issues regarding the divine name do not carry over in the same manner in either the deuterocanonical texts or the New Testament because the texts within each of these sections of the Catholic Scriptures were handed down originally in Greek.

red,/Your garment like his who treads grapes [in a winepress]?" asks the prophet. The LORD replies,

> I trod out a vintage alone,
> Of the peoples, no man was with Me.
> I trod them down in My anger,
> Trampled them in My rage;
> Their life-blood bespattered My garments,
> And all My clothing was stained.
> For I had planned a day of vengeance,
> And My year of redemption arrived.
> Then I looked, but there was none to help;
> I stared, but there was none to aid—
> So My own arm wrought the triumph,
> And My own rage was My aid.
> I trampled peoples in My anger,
> I made them drunk with My rage,
> And I hurled their glory to the ground (Isa. 63:2–6).

Important to note is that Isaiah 63 is *not* an example of apocalyptic literature. It rather is what the respected biblical scholar John L. McKenzie calls "the verge of apocalyptic literature" in its reliance on historical context in order to envision a world transforming act of divine restoration (1968: 6–8, 187). To put this another way: while the passage obviously uses metaphor to describe the violence enacted by the LORD, the violence described is not symbolic of spiritual warfare. Instead, for ancient Israel these were promises to be fulfilled in history and in the flesh.

This imagery in turn draws up one of the oldest images of the LORD offered in the Hebrew Bible. Exodus 15 and Judges 5 contain very ancient poems that most biblical scholars date to the late thirteenth or early twelfth century BCE, making them likely the oldest extant writings in the Hebrew Bible (Cross, 1973: 91–144).[4] The poem in Exodus 15, known today as the "Song of the Sea," recounts the LORD's defeat of the

---

4. Frank Moore Cross' *Canaanite Myth and Hebrew Epic* (Harvard University Press, 1973) remains one of the standard and indispensible texts among biblical scholars

An Unpleasant Little Jolt: Flannery O'Connor's *Creation ex Chaos*

Egyptian army at the Sea of Reeds after the Israelites' escape from Egypt. Early in this celebration of divine battle, the poet proclaims,

> YHWH the warrior—
> YHWH is His name!
> Pharaoh's chariots and his army
> He has cast into the sea;
> And the pick of his officers
> Are drowned in the Sea of Reeds (Exod. 15:3–4).

Unlike later additions to the book of Exodus,[5] this most ancient poem is not clear as to what exactly happened at the Sea of Reeds. The Egyptians pursing the fleeing Israelites alternately were cast into the sea (presumably from either the shore or from boats they were using to cross the sea as the Israelites fled around the body of water, vv.4–6), or they were caught up in a tidal wave (the "heaped" water of vv. 8–10) or even "swallowed" by the earth in an apparent earthquake (vv. 11–12). Regardless of the method by which the Israelites were delivered, it is clear that the poet of Exodus 15 affirms that the LORD alone brought about this military victory, not through spiritual battle but through overt physical might expressed through extreme natural forces.

Judges 5 portrays another battle with Israel's enemies, this time in the Promised Land. In this case, the poet shows a majestic vision of the LORD as the Divine Warrior fighting alongside the Israelite army in a manner identical to Revelation 19.

> Hear, O kings! Give ear, O potentates!

---

interested in exploring the ancient roots of early Israelite understandings of their God as warrior and protector.

5. It is Exodus 14, a later commentary inserted into the book of Exodus, in which the reader finds the story of the miraculously parted sea with "walls of water to the right and to the left" and instantaneously dry ground on which the Israelites flee the pursuing Egyptians, the latter then destroyed by drowning when the sea crashes down on top of them. In Exodus 14, the LORD is also overtly present in the pillar of cloud and fire that travels with the Israelites once they leave Egypt.

> I will sing, will sing to YHWH,
> Will hymn to YHWH, the God of Israel.
> O YHWH, when you came forth from Seir,
> Advanced from the country of Edom,
> The earth trembled;
> The heavens dripped,
> Yea, the clouds dripped water,
> The mountains quaked—
> Before YHWH, Him of Sinai,
> Before YHWH, God of Israel.
> ………………………………......
> Then was the remnant made victor over the mighty,
> YHWH's people won my victory over the warriors (Judg. 5:3-5, 13).

The poem then goes on to assess which of Israel's tribal groups fared valiantly in the battle and which chose to remain behind, to the latter's shame (vv. 14-23) "[b]ecause they came not to the aid of the LORD,/ To the aid of the LORD among the warriors" (5:23). Notice the contrast with Exodus 15 that we see in Judges 5: as with the vision described in Revelation 19 (and repeated in O'Connor's story), the God of Israel in Judges 5 is accompanied by his people in physical warfare. Divine warfare, it seems, not only permits, but sometimes requires, human cooperation on the battlefield.

The image of the Divine Warrior is neither isolated to these passages within the Bible, nor unknown in the cultural context of the Ancient Near East (ANE) from which the biblical texts emerged. Common throughout the region, likely for a millennium or more before the composition of the earliest biblical texts, was a theological understanding of creation that modern biblical scholars call either the Divine Warrior myth or the Divine Combat myth.[6] Briefly stated, this myth poses the events of

---

6. Readers interested in further understanding the Divine Warrior mythology of the Ancient Near East might consult Richard J. Clifford's *Creation Accounts in the Ancient Near East and in the Bible* (Catholic Biblical Quarterly Monograph Series, 1994); or the collected essays in *Creation in the Biblical Traditions* (ed. Richard J. Clifford and John J. Collins. Catholic Biblical Quarterly Monograph Series, 1992). For

creation not as a process of divine fiat or as occurring peacefully through divine speech; rather, creation is the result of a battle. In the days prior to the creation of the cosmos, an ancient chaos deity rose up against the divine council of the gods and threatened them with annihilation. This chaos deity, usually associated with femininity (or androgyny), water, rivers, seas, serpents, and death, went by various names in the ANE myths: Leviathan, Rahab, Yam, Mot, Tiamat, or Tehom. In response to the chaos deity's threat, a young storm god arose and offered to wage war on it and its minions.[7]

Not surprisingly, the storm deity defeated the chaos deity, in some versions by killing the chaos deity outright, while in other versions strictly regulating or limiting its powers. Upon this victory, the storm deity not only assumed leadership of the divine council but likewise utilized the body and/or remnant elements of the chaos deity, and with his minions, the storm deity created the ordered universe from this chaotic material. This truly is *creation ex chaos*: the totality of our cosmos derives from uncreated stuff that retains a chaotic substratum, rendering the whole of creation unstable and prone to disorder. Creation, when not overseen carefully by the divine warrior and his servants, tends to revert to chaos in ways great and small. Preserving creation is an ongoing effort to impose divine order onto creation; it is a real battle, both physical and spiritual, against conscious and unconscious forces of chaos.

The biblical texts in numerous passages affirm this account of creation, not only revealing various references to the chaos deities of the cultures surrounding ancient Israel, but likewise showing the God of Israel as the Divine Warrior who overpowers them in battle. Psalm 74

---

a theological exploration from a Jewish perspective, see Jon D. Levenson's *Creation and the Persistence of Evil: The Jewish Drama of Divine Omnipotence* (revised edition, Princeton University Press, 1994).

7. In return for his victory, the storm god would be declared head of the divine council and would be worshiped as the "god of gods and lord of lords." This phrasing finds a clear echo in the description of the Jesus as the Rider on the White Horse in Revelation 19, the passage central to our discussion of "Why Do the Heathen Rage?"

offers an account of God defeating the monsters of the sea in a primordial battle, naming Leviathan in particular:

> O God, my King from of old,
>   who brings deliverance throughout the land;
> it was You who drove back the sea [Hebrew, *yam*] with Your might,
>   who smashed the heads of the monsters in the waters;
> it was You who crushed the heads of Leviathan,
>   who left him as food for the denizens of the desert;
> it was You who released springs and torrents,
>   who made mighty rivers run dry (Ps 74:12–15).

Isaiah 27, in contrast, places the supernatural battle in the future, as part of the work of returning creation to its intended order:

> In that day the LORD will punish
> With His great, cruel, mighty sword
> Leviathan the Elusive Serpent—
> Leviathan the Twisting Serpent;
> He will slay the Dragon of the sea (Isa 27:1).

Tellingly, both passages pivot unexpectedly (at least from a modern standpoint) from divine warfare to an account of creation. In Isaiah 27, for instance, the very next verse celebrates the "Vineyard of Delight" that the LORD will bring about, so much so that through Israel, "the face of the world [in the days to come]/Shall be covered with fruit," here meant both literally and metaphorically (Isa 27:2–6). And in Psalm 74, the pivot is even more overt; immediately upon finishing his description of God's battle with Leviathan, the psalmist notes,

> [T]he day is yours, the night also;
> it was You who set in place the orb of the sun;
> You fixed all the boundaries of the earth;
> summer and winter —You made them (Ps 74:16–17).

An Unpleasant Little Jolt: Flannery O'Connor's *Creation ex Chaos*

Creation, and specifically the ordered nature of creation, is seen here as the direct outcome of the divine defeat of the chaos deity.

Rahab, in contrast, is the "raging sea" defeated by the LORD in Psalm 89; significantly, the Hebrew word for sea again is Yam, yet another name by which the chaos deity was known in neighboring cultures.

> O LORD, God of hosts,
>   who is mighty like You, O LORD?
> Your faithfulness surrounds You;
>   You rule the swelling of the sea;
>   when its waves surge, You still them.
> You crushed Rahab; [she] was like a corpse;
>   with Your powerful arm You scattered your enemies (Ps 89:9–11).

Immediately after the defeat of Rahab, the psalmist intones,

> The heaven is yours,
> the earth too;
> the world and all it holds—
> You established them (Ps. 89:12).

In each of these poems, the shift in description from battle to the created order is not a *non sequitur* but rather an assertion: combat is a necessary part of creation. This too is the reason that the vision of the new heaven and new earth described in the book of Revelation notes that in the restored creation, there will be only "living waters" that come forth from the throne of God in Jerusalem; "the sea [will be] no more" because the chaos that it embodies will have been defeated (Rev. 21–22). Just before this scene, yet another chaos deity was defeated: in this case, Death, whose name in Hebrew is *Mot*, the final element of chaos defeated in the conflict described in Revelation 19.

Perhaps most interesting of all are the references to Tiamat and Tehom (variants of the same name), a chaos deity defeated in Psalm 77:

The waters saw You, O God;
   the waters saw You and were convulsed [in terror];
   the very deep [Hebrew, *tehom*] quaked as well.
Clouds streamed water;
   the heavens rumbled;
   Your arrows [i.e., lightning] flew about;
Your thunder rumbled like wheels;
   lightning lit up the world;
   the earth quaked and trembled (Ps. 77:17–19).

Not only is this a clear description of the Divine Warrior as a storm god defeating chaos, but this psalm ends with a reference back to Exodus 15: the parted carcass of the sea (Hebrew *yam*) is not only the way of God toward creation, but also the way by which the God of Israel re-created and led his people through the sea "in the care of Moses and Aaron" (Ps 77:21). Creation is again an ongoing process; what was begun in the primordial battle is renewed and re-engaged in the formation of the people Israel during the exodus.

Tehom, the primordial abyss, remains as a chaotic substratum, however. Indeed, it is the exact same Hebrew word mentioned in Genesis 1:2 as the abyss over which God begins creation; it is one of the few elements present before the work of creation even begins: "When God began to create heaven and earth—the earth being unformed and void, with darkness over the surface of the deep [Hebrew, *tehom*] and a wind from God sweeping over the water" (Gen 1:1). The abyss remains present in the book of Revelation (now called *abussos* in the Greek); only here, it is the volcanic chaotic substratum underlying the cosmos: "Then the fifth angel blew his trumpet[...]. It was given the key for the passage to the abyss. It opened the passage to the abyss, and smoke came up out of the passage like smoke from a huge furnace. The sun and the air were darkened by the smoke from the passage" (Rev 9:1–2). Later, it is this same abyss into which the Devil, the forces of evil, and Death and Hades themselves, are thrust once chaos is formally banished from creation at the end of time:

An Unpleasant Little Jolt: Flannery O'Connor's *Creation ex Chaos*

> Then I saw an angel come down from heaven, holding in his hand the key to the abyss and a heavy chain. He seized the dragon, the ancient serpent, which is the Devil or Satan, and tied it up for a thousand years and threw it into the abyss[. . .]. After this, it is to be released for a short time.
>
> ....
>
> When the thousand years are completed, Satan will be released from his prison [and in turn will wage a great final battle against the holy ones]. The Devil who led them astray was thrown [back] into the pool of fire and sulfur, where the beast and the false prophet were. There they will be tormented day and night forever and ever. [...] Then Death and Hades were thrown into the pool of fire (Rev 20:1–14).

The conscious and recalcitrant forces of chaos, along with the final concrete markers of chaos in the created order, are in this vision forcibly returned by the divine powers to the raw chaotic substratum from which they came.

Forces of chaos abound in O'Connor's fictional world, but in several instances, there are strong connections with the watery chaos deity of the Divine Warrior myth. In *The Violent Bear It Away*, for instance, Tarwater dreams a nightmarish memory of the drowning of Bishop, and the narrator describes the lake and its bank in monstrous terms: the bank rises near him in the dream, "like the brow of some *leviathan* lifted just above the surface of the water" (O'Connor, 1988: 462, emphasis added). The image includes the watery chaos itself: "The water slid out from the bank like a broad black tongue," and the narrator describes Tarwater's thrashing as though "[h]e might have been Jonah clinging wildly" to it. Even the waking world takes on for Tarwater the appearance of a great primordial beast, caged by a "fence of light to keep it in" (O'Connor, 1988: 464). This image echoes distinctly the LORD's challenge in the book of Job, when he rhetorically asks whether Job possesses divine powers like his own:

> Who closed the sea [Hebrew, *yam*] behind doors
> When it gushed forth out of the womb,

> When I clothed it in clouds,
> Swaddled it in dense clouds,
> When I made breakers My limit for it,
> And set up its bar and doors,
> And said, "You may come so far and no farther;
> Here your surging waves will stop"? (Job 38:8–11).

If this association is correct, it foreshadows that this chaos invading Tarwater's world is already controlled and limited, significantly by the power of light (which in Genesis is the result of the first act of divine creation: creating light and in doing so, limiting the realms of darkness and disorder).

In another story, "The River," we see the deformed and disordered Mr. Paradise, a likely pedophile, chase Harry Ashfield as the little boy makes his way back to the scene of his river baptism the previous day. As Harry disappears under the river, Mr. Paradise lurches into the water after him, but "[f]inally, far downstream, the old man rose like some ancient water monster and stood empty-handed," his prey eluding him (O'Connor, 1971: 174). In "A View of the Woods," the escape is not successful: Mary Fortune's grandfather collapses after crushing his granddaughter's skull in rage. But as he tries to escape the woods that are the scene of his crime and the source of his family's anger at him, he feels as though his body flees toward the nearby lake —perhaps in hope of the baptismal-like release Harry Ashfield gained— but finding instead only a sense of imminent death, observed by a steamshovel at work near him, now transmogrified into "one huge yellow monster which sat to the side, stationary as he was, gorging itself on clay" and destroying the natural order of the woods (O'Connor, 1971: 356).

Given that *Wise Blood* is filled with references to B-Picture monsters, it is no surprise that Enoch Emery's encounter with Hazel Motes is likewise nearly defeated by the intervention of a chaos creature. In this case, the chaotic force is the woman with two young boys who visits the public swimming pool in the park where Enoch works. She arrives at the sickly "bottle-green" water of the pool, dressed in a "stained white bathing suit that fit her like a sack" (O'Connor, 1988: 45). Enoch clearly views her as a bathing beauty and wolfishly follows her visits, but the narrator's description sounds more like something from an early horror movie. As Hazel Motes approaches in the distance, the woman dives into the pool and then emerges at the water's edge. O'Connor then sets up what appears to be a classic movie trope: the shimmering wet siren who emerges poolside in sleek, seductive, and scantily-clad slow motion. Instead, though, we see a "cadaverous" face, wrapped like a mummy in its "bandage-like bathing cap[,] sharp teeth protruding from her mouth." A "large foot and leg" heave out of the water, and like some sea monster, the woman squats panting at the pool's edge, revealing matted hair run through with the colors of rust and a greenish yellow (O'Connor, 1988: 47). After her emergence, she and her offspring will engage in a slow-motion pursuit of Haze and Enoch through the park, nearly disrupting Enoch's secret revelation at the museum before the chapter's end.

Perhaps most overtly connected to the chaos deities is General Sash's death in "A Late Encounter with the Enemy." Centered on an ancient and dying Confederate soldier bearing a Tinseltown rank given decades earlier to increase his prestige at a movie premiere, the old man sees in the graduation procession before him a vision of "a black pool" that "began to rumble and flow toward him" (O'Connor, 1971: 142–43) and that ultimately claims him when he recognizes what it is: "it had been dogging him all his days. He made such a desperate effort to see over it and find out what comes after that his hand clenched the sword in his lap until the blade touched bone." The black pool is that ultimate chaos, the ultimate enemy from the book of Revelation whom the General has avoided his entire life: death.

One could continue to catalog the chaos churning below the surface of the universe described in O'Connor's fiction, but these examples are sufficient to make the case that O'Connor's narrators appear fully aware of the Divine Warrior mythology. The mechanics of O'Connor's fictional universe are those of chaos continually threatening alike the authentic divine order and the artificial order of human society, a chaos limited only by the forceful intervention of the Divine Warrior. Yet very much *unlike* the apocalyptic intensity of the biblical books of Daniel, Ezekiel, or Revelation, O'Connor's fictional universe lacks any correspondingly overt imagery to describe the divine presence at war with chaos in the cosmos.

In and of itself, this is not surprising. In large swaths of biblical literature, the spiritual and physical realms openly overlap: angelic messengers and diabolic figures appear in physical form with regularity, and even the LORD at times is manifest. There exists, however another theological line of thought in biblical literature, seen most clearly in narratives like the Joseph story, the books of Esther, Ezra, and Nehemiah, and likewise the deuterocanonical texts of Judith and 1 Maccabees. In each of these narratives, God does not appear, he does not speak, and there is an absence of any sense of an overt supernatural order intruding into the physical realm. For example: how does Joseph, not to mention the reader, know that God was with Joseph throughout his dreams, his conflict with his brothers, his experience of slavery, his imprisonment, and his rise to power in imperial Egypt? The answer —within the biblical text itself— is surprising to some readers: Joseph does not encounter God personally; instead, he intuits the presence of God as the force behind his ability to interpret dreams and as the guide who led him to a place where he could act to save Israel from famine. The same understanding applies for Ezra and Nehemiah. As deliverances from enemies pile up and obstacles are overcome in the restoration of the Promised Land, Ezra and Nehemiah credit these actions to divine interventions motivated in response to prayer and Torah observance because, in the wake of these events, chaotic threats have been brushed back and the divine order has been restored.

We draw even closer to the sensibility informing O'Connor's fiction, however, as we turn to the deuterocanonical texts, those biblical texts that are canonical for Catholics and the Orthodox Church but that are considered apocryphal by Jews and Protestants. In Judith and 1

Maccabees,[8] the threat to the existence of the Jewish people is specifically annihilation at the hands of an enemy military. In each narrative, groups of devout Jews engage in prayer, fasting, and sacrifices —and then violence erupts. And while God does not appear or speak in either narrative, and while there is no evidence of angelic forces or miraculous interventions, the presence of the Divine Warrior is intuited in each narrative. In these cases, though, it is the military victory of God's chosen people that is lifted up as evidence that God has acted; the violent assertion of divine order *through his people's warfare* is offered as proof of the divine presence.

This theology of what I call "the hidden Divine Warrior" is described overtly in the deuterocanonical additions to the Greek versions of the book of Esther. In the Hebrew version of the story, not only is there no overt divine manifestation, but there is no mention of God whatsoever. It is truly a world of *deus absconditus*, God apparently missing from the universe. The Jews are delivered from seeming inevitable genocide through a battle that ends with the deaths of more than 75,000 gentile anti-Semites. The deuterocanonical additions clarify what the Hebrew text leaves unsaid. According to Mordecai the Jew, the Jewish victory itself is evidence of divine presence and divine action:

> The nations [...] assembled to destroy the name of the Jews, but my people is Israel, who cried to God and was saved. The Lord saved his people and delivered us from all these evils. God worked signs and great wonders, such as have not occurred among the nations.[...]

---

8. Unlike these texts, 2 Maccabees revels in the portrayal of numerous supernatural events, including two brawny angels who flog a pagan government official who attempts to ransack the Jerusalem Temple (2 Macc 3:12–40); as well as a vision in which the prophet Jeremiah presents a supernatural sword to Judas, the leader of the Maccabean forces retaking the Promised Land from the Seleucid occupiers (15:7–16). My point in noting this contrast between these two books of Maccabees lies in the point that we do not see a simple evolution of biblical thought in the portrayal of divine interventions in history; rather, the biblical authors and editors choose to leave conflicting portrayals within the biblical canon itself, encouraging the reader to embrace multiple perspectives within one's interpretive field.

God remembered his people and rendered justice to his inheritance (Esth. F:5–6, 9).[9]

The narrative of Jewish military victory has not changed in the deutero-canonical version of the Esther story; instead, Mordecai has stated here overtly what this line of biblical thought typically leaves implicit: God acts *through* violence to deliver his people from looming chaos. This is an especially strong point when one considers that the biblical concept of justice (particularly in the Hebrew Bible) relies fundamentally on a sense of right order in society. Injustice is, by definition, a disorder in society and ultimately in the cosmos. The presence of God is *marked* by the way in which liturgically activated violence leads to the restoration of divine order.

This appears to be the method O'Connor uses to mark divine presence in her fictional universe. We can briefly note a few. As we have already seen, Harry Ashfield's drowning saves him from Mr. Paradise; we have not emphasized sufficiently, however, that Harry drowns in the same location in which he had been baptized only a day earlier—and while he was seeking to return to that baptismal state. Most readers of *Wise Blood* also will quickly remember that Hazel Motes only begins to see truly once he blinds himself; but as his landlady Mrs. Flood ponders his state, her thoughts reveal that his self-blinding does not reflect the isolated psychological or spiritual revelation of Oedipus. Instead,

> [s]he imagined it was like you were walking in a tunnel and all you could see was a pin point of light. She had to imagine the pin point of light; she couldn't think of it at all without that. She saw it as some kind of a star, like the star on Christmas cards. She saw him going backward to Bethlehem and she had to laugh (O'Connor, 1988: 123).

---

9. In order to clarify where the deuterocanonical version of the Esther story differs from the Hebrew text—as well as to clarify where the versions agree—biblical scholarship has adopted the decision to use consistent chapter numbers for those chapters that are shared by the versions; the six additional chapters of the Greek versions are indicated by the respective letters A-F.

Mrs. Flood has to laugh, of course, because she is a good Southern Protestant, who fears that Hazel "might as well be in a monkery" or "some kind of agent of the pope" and whose mortifications are "something that people have quit doing" because such liturgically-informed acts are appalling (O'Connor, 1988: 123, 127). Similarly, Ruby Turpin in "Revelation" finally can pray in earnest and see the true heavenly procession only after Mary Grace (hued in the symbolic blue of the Virgin Mary) has struck her with a book and physically assaulted her. And most notoriously of course, the Misfit reminds us that Bailey's mother "would of been a good woman [...] if it had been somebody there to shoot her every minute of her life" (O'Connor, 1971: 133).

Now seen through the lens of the ending of "Why Do the Heathen Rage?", this connection between violence and divine presence emerges most powerfully among O'Connor's works in *The Violent Bear It Away*. Here, the transforming hunger for the "Bread of Life" drives Tarwater's increasingly violent responses to the chaotic world he encounters after his grand-uncle's death, even as Tarwater resists his call. Violence permeates the novel: its opening unveils a death and a burning house, and it ends in a vast conflagration. Along the way, characters encounter vicious words, racial hatred, gunfire, physical abuse, kidnapping, rape, and death by human hands. There is perhaps not a single page of the novel untouched in some way by what we today call violence. Yet the words *violent* and *violence* appear within its pages less than a dozen times in the entire novel, and in every single case, these two words refer exclusively to the divine presence in the novel's world, describing the results of baptism and the life shaped by Jesus and the prophets, those "strangers from that violent country where the silence is never broken except to shout the truth" (O'Connor, 1988: 478).

Shortly after Old Tarwater baptized young Tarwater as a baby, Rayber returned to the baby's room and denounced what Old Tarwater's baptism had done to him: "You pushed me out of the real world and I stayed out of it until I didn't know which was which. You infected me with your idiot hopes, your foolish violence" (O'Connor, 1988: 377); later,

Rayber will call his baptism a violent wound that "made a lasting scar" (O'Connor, 1988: 437). Both Tarwater and his grand-uncle have "violent" eyes, made so "with their impossible vision of a world transfigured" by what Rayber can only call a "horrifying love" (O'Connor, 1988: 401). Rayber, reflecting on his own life and will, sees with "a peculiar chilling clarity of mind" that his baptism has left him divided, "a violent and a rational self" that now battle within his soul (O'Connor, 1988: 417). As Jill Baumgaertner notes concerning this latter example, "His violent side loves; his rational side does not. In like manner [Rayber] establishes a dichotomy between baptism and intelligence, thus linking baptism with violence" (1999: 200).

Young Tarwater's experiences bring this divine violence into the clearest relief. His eyes are "still shocked by some violent memory" early in the novel (O'Connor, 1988: 396), and while one might mistakenly infer this to be the memory of his uncle's death and the ensuing arson, we see later that this memory is tied to his uncle's prophetic teaching. When Tarwater sees his reflection in the city's shop windows, he sees "his own form [...] mov[ing] beside him like some violent ghost who had already crossed over and was reproaching him from the other side" (O'Connor, 1988: 429), and near the novel's end, he "move[s] off [...] through the dark forest toward a violent encounter with his fate" (O'Connor, 1988: 456). Leaving aside the overt preaching of the various evangelists in the story, the narrative ties the fate of young Tarwater into the stories of Jonah, Elijah and Elisha, Moses, and Ezekiel, while revealing embodiments of Christ's passion and Catholic baptismal and eucharistic theologies. For O'Connor, the violence of Matthew 11:12 (the source text for the novel's title) is itself part of the kingdom of heaven, and not only does the kingdom compel by violence, but the violent themselves will reach the final reward: she notes in one of her letters that "more than ever now[,] it seems that the kingdom of heaven has to be taken by violence, or not at all" (O'Connor, 1979: 229).

An Unpleasant Little Jolt: Flannery O'Connor's *Creation ex Chaos*

Lest the reader mistake this divine violence for something evil or broken, O'Connor makes clear its nature in a soaring revelation near the novel's end:

> He felt his hunger no longer as a pain but as a tide. He felt it rising in himself through time and darkness, rising through the centuries, and he knew that it rose in a line of men whose lives were chosen to sustain it, who would wander in the world, strangers from that violent country where the silence is never broken except to shout the truth. [...] He knew that this was the fire that had encircled Daniel, that had raised Elijah from the earth, that had spoken to Moses [...] (O'Connor, 1988: 478).

The prophetic message that accompanies this revelation is a warning and promise of the intense power of divine love: "GO WARN THE CHILDREN OF GOD OF THE TERRIBLE SPEED OF MERCY." The exact same message had come to Old Tarwater years earlier with one crucial change; it then was a warning of the terrible speed of justice. O'Connor herself heard far too many readers remain convinced that such images were tied solely to the Old Testament. In response to a letter writer's thoughts about the novel's title, O'Connor says:

> One thing I observe about the title is that the general reaction is to think that it has an Old Testament flavor. Even when they read the quotation, the fact that these are Christ's words makes no great impression. That this is the violence of love, of giving more than the law demands, of an asceticism like John the Baptist's, but in the face of which even John is less than the least in the kingdom —all this is overlooked (O'Connor, 1979: 382).

This comment is a powerful rejoinder to the false dichotomy split between Law and Gospel, on one hand, and the "old age" of divine wrath and the "new age" of divine love on the other. For O'Connor, the violent land of Tarwater's vision *is* the kingdom of heaven, where justice and mercy are both terrible and frightful things for people who must bear that hard discipleship necessary to achieve the kingdom.

Most decidedly, not all the violence in O'Connor's stories is divine violence. Still, this theology offers a criterion by which to evaluate that narrative violence and to discern where moves the hand of the Divine Warrior. Most importantly to O'Connor studies, this criterion of evaluation moves in accordance not only with the narratives themselves but also with the biblical sources on which O'Connor's narratives frequently depend, allude, and appear to find their theological support. The Divine Warrior silently and surreptitiously travels the roads and byways of Flannery O'Connor's fictional universe. Turning back to yet another biblical allusion in her fiction, it is precisely the presence of this Divine Warrior that explains "why the heathen rage." The story's title is an allusion to Psalm 2, in which the LORD "has installed his king on Zion," a son who "[w]ith an iron rod [...] will shepherd [the nations]" and "like a potter's vessel [....] will shatter them" (Ps. 2:1–9). This son, according to the Church, ultimately is Jesus, the General marching to do violence with a sword in mouth and blood-drenched robes, he who battles chaos in a world not yet fully restored and fully healed, but whose victory is sure.

Bibliography

Baumgaertner, Jill Peláez (1999). *Flannery O'Connor: A Proper Scaring.* Chicago, IL: Conerstone Press.

Burns, Marian (1985). O'Connor's Unfinished Novel. In Melvin J. Friedman and Beverly Lyon Clark (Eds.), *Critical Essays on Flannery O'Connor.* Boston, MA: G.K. Hall and Co., pp.169–80.

Clifford, Richard J. (1994). *Creation Accounts in the Ancient Near East and in the Bible.* Washington, DC: Catholic Biblical Quarterly Monograph Series.

Clifford, Richard J. and John J. Collins (Eds.) (1992). *Creation in the Biblical Traditions.* Boston, MA: Catholic Biblical Quarterly Monograph Series.

Cross, Frank Moore (1973). *Canaanite Myth and Hebrew Epic: Essays in the History of the Religion of Israel.* Boston, MA: Harvard University Press.

Desmond, John F. (1997). "Violence and the Christian Mystery," in *Literature and Belief*, 17, 1 & 2: 129–47.

Fowler, Doreen (2011). "Flannery O'Connor's Productive Violence," in *Arizona Quarterly: A Journal of American Literature, Culture, and Theory*, 67, 2: 127–54.

Hewitt, Avis, and Robert Donahoo (Eds.) (2010). *Flannery O'Connor in the Age of Terrorism: Essays on Violence and Grace*. Knoxville, TN: University of Tennessee Press.

Levenson, Jon D. (1994). *Creation and the Persistence of Evil: The Jewish Drama of Divine Omnipotence* (revised edition). Princeton, NJ: Princeton University Press.

McKenzie, John L. (1968). *Second Isaiah*. New York, NY: Doubleday & Company.

O'Connor, Flannery (1988). *Collected Works*. Edited by Sally Fitzgerald. New York, NY: Library of American/Penguin.

--- (1971). *The Complete Stories*. New York, NY: Farrar, Straus and Giroux.

--- (1979). *The Habit of Being: Letters of Flannery O'Connor*. Edited by Sally Fitzgerald. New York, NY: Farrar, Straus and Giroux.

Senior, Donald; John J. Collins, and Mary Ann Getty (Eds.) (2013). *The Catholic Study Bible*. Third Edition. New York, NY: Oxford University Press.

Shinn, Thelma J. (1968). "Flannery O'Connor and the Violence of Grace," in *Contemporary Literature*, 9, 1: 58–73.

Srigley, Susan (2007). "The Violence of Love: Reflections on Self-Sacrifice through Flannery O'Connor and René Girard," in *Religion and Literature*, 39, 3: 31-45.

Stein, David E. Sulomm (Ed.) (1999). *JPS Hebrew-English Tanakh*. Revised Edition. Philadelphia, PA: Jewish Publication Society.

Co-Editors

Mark Bosco is Professorial Lecturer in English and an administrator at Georgetown University. His research focuses on literary aesthetics and the intersection of religion and art, especially the 20th century Catholic literary tradition. He is the author of *Graham Greene's Catholic Imagination* (Oxford, 2005) and *Academic Novels as Satire: Critical Studies of an Emerging Genre* (Edwin Mellen, 2007), and co-editor (with Brent Little) of *Revelation and Convergence: Flannery O'Connor and the Catholic Intellectual Tradition* (Catholic University of America Press, 2017). He is a producer and director of the full-length documentary film, *Flannery*, on the life and work of Flannery O'Connor.

Beatriz Valverde is an Assistant Professor at Universidad Loyola Andalucía, Spain. She holds a Doctorate in English Philology from Universidad de Jaén, Spain. In addition, she holds a MA in Spanish Literature from Loyola University Chicago. In both fields, English and Spanish Literature, she has published articles in various national and international journals, mainly on theological and political aspects in the work of Graham Greene.

List of Contributors

Anabel Altemir Giral, is a PhD candidate at the University of La Rioja, Spain. She is currently researching on the Gothic and fantastic elements in the work of Scottish writer Muriel Spark. Other interests include Catholic writers and Horror Literature and Film. She teaches at the School of Modern Languages at the University of Zaragoza.

Guadalupe Arbona Abascal is a professor of Spanish Literature at Universidad Complutense de Madrid and has served as visiting Professor at Harvard University, the University of Tampere, and the University

"Sedes Sapientae" in Lima. Her research focuses on 20th-century and 21st-century Spanish Literature and its relations with other literatures.

Michael Bruner is a professor of Practical Theology at Azusa Pacific University in California. He was born and raised in the Philippines, received his Bachelor's degree in English from the University of Washington, an M.Div. from Princeton Seminary, and a Ph.D. in Theology & Culture from Fuller Theological Seminary. He is a resident scholar at the Huntington Library in San Marino and an ordained minister in the PC(USA). He lives in Pasadena with his wife Jenna and their two children, Arabelle and William.

Xiamara Hohman is a PhD student at Loyola University Chicago. In 2010, she received her MA in English from the University of Dayton. Her current research interests include 20th century American literature, religion and literature, and the influence of translation on Modern poetry. Her most recent publication, "Lessons from the Middle Kingdom: Pedagogical Approaches to Fostering Greater Classroom Participation among Chinese Learners of English," appeared in the Fall/Winter 2015 edition of the *Ohio Journal of English Language Arts*.

Ismael Ibáñez Rosales teaches Language and Literature at the University of Zaragoza, Spain. His research focuses on Catholic aesthetics and sensibility, the study of baroque aesthetics in Literature and Film and contemporary Horror Film studies.

Michael Kirwan is a British Jesuit theologian, currently attached to the Loyola Institute, Trinity College Dublin. Before this, he taught systematic theology at Heythrop College (University of London) for twenty years. He is the author of *Discovering Girard* (2004), and *Girard and Theology* (2009), and the co-editor of several collections on Girard's mimetic theory and religion. He has also written on political theology.

José Liste-Noya teaches American Literature at the Universidade da Coruña (University of Corunna) in northwestern Spain where he is a tenured professor in the Departamento de Letras. He specializes in contemporary American fiction, with specific interests in postmodernism, speculative fiction and literary theory. He has published on diverse authors in his field in national and international journals such as *Contemporary Literature, Studies in the Novel, Western American Literature, Atlantic Studies, Journal of Narrative Technique* and *JTAS (Journal of Transnational American Studies)*. He has also co-edited *Ethics and Ethnicity in the Literatures of the United States* (Universitat de València, 2006) and *American Secrets: The Politics and Poetics of Secrecy in American Culture* (Rowman & Littlefield, 2011).

Brent Little is an Assistant Lecturer in the Department of Catholic Studies at Sacred Heart University in Fairfield, CT, and holds a Ph.D. from Loyola University Chicago. He is the co-editor (along with Mark Bosco, S.J.) of *Revelation and Convergence: Flannery O'Connor and the Catholic Intellectual Tradition* (Catholic University of America Press, 2017). His articles have appeared in *The Heythrop Journal, Renascence,* the *Toronto Journal of Theology*, and the *Flannery O'Connor Review*.

Anne-Marie Pouchet holds a PhD in Hispanic Literatures and Cultures from The Ohio State University. Her dissertation treats with the Catholic sensibility of Spanish author, Juan Manuel de Prada. She is currently faculty at the University of the West Indies, St. Augustine where she teaches Spanish Language and Hispanic Literature to undergraduate and graduate students. Her main area of research is Modern Hispanic Literature and has published on history and memory in the post-Franco Spanish novel, dictatorship and its vestiges in the Hispanic narrative and religion in Hispanic literature. Other interests include migration and drug trafficking in the Hispanic narrative.

Thomas Wetzel is assistant professor of Hebrew Bible/Old Testament at Loyola University Chicago, where his work focuses on the intersections between theology and literary studies, as well as Jewish-Christian dialogue. He holds a doctorate in English and literary studies from the University of Wisconsin-Milwaukee and a doctorate in Hebrew Bible from Harvard Divinity School. He is currently working on a book tentatively entitled *The Hidden Covenant: God, Violence, and the Survival of Israel in the Book of Esther.*

www.ingramcontent.com/pod-product-compliance
Lightning Source LLC
Chambersburg PA
CBHW050310010526
44107CB00055B/2180